The Connecticut Town

The Connecticut Town

GROWTH AND DEVELOPMENT,

1635–1790

BRUCE C. DANIELS

WESLEYAN UNIVERSITY PRESS

MIDDLETOWN, CONNECTICUT

Copyright © 1979 by Wesleyan University

The publisher gratefully acknowledges support of the publication of this book by the National Endowment for the Humanities.

Maps: Milt Johnson

Library of Congress Cataloging in Publication Data

Daniels, Bruce Colin.
  The Connecticut town.

  Includes bibliographical references.
    1. Cities and towns—Connecticut (Colony)—
History.   2. Urbanization—Connecticut (Colony)—
History.   I. Title.
HT123.5.C8D35   301.36'09746   79-65331
ISBN 0-8195-6065-0
Distributed by Columbia University Press
136 South Broadway, Irvington, NY 10533

Manufactured in the United States of America
First paperback edition, 1981

With Love To
My Three Daughters
Elizabeth
Abigail
Nora

CONTENTS

MAPS

TABLES

ACKNOWLEDGMENTS

It is a source of profound amazement and warmth to me that so many friends and professional acquaintances freely devoted their time and knowledge to improving this book. One would have to be a hardened cynic to be skeptical about human nature after receiving such generous aid. I am neither a cynic nor a skeptic and it gives me great pleasure to thank the following people for their unselfish assistance.

Professors Robert Calhoon of the University of North Carolina at Greensboro, R. Kent Newmyer of the University of Connecticut, and John Waters of the University of Rochester all read first drafts of the manuscript and offered valuable advice on both style and substance. Professor Anthony Philpotts of the University of Connecticut showed me how to calculate the square mileage of towns from a map by using an analytical balancer. I am greatly indebted to Professor Albert E. Van Dusen of the University of Connecticut for sharing his unrivaled knowledge of Connecticut source material with me. As is the case with nearly everything I have written, Professor Fred Cazel, Jr., of the University of Connecticut, went over every part of this book testing its use of evidence and logic and pointing out weaknesses in the prose. My father, Howard Daniels, who has been a businessman all his life but who would have made a magnificent editor, similarly devoted dozens of evenings to eliminating infelicities in my style. Professor Edward Cook, Jr., of the University of Chicago, who is among the most distinguished students of the New England town, read two drafts of the book and gave me the kind of assistance that only a scholar deeply involved in the sources and methodologies of community studies could give.

My debts to the staff at Connecticut State Library, a marvelously rich and well-run research center, are many. I wish especially to thank Kristin Woodbridge, reference librarian, who combines professional knowledge with good cheer and personal charm in serving library patrons better than anyone I know; Marvin Thompson, Associate Editor of the Jonathan Trumbull Papers, who always knew where some piece of information could be found when I was stumped; and Robert Claus, Head of Archives, who has brought order and structure to the library's source materials in a way that has benefited me and will benefit all future scholars who use them.

Several lunches at the Connecticut State Library with Professor

Jackson Turner Main of the State University of New York at Stony
Brook immeasurably improved my knowledge of colonial history,
colonial Connecticut, and quantitative methodology. At several
dinners at their house in Orange, Connecticut, Bonnie Collier of
the Sterling Library at Yale University and Christopher Collier of
the University of Bridgeport gave me the benefit of their thorough
knowledge of early Connecticut (and also fed me well). Jo Ann
Thompson of Middletown, Connecticut, typed the first draft of the
manuscript faster and better than I thought possible; not inciden-
tally, she is a better speller than I am, for which I am grateful. My
parents, Willa and Howard Daniels, provided me with a warm and
comfortable place to work and live while I wrote this book during a
sabbatical leave.

People who know me well, know how much motivation I derive
from the faculty, students, and administration of the University of
Winnipeg. In particular I wish to single out my colleagues in the
Department of History for setting me examples as scholars and for
providing me with friendship, Professor David Cheal of the Department of Sociology, Professors Robin Armstrong and James
Richtik of the Department of Geography, and Professor Shirley
Mills of the Department of Mathematics and Statistics, for assistance in their respective areas of specialization. Two former colleagues of mine, Colin Read, now of Huron College in the University of Western Ontario, and James Pitsula, now of the University
of Regina, gave me the benefit of their insight into social and urban
history. I wish also to thank Robert Belfield, Evelyn Drescher,
Robin Finlayson, Jaye Goosen, Brenda Keyser, Linda Lee, Brent
Stewart, and Charles Wiebe, all distinguished students, who have
sharpened my perceptions of history and the historical process.
The Research and Travel Committee of the university was generous as usual in its financial support of my research.

I wish also to thank the Canada Council for its support in the
form of a leave fellowship for the academic year 1976–77 and the
William and Mary Quarterly for permission to use parts of chapter
III which appeared as an article in its January, 1977 issue.

And finally, I wish to thank the three people whose names appear on the dedication page for providing me with a personal life
that sustains me in my professional one.

                                                    BRUCE C. DANIELS
Winnipeg, Manitoba
January, 1979

The Connecticut Town

INTRODUCTION

THE colonial New England town has always intrigued American historians but, paradoxically, few historians until recently have placed the colonial town under a microscope and studied it in detail. Most, instead, like George Bancroft and Herbert Baxter Adams, simply heaped accolades upon it. Even the Progressive historians, writing in an age of scientific history and seeking to debunk the myth of town-meeting democracy, still did not apply a close scrutiny to the actual sources but instead also talked in generalities. The only real exceptions to this pattern and the only persons to delve deeply into local sources were Charles Andrews in his *River Towns of Connecticut* and G. E. Howard in his *Introduction to the Local Constitutional History of the United States*, both published in 1889. The next serious professional local study did not appear until 1961. In the intervening seventy-two years hundreds of local histories were written, but by antiquarians who frequently wrote with intelligence and felicity but seldom asked the significant questions that a professional historian would ask. Indeed, to be involved in local history implied, to professional historians living in this era, that a person was an antiquarian and not a true historian. However, since 1961 a number of historians have attempted to put the New England town under a microscope and ascertain some specifics to replace the generalities.

The corpus of work produced by this new wave of professional local historians is prodigious; twelve major books published by national presses, several lesser but still important books published by local presses, a multitude of journal articles and conference papers, and numerous master's theses and doctoral dissertations have focused explicitly on community analyses;[1] taken together, they have so vastly expanded our knowledge that it would be neither an exaggeration nor an arrogance to say that the study of the colonial New England town in the 1960s and 1970s took a quantum leap beyond that of the preceding generation. It would be smug, however, to think that we now *know* the colonial New England town. The act of writing history is essentially Sisyphean and productive of humility, not arrogance. Along with quantum leaps go new problems.

The basic problem arising from the recent community studies is that we are now bogged down in too many specifics and have not developed secure new generalizations to replace the discarded ones. Almost all of the recent studies have been of the case-study genre — each an exhaustively researched analysis of one community; frequently the analysis has covered a relatively short period of time that does not embrace the entire colonial and Revolutionary periods. The microscope has been so finely focused by the practicing historians that we no longer have a picture of a region or a colony or an era; we have instead a series of slides, each of which shows us only a magnified fragment of the whole. To be sure, most of the recent local historians are fine social scientists who show what theoretical models of behavior their data support. The result is a number of provocative hypotheses about the New England towns — they were "frontier democracies," "closed, corporate, utopian, peasant communities," "peaceable kingdoms," "East Anglian oligarchies," "covenanted communities," and so on. But in each case, the author must enter the disclaimer of many exploratory social scientists — the data base is sufficient to establish only a working hypothesis, not a firm conclusion. The standard cliché in reviews and other critiques of these works is to cast doubt on the typicality of the community under study. But these comments, although becoming tiresome, are absolutely justified, as all the practicing local historians know — we do not know how typical each community was. If the response to the case-study approach is cliché-ridden, it is no more so than the invariable call of the local historian for his fellow historians to test the hypotheses he has developed by applying his model to other communities. This call for collecting new data to test preexisting models is eminently rational but it is a peculiar bent of the new social historians that no one above the level of graduate student wants to use anyone else's model. This insistence on developing a new theoretical framework for each new case study may not be as egocentric or idiosyncratic as it first appears — major journals and presses want only to publish work that is a "major methodological breakthrough"; other work is stigmatized as "derivative." Hence, studies that do not ask new questions in new ways are relegated to graduate seminars, state journals, and local presses. Most of the best historians have higher hopes than that for marketing their work, and consequently new methodologies and models that generate new hypotheses proliferate. But this multiplicity of approaches does not make for meaningful comparability and the tentative generalizations of several dozen historians remain precisely that — tentative generalizations, not adequately tested by researchers and not capable of being fully tested by readers.

I believe that the study of the community in colonial New England is now ready to move to the next level — that we need to take a step back from the microscope and integrate the separate slides into a whole picture. We must do so, however, without sacrificing the quality of the in-depth studies; we must not spread a gloss of hazy generalities over the clear specifics. Rather we must start taking our new pictures with a lens wide enough to encompass an area of some significance but sharp enough to held up under microscopic analysis.

This call for a wider field of vision is certainly not entirely original with me; a few pioneering studies have started to reintegrate our knowledge of the colonial New England town and several more such studies are in preparation.[2] At the present time, however, it is not possible to produce a synthesis that will embrace all of the many experiences of the communities of colonial New England. Despite the fact that the secondary literature is extensive, because of the wide variety of evidence and methodologies it employs, one cannot rely on secondary materials alone for a comprehensive study. Much primary research still is required to get uniform materials that allow for comparability. Hundreds of man-years still remain to be spent in data collecting before a holistic synthesis will be written.

What I offer in the following pages is a picture somewhere between the magnificent panorama of a full synthesis and the sharply focused slide of a community case study. I attempt to trace the phenomenon of the growth and development of Connecticut's towns between the founding of the colony and the federal census of 1790. This period embraces the entire colonial and Revolutionary experience of one colony. Though it may sound banal, the most obvious feature of this experience is that Connecticut towns grew and developed from nothing to something, and it is this phenomenon that I wish to explore. In separate chapters on town settlement and formation, population, town-meeting government, ecclesiastical societies and their government, other important local institutions, and central places, I wish to examine and discuss the various dimensions of growth and development. How much took place? Why did it take place? What forms did it take? What factors influenced it? How did it respond to ideological currents, economic trends, and political events? And finally, in what did it result? That is, what was the state of Connecticut's towns in 1790?

It is my hope, however, that this book goes beyond merely recounting how a large number of towns increased all of their vital statistics. Within the story of growth and development, I wish to focus on the process of institutional elaboration and economic interconnection within and among towns. Towns did not merely grow in number and size to the point where, in 1790, there were just more of them that were just larger versions of their 1635 predecessors. Rapid growth in the number and size of towns caused them to grow in political, economic, and social complexity also; the towns of 1790 had developed sophisticated institutional and economic arrangements that would be largely unfamiliar to the founders of the first communities. This is hardly surprising when one considers that the period under study is 155 years long, but too often historians have been so impressed by the quantity of growth and development that they have not appreciated the dynamics of the process. Moreover, although it is a commonplace for historians of New England to discuss attitudinal and ideological changes in towns over the colonial and Revolutionary periods, virtually no one has investigated these very real changes in light of local political and economic institutions that were undergoing constant change. This present study, then, is not just a case study of the growth and development of towns in one colony — it attempts to integrate institutions and attitudes into an interpretation of early American history and in many ways is as much a synthesis of the older political history and the new social and economic history as it is a synthesis of the many varieties of local history.

As the title of the final chapter indicates, this book contends that the process and dynamics of institutional elaboration and economic interconnection were moving Connecticut toward urbanization. The new state certainly was not an urban society in 1790, but it was much closer to the urban condition than it had been in the mid-colonial period.[3] Demographers argue that a society is entering the urbanization process when a "multiplicity of points of concentration" develops among a population. Political scientists, economists, and sociologists argue that a society is entering the urbanization process when "units of organization become more specialized . . . and the sum of units becomes more complex."[4] By either or both of these definitions, Connecticut, as was much of the colonial world, was moving toward urbanization throughout the preindustrial period. The growth and development of the towns that this book examines produced an ever-larger number of points of concentration with an increasingly specialized and complex governmental, economic, and social structure: thus, it is a process and the effects of the process that I describe, measure, and analyze in the following pages.

My story of growth and development in Connecticut towns is heavily dependent not only on the recent community studies of professional historians and the extensive primary sources for the colony and new state but also on the hundreds of local histories written by amateurs and hundreds of monographs and articles written on particular subjects by amateurs and professionals alike. I draw upon all of these for a data base that is sufficient to enable me to make generalizations about towns over time in early Connecticut. The questions I ask of my data are frankly designed for the professional historians and social scientists who seek to establish general principles and themes. Many of the questions were suggested by the case studies of the 1960s and 1970s, and most of the questions in some way relate to issues raised by this scholarship. Yet, I believe that the overall product is unique and in a modest way makes a significant contribution to a new level of knowledge in our quest to understand the New England town. Although the influence of the recent professional local historians will be seen on almost every page of this book, and although I comment explicitly on the major theses of the secondary literature, I do not intend continuously to measure my general conclusions against the hundreds of current ones and "accept" or "reject" every specific extant hypothesis. This kind of ongoing testing would mar the narrative and become tedious. For similar reasons I have put as much of the raw data as is possible into appendices.

[I]

THE PROCESS OF TOWN
SETTLEMENT AND FORMATION

FROM 1635, when Massachusetts men first traveled over the "Connecticut Path" to form a new colony, to 1790, when the first federal census was taken of the American nation, Connecticut's communities progressed from isolated enclaves on the Great River to 101 thickly settled towns comprising the same territory as the present state. No one in 1635 could have foreseen the future extent of Connecticut's borders as they took final form in the mid-eighteenth century: they were hammered out at the English Court and in negotiations with the three neighboring colonies.[1] Nor could anyone in the early seventeenth century have predicted accurately the rhythm and pattern of town formation; the process by which the first settlements grew to the 101 early national towns was unplanned and irregular, usually orderly but occasionally chaotic, and significantly different by time and region. The disjointed nature of the growth of communities, besides being fit material for an exciting and varied narrative, lends itself well to classification and analysis. Although they could change if one selected other variables to measure, and although they permit several exceptions and some internal variation, four separate periods with clearly distinct characteristics can be fashioned from this disparate whole: (1) settling the coastline and the major river valleys, 1635–75; (2) settling the interior uplands and the secondary river valleys, 1686–1734; (3) settling the northwest and rounding out the borders, 1737–61; (4) carving new towns out of old ones, 1767–89.

Traditionally, historians ask who, when, why, where, and how of their sources, and these are the salient questions to answer when classifying eras of town settlement and formation. The "when" is the most important of these questions for the present analysis, and the classification scheme propounded here is essentially chronological; but as students of the past know well, eras do not end precisely on last years of centuries, nor do they come in neat, even packages of time. Hence, four other variables — origins of first settlers, geographic location of new communities, reasons for migration, and methods of settlement — basically determine when a crossline is drawn on the continuum between 1635 and 1790, and one period is designated as over and another as beginning. These segments delineated by the crosslines on the continuum have certain clusters of similar traits that give each period a unity permitting description as an historical entity.

PERIOD 1:

Farmers, Traders, and Purists: Settling the Coastline and the Major River Valleys, 1635–1675

CONNECTICUT'S first period of settlement, from 1635 to 1675, witnessed the planting of twenty-five towns that stretched along the entire coastline from Stonington in the east to Greenwich in the west and inland along the three major river valleys of the colony, the Thames in the east, the Connecticut in the center, and the Housatonic in the west. These towns occupied farming land that was fertile relative to the rest of the colony, were situated well for trade and communication along water routes, and, once their boundaries were firmed up and clearly laid out, possessed amounts of land best described as huge, considering the present folk-cultural view of the size of an early New England town and considering the ability of the settlers to bring the land under cultivation. Farming, trade, and religious purity all were factors motivating the settlement of these twenty-five towns. Many of the first settlers came directly from Massachusetts and England, although the towns founded after 1650 were settled primarily by families already living in a Connecticut town.

The distinction of being the first Connecticut towns goes to the three River Towns of Windsor, Wethersfield, and Hartford. The founders of these towns, who, beginning in the summer of 1635, trekked overland on the Connecticut Path from Massachusetts, derived their claims of ownership from three separate sources: the General Court of Massachusetts, the Warwick Patent, and the local Indians. Most of the founders of the River Towns had been recent arrivals from England in the Bay Colony towns of Cambridge, Dorchester, and Watertown and had experienced the fate of many newcomers to Massachusetts' towns — small lots of poor quality land with little likelihood of significant future additions. Goaded by the fact that, as John Winthrop stated, "their cattle and towns were so near to one another" and lured by the "fruitfulness and commodiousness of Connecticut," they secured a grant from the Massachusetts General Court to land in the Connecticut River Valley. Although the River Towns settlement was thus authorized by the Massachusetts General Court, rival claims to ownership of the valley were advanced by a group of Englishmen known as the Warwick Patentees, who had been deeded the land by the Crown. The Warwick Patentees were not hostile to the three River Towns — indeed, they welcomed them in the hope that settlers would establish the legality of the Patentees' claims to the lands and increase their value — and in the winter of 1635–36 the River Towns entered into an agreement with the Warwick Patentees whereby they claimed ownership of the lands they were occupying by virtue of the authority of the Patentees. The emigrants did not mind being freed from the restraining hand of Massachusetts and were pleased with the new agreement, "the Commission for a Provisional Government," which gave them the right to create their own government and to be an independent colony instead of an adjunct to another colony. Massachusetts did not protest the agreement's legality and, with the purchase of the lands from the Indians, the River Town settlers found themselves owners of a colony they named Connecticut, whose legality was recognized by their colonial neighbors, the English Crown, and the natives of the area.[2]

The strong potential for trade offered by the location on New England's greatest river and the excellence of the surrounding lands for farming motivated the founders of these three towns — not any desire to begin a religious experiment contrary to the Massachusetts one. These settlers were farmers who wanted an ample supply of fertile land and hopeful traders who wanted accessibility to markets; except for minor variations they duplicated the Massachusetts religious and political model. The largest party of Massachusetts families to emigrate, the congregation led by Thomas Hooker in 1636, drove with it from Cambridge to Hartford 160 head of cattle and large numbers of sheep, swine, and fowl. The location of the three towns was no fortuitous accident; the river was ideal for trade — it had few rapids and many tributaries going inland that could be navigated by canoes and small boats, and the main channel was deep enough to admit seagoing vessels. The settlers also realized how abundant a supply of good fish the river furnished.[3]

The second pocket of settlement within the borders of present-

day Connecticut developed nearly simultaneously with the formation of the River Towns, when in July of 1635 the Warwick Patentees commissioned John Winthrop, Jr., to locate a good harbor at
the mouth of the Connecticut River, build a fort there to guard the
entrance from Long Island Sound to interior Connecticut, and
settle a community. All of this he did later in that year, but the best
available harbor was blocked by a sand bar and the land in the
immediate vicinity was not fertile. Hence, while Saybrook, as the
settlement was named, occupied a crucial strategic position and
quickly became important as a military post, it never developed
into a commercial entrepôt and did not become a productive farming community until the 1650s and 1660s, when new settlers
pushed inland within its boundaries to more fertile soil. Saybrook's
economic weaknesses prevented it from becoming a serious rival to
the River Towns as a competing colony, and in 1644 the Saybrook
Patentees negotiated an agreement with Connecticut in which their
settlement was in effect sold to the River Towns and submitted to
their jurisdiction.[4]

South of the River Towns and west of Saybrook another pocket
of settlement, which began with the founding of a mercantile trading post in 1638, did ultimately challenge the hegemony of Connecticut Colony. New Haven, the name given the post, was settled
by Puritan merchants looking for a trade center site, and seemed
ideally located for commercial purposes; it had friendly surrounding Indians, possessed a fine harbor and navigable rivers running
to a fertile backcountry, and was situated 134 miles south of Boston
and 76 miles north of New York. While farming was not completely ignored, New Haven in its first years placed its emphasis on
trade, though it initially failed to become the entrepôt envisaged by
its founders. New Haven's undeveloped hinterland gave the
founders no products for export, and they were unable to compete
with the direct trade of New York and Boston with England.
Primarily, the approximately three hundred first settlers of New
Haven came directly from England and were led by men who
enjoyed more social position in the home isles than the founders of
any other New England enterprise. Much criticized by other colonists for putting "too much of their stock and estates in building
of fair and stately houses," the New Haven leadership, while not
entirely giving up its dreams for commerce, changed the preponderant emphasis in the colony to agriculture in 1640. This activity
also floundered initially, because many of the people and most of

the leaders lacked agricultural skills, but over the course of the decade of the 1640s New Haven became a successful farming community. The New Haven settlers had no legal claim to the area in English law; they purchased their lands from the local Indian sachem in two separate transactions and received from him title to a large but vaguely defined territory.[5]

On either side of New Haven, Guilford in the east and Milford in the west, two plantations independent of any colonial jurisdiction, were formed in 1639 by groups emigrating primarily from England. The Guilford founders, mostly farmers, unlike their New Haven neighbors, sought a plantation in the New World in order to be free to enjoy the ministry of a brilliant divine, Henry Whitfield. Milford similarly was founded by families from Herefordshire, England, from Wethersfield, and from Dorchester and Roxbury, Massachusetts, who wanted to form a settlement around the ministry of one man, Peter Prudden, a figure of inspiring religiosity who had preached in all of these locations. These two short-lived colonies gave up their independence and became towns in the New Haven Colony in 1643, against the wishes of some of their residents; a majority in each of them sought the benefits of the New England Confederation formed in 1643 by Massachusetts Bay, Plymouth, Connecticut, and New Haven. Fearful of Dutch claims to their lands and of Indian raids, Guilford and Milford thought amalgamation with New Haven would afford them the protection of a united front of northern English colonies.[6]

The next independent enclave that would become part of Connecticut was at the mouth of the Thames River near where Long Island Sound meets the ocean. In 1644 the General Court of Massachusetts granted that tireless colonizer John Winthrop, Jr., "a plantation at or near Pequod for iron works." Massachusetts wanted not only to reward the younger Winthrop for his rich services to the colony and to start an iron works but also to settle a plantation near this good harbor and gateway to the interior and claim it for Massachusetts before the settlers of the Connecticut River Towns might attempt a similar establishment. Under Winthrop's personal direction, twelve to fifteen families formed a plantation called Pequod on the west bank of the Thames in the summer of 1645 and began the work of clearing the land and laying out the town. More settlers from Massachusetts arrived in 1646, perhaps doubling the existing population; when an entire congregation of at least a dozen families arrived in 1651 from Gloucester,

Massachusetts, Pequod's permanency was assured. The area, however, was also claimed by the Connecticut Colony under the authority of the Warwick Patent, and even Winthrop acknowledged that it was unclear under whose jurisdiction the new plantation should be. Connecticut obtained a favorable imperial court decision in 1646 and again in 1647, and although Massachusetts did not accept either decision, the Pequod settlers did, and the plantation was organized as a town in Connecticut Colony. The name New London replaced Pequod in 1658.[7]

The four clusters of settlement — the three River Towns of Windsor, Wethersfield, and Hartford which constituted the original colony of Connecticut; Saybrook; New Haven, Guilford, and Milford; and New London — all settled independently of one another, were brought together under the leadership of the River Towns to form the enlarged colony of Connecticut. Saybrook recognized the superior economic and political power of the River Towns, and New London recognized their superior legal claims; only New Haven colony maintained a lengthy independent existence — when England included it in the lands granted to Connecticut Colony in the Charter of 1662, it resisted the process with all its energy until resistance literally would have meant rebellion against the Crown. Each of these four areas of settlement served as a nucleus from which other towns were peopled until by 1675 the entire coastline and major river valleys were settled. Emigrants from the three River Towns settled Fairfield, Stratford, Farmington, Middletown, Norwalk, Killingworth, Haddam, and Woodbury; Saybrook emigrants founded Lyme and Norwich; New London emigrants founded Stonington and aided in the settling of Norwich; New Haven emigrants settled Wallingford and Derby. Branford and Stamford, settled by residents of the three River Towns, were incorporated as towns in New Haven Colony before it was absorbed by Connecticut.* The southernmost and westernmost town in present-day Connecticut, Greenwich, settled by drift-

---

* I use the term "incorporation" to designate the status New Haven and Connecticut gave towns when it legally recognized them. One corporation, which is what each colony was, cannot incorporate another, and hence technically the communities were not incorporated. This distinction is only theoretical, however, since no one questioned the towns' status and they always functioned as incorporated entities. Briefly, during the period of the Dominion of New England, when colonial governments were being challenged by England, this anomaly worried Connecticut authorities.

ers of questionable reputations and unknown origins, was the only Connecticut town not peopled from one of these four sources; it was successively under the jurisdiction of the Dutch, Stamford, New Haven Colony, and ultimately Connecticut in 1656.

With the exception of Greenwich, and to a lesser extent Derby, Saybrook, and Stonington, the method of town planting in this period was the same in each community. Towns were founded by groups of families averaging 31.0 families per town, who moved en masse to the town site, and town government or legal incorporation quickly followed settlement; the twenty-five towns averaged 2.9 years between first settlement and the creation of the town, if one excepts Derby, whose settlement and incorporation were delayed by conflicting claims of land ownership. Similarly, the motivation for town planting displays some consistency. Although several towns were founded by congregations who specifically moved to enjoy the ministry of one man, and although trade considerations were uppermost in the minds of the founders of a few towns, the overwhelming desire for fertile land motivated the vast majority of these early settlers.[8]

This quest for land to farm can best be seen by examining another distinguishing characteristic of the towns settled in this time period — the large area each town encompassed. Almost none of the towns had firm borders when settled and most sought to enlarge their original claims through additional purchases from the Indians. Most stopped extending their boundaries only when they came in conflict with neighboring towns, and the endemic boundary disputes among the towns reveal the depth of the desire of town planters to secure all the land possible. This quest for land reflects an attempt by Connecticut town founders to establish an agricultural base sufficiently large to sustain the needs of future generations. The twenty-five towns averaged 106.3 square miles each when the final borders were clearly outlined and ranged from the huge tracts of the three largest — Farmington, Woodbury, and Windsor, with 224.1, 183.8, and 173.8 square miles, respectively — to the more modest holdings of Branford, Killingworth, and Greenwich, with 53.7, 53.2, and 50.6 square miles, respectively. Even the smaller areas of these latter three towns were large when compared to the 6 x 6-mile towns (36 square miles) laid out in the nineteenth-century Middle West and supposedly patterned on the New England system. When measured by region, the seven towns along the Connecticut River that averaged 117 square miles were the largest ones, and the towns east and west of the river were nearly equal in average size, 95 square miles. A major difference in size existed between inland towns, which averaged 130 square miles, and coastal towns, which averaged 88 square miles, reflecting a keener competition for the coastal lands, perceived to be potentially more valuable.

Still another distinguishing feature of the period, the importance early settlers attached to location on accessible waterways, is evident from the sites of these twenty-five towns. Even the four towns removed from the coastline and the major river valleys were located on rivers of significant secondary potential for transportation: Farmington and Simsbury on the Farmington River, Wallingford on the Quinnipiac, and Woodbury on the upper reaches of the Housatonic. Water transportation was important not only to settlers interested in extensive trade; at the most one-fourth of the towns settled in the period had visions of becoming mercantile centers. Farmers valued access to the outside world and viewed waterways as their natural link to it. Americans of the nineteenth and to a somewhat lesser extent the eighteenth century saw water as a buffer zone — as an isolating factor — but to the seventeenth-century colonists it was a highway — an integrating factor. The inland towns founded on rivers always settled on both banks and encompassed the river within their boundaries. The conception that rivers united, not divided, began to erode, however, as early as 1667, when Saybrook divided into two separate towns with the Connecticut River as their boundary. This process would be repeated frequently in colonial and Revolutionary Connecticut until all the towns on major rivers were divided into separate communities bounded by the rivers.

The importance of being located on a major waterway, however, may not have been as *overwhelming* as the twenty-five locations would at first suggest, for it must be remembered that the land along the major rivers and the coastline was generally the most fertile; hence even if there had been no preponderant desire for communication, these areas still would have been the best sites for farmers to occupy. Moreover, they were easily accessible as sites for new towns; the places removed from waterways had yet to be explored thoroughly by the Connecticut Puritans. At times a location on water clearly was the operative factor in planting a town;

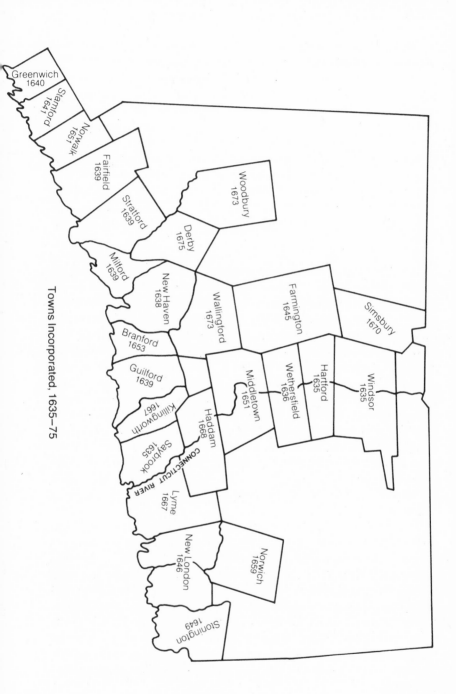

Towns Incorporated, 1635–75

Greenwich 1640
Stamford 1641
Norwalk 1651
Fairfield 1639
Stratford 1639
Milford 1639
Woodbury 1673
Derby 1675
New Haven 1638
Wallingford 1673
Farmington 1645
Simsbury 1670
Branford 1653
Guilford 1639
Killingworth 1667
Saybrook 1635
CONNECTICUT RIVER
Middletown 1651
Wethersfield 1636
Hartford 1635
Windsor 1635
Haddam 1668
Lyme 1667
New London 1646
Norwich 1659
Stonington 1649

New London, Saybrook, Lyme, and Stonington, for instance, did not have land especially conducive to farming, yet were among the early towns settled. At other times soil conditions and the terrain seemed to be the operative factors: colonists chose Farmington over Middletown as a site because of Middletown's allegedly poor land, even though Farmington had a much less advantageous location; Haddam, with the poorest land for farming in the Connecticut River Valley, was the last town settled there; and Killingworth, with the poorest soil on the coastline, was the last town established there.

PERIOD 2:

Farmers and Speculators: Settling the Interior
Uplands and the Secondary River Valleys, 1686–1734

IN THE forty-eight years between 1686 and 1734 twenty-nine new towns were incorporated; twenty-four of them were newly settled and five of them were formed by hiving off from older communities. Most of the newly settled towns were situated on small rivers, unnavigable except for small canoes and flatboats but useful for power for mills and a supply of fresh water; and many of them were on the less fertile soil and less easily farmed terrain loosely termed "uplands" by the colonists. This desire to be near water is not surprising; as geographers have found in analyzing the locations of peasant villages around the world, a readily available supply of water is always sought by farmers siting a settlement. The geographer James Lemon shows that accessibility to water was the single mose important criterion in selecting village sites in colonial Pennsylvania.[9]

Connecticut's topography consists of four main areas: the Connecticut River Valley, which bisects the colony and ranges from six to thirty-five miles wide; the coastal strip of lowlands extending eight to thirty miles inland; and the eastern and western hill country. Both the sections of hill country do have small and medium-sized valleys of lowlands within them. The towns settled before 1675 occupied the Connecticut River Valley and coast, and what remained for settlement were the eastern and western sections of hill country. The physical nature of these areas was not nearly as conducive to settlement as that of the sections settled earlier. The

General Court in 1680, when writing the Committee for Trade and Foreign Plantations in England, commented: "Most land that is fit for planting is taken up. What remains must be subdued, and gained out of the fire as it were by hard blows and for small recompense."[10] Yet, if title to the land was secure, the new towns had little trouble attracting settlers willing to exert these "hard blows." The heaviest concentration of new towns was in the eastern part of the colony; twenty-two were planted east of the Connecticut River, while only seven were planted west of it. The rhythm of creation was reasonably even; after an eleven-year hiatus in town formation between 1675 and 1686, no period of more than five years elapsed between the creations of towns until 1727. Almost exclusively the desire for lands to farm attracted settlers to these towns; none of them possessed particularly advantageous locations for trade and none was settled for specifically religious purposes. Speculation for profit and the resultant absentee ownership of land, lacking in the founding of towns in the first period except in the cases of Farmington and Simsbury, became factors in the founding of many of these towns. After the Narragansett War the General Court became persuaded that the lands under its jurisdiction were fit subjects for individual speculation, good sources for colony revenue, and a handy means of rewarding soldiers and statesmen.[11] Even with this willingness to assign some of the responsibility for starting new towns to land profiteers, the colony government still attempted to supervise the process of town formation and keep it orderly. In most cases they were successful; in a few cases they were not.

All of the new towns created in the west maintained the orderly processes that characterized the founding of the first towns, and three of them, Waterbury, Danbury, and Ridgefield, maintained the earlier communal spirit.[12] Durham, New Milford, Newtown, and Litchfield, also settled with little contention or division, differed sharply, however, from the western towns just listed in one important respect and reflected the new era of the speculator town. All four of these towns had original owners interested in profiting from the land, not settling on it, and three of the four, Durham, New Milford, and Newtown, were settled by people who were unknown to one another and not by group migration. The original owners of these three towns were granted the land for either cash payment or meritorious service rendered the colony and in turn

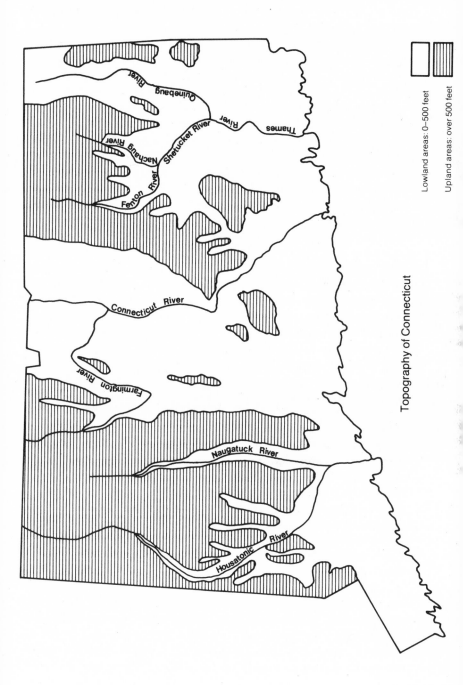

Topography of Connecticut

Lowland areas: 0–500 feet

Upland areas: over 500 feet

sold it to men who moved to the towns as separate individuals who had purchased shares in a land company.[13]

Through a peculiar set of circumstances, the area that was to be the future town of Litchfield was owned by the towns of Hartford and Windsor and not by the General Assembly. In 1687, when Connecticut was ordered to surrender its charter as a self-governing colony and become part of the imperial unit the Dominion of New England, it feared the loss of its jurisdiction over the ungranted and unsettled lands in the northwestern part of the colony and in an act of chicanery deeded this huge tract of wilderness to the towns of Hartford and Windsor. The colony could then claim that the northwest was part of two established towns, not mere wilderness but an integral part of already settled communities. The Dominion of New England, short-lived and beset with problems, never sufficiently grasped the reins of government in Connecticut to challenge this legal fiction, and hence Hartford and Windsor remained proprietors of what were called the "western lands." The ownership, existing only on paper, meant little until 1719, when the two established towns, after commissioning a survey of their domain, divided a portion of it into sixty land rights and sold fifty-seven of them to purchasers interested in starting a new plantation; they reserved the remaining three for religious purposes in the proposed new town.[14]

Most of the settlement in the east occurred in the future Windham County, and much of this was on land owned by one man, James Fitch, Jr., whose claim to parts of the area was challenged by the heirs of John Winthrop, Jr. In 1653 Winthrop had bought from the Indians, without the permission of the General Court, a large, vaguely defined tract of land in the area. This omission of consent by the colony government made the legality of the transaction dubious, but in 1671 Winthrop, who was then governor of the colony, by dint of great personal effort persuaded the General Court to validate the deed. In 1680 Fitch assumed ownership of his huge tract of land, which partially overlapped the land claimed by Winthrop, when the Indian sachem Oweneco, in order to stop men from "taking advantage of me when I am in drink, by causing me to sign deeds," sold him all of present Windham County, excluding an area called "Joshua's Tract" already sold to a group of men from Norwich. Having secured the General Assembly's recognition of this purchase as legal, Fitch personally became almost as important a force in town planting in Windham County as the General Assembly itself. Inevitably, disorder surfaced as a result of the overlapping claims of Fitch and the Winthrop heirs.[15]

The first town created in Windham County in this period, the shire town of Windham, was not adversely affected by the grandiose land purchases of Fitch and Winthrop, inasmuch as it was located on Joshua's Tract, that area excluded from Fitch's holdings. However, settlement of Plainfield, the second town in the county, engendered bitter conflict lasting over a decade. The area in which Plainfield was settled, the so-called Quinebaug Country located within the overlapping claims of Fitch and the Winthrops, had its settlement delayed because no one wanted to hazard planting a town on land disputed by rival owners. However, in the early 1690s, sixteen Massachusetts families moved to the area after purchasing lands from the Winthrops. They were followed by about an equal number of Connecticut families, some of whom had purchased their lands from Fitch, whose claims they regarded as superior. Few details are known of the first years of Quinebaug; the scanty evidence indicates that the settlers lived a chaotic life, staunchly resisted outside authority, and governed themselves in vigilante fashion. Holdings of individuals who had purchased land from either Fitch or the Winthrops overlapped, with resultant occasional violence. Despite the confusion, Quinebaug grew and became extended several miles on both sides of the Quinebaug River. In 1699 the settlement contained about thirty families, two-thirds of whom petitioned the General Assembly to make them a town and, because "this place lyeth under many pretended claims," to designate a committee of "indifferent, uninterested persons to lay out allotments and to equalize such as have been in part laid out." The Assembly granted the petition, Quinebaug became a town, and the committee appointed held a meeting in May of 1701 in Quinebaug to settle the conflicting claims. All interested parties were present: Wait Winthrop and his counselors, Fitch and his, Oweneco and other sachems, and the residents of the new town who espoused the rival claimants. The committee took testimony, spent four days exploring the area, and then reported back to the General Assembly the bounds of the Fitch and Winthrop purchases, confirming that both purchases did have claims to validity and that they did overlap. This investigation and further negotiations with the townspeople resulted in the division, in 1703, of

Quinebaug into two separate towns — Plainfield on the east bank of the river and Canterbury on the west; generally, settlers on the west bank had purchased their lands from Fitch and those on the east had purchased theirs from the Winthrops. Canterbury contained ten families at its inception and the Assembly thought its creation the only way to solve the thorny problem and promote peace. To everyone's chagrin, dividing the town did not settle the controversy, and after three more years of local contention the Assembly appointed a six-man committee to try once again to end the difficulties. This committee took a strong stand and concluded that the Winthrops' claims were not tenable. It successfully persuaded the Winthrops to renounce their claims in return for receiving one thousand acres in each of the two towns and assurances that the people who in good faith had purchased lands from the Winthrops would have their titles confirmed. Fitch adherents reacted angrily to this agreement, protesting, with some justice, that while the committee ruled the Winthrop purchase invalid, the terms of the settlement acted as if the purchase were indeed legal. Still, excepting the two thousand-acre tracts, the remaining undivided lands were in the hands of Fitch and those settlers who had purchased their rights from him, and this substantial source of future wealth was eventually enough to assuage their feelings and quiet the protest; peace came to Plainfield and Canterbury and they assumed the normal temper of lawful towns.[16]

In another controversial town founding, Ashford, also located on land purchased from Fitch, had its settlement and incorporation marred by two bitter disputes. The first one arose out of Fitch's sale in 1708 of overlapping tracts of land in Ashford to two groups, one led by a James Corbin and the other by a John Chandler. The two groups of speculators each sold land to prospective settlers, and when families began to arrive to claim their lands in 1711, a situation developed like that in Plainfield, wherein purchasers from two rival groups of speculators disputed ownership of the same land. Unlike the earlier Plainfield residents, however, those of Ashford managed, over a three-year period of acrimony, to sort out their problems; in 1714 they presented a united front to the General Assembly and asked for town status, which was granted. A new dispute surfaced in 1716 when the then-united townspeople of Ashford fought the speculator proprietors over control of the undivided lands remaining in the town. The Corbin and Chandler groups of speculators, former rivals, banded together to fight what they regarded as an illegal attempt to deprive them of their ownership of Ashford's lands in the first titanic battle in Connecticut history between resident and absentee proprietors. The dispute reached the General Assembly, where an act "giving the land to the inhabitants" passed the lower house but was defeated in the upper chamber. Rebuffed by this loss, the townspeople fought off an attempt by the speculators to gain control of the town government; the absentee proprietors demanded the right to vote at town meetings and when the inhabitants denied it, the town briefly split into two meetings, each one of which claimed to be the legitimate government. The controversy went through several General Assembly appeals and was finally decided by a compromise arranged by the Assembly in 1719, whereby the town paid the Chandler speculators three pounds per hundred acres to quit their claims to the land and allowed the Corbin speculators uncontested claim to twenty-five hundred acres, provided they deeded over to the town the other thirty-five hundred acres they claimed. The Ashford controversy forced the Assembly to consider for which purpose new towns were created — family settlement or speculator profit. Unable to endorse one principle to the exclusion of the other, the colony government wavered and compromised.[17]

One should not be misled, however, by a few highly visible battles into believing that controversy surrounded all the new towns in this period. Between 1698 and 1734 twelve additional towns were settled and incorporated in relative peace, filling in most of the uninhabited eastern part of the colony. Although developed and settled separately, their evolutions were nearly identical. Despite some conflicting claims, no heated controversy surrounded their foundings and no serious acrimony disturbed their original settlers. Small groups of speculator proprietors interested in profits bought the land from the Indians, or obtained it as a reward for civic or military service, and sold it in lots and rights to those who would become resident proprietors, interested in settling and farming the land. It was not a group migration. Residents from throughout Connecticut and Massachusetts, strangers to one another, moved in by piecemeal and assumed ownership of their land. The process was monitored by the General Assembly — in some cases committees of the Assembly supervised the laying out of the town — and resulted in a slow but orderly founding devoid of any early feelings of communalism. The towns were thinly populated at the time each was incorporated, ranging from nine families in the least populous to twenty-three in the most.[18]

Preston, Glastonbury, Mansfield, Groton, and East Haddam, five towns that hived off from earlier settled ones, round out the towns created in this period. Each requested separation from an older town because of attendant difficulties in traveling to church worship and town meetings. In all five cases the transportation problem involved crossing water. Preston, incorporated in 1687, technically was a new town, not a hived-off one, but in reality it had always been a part of the Norwich settlement known as East Norwich. Its residents applied to the General Court for incorporation as a town, citing the distance that separated them from the main settlement and the fact that they had to "hazard their lives over water" to get to Norwich's center.[19] Fifteen years later, in 1702, the residents of the village in northwest Windham that was to become Mansfield echoed these same sentiments in their petition for town status and complained of "the great difficulties, inconveniences, and hazards . . . by reason of . . . being settled so remote from the south part of said town and the deep and dangerous river lying between."[20] For similar reasons, Glastonbury and East Haddam on the east bank of the Connecticut separated from Wethersfield and Haddam in 1693 and 1734, respectively, and Groton on the east bank of the Thames separated from New London in 1705. Glastonbury, Mansfield, Groton, and East Haddam had each received status as an independent church society previous to becoming an independent town. Preston did not go through this intermediate step on the way to townhood because it was discovered that its lands lay outside Norwich's legal bounds; hence, there was no need to separate from the mother town in stages.[21]

By the end of the second period of town formation all of the land in Connecticut except for approximately eight hundred square miles in the northwest corner was settled and under the local jurisdiction of town government. The towns constituted in this period were usually much smaller in population at the time of their incorporation, averaging 20.4 families, than the towns of period one had been. The physical size of towns in period two was also substantially smaller, averaging 64.9 square miles. The average size of towns east of the Connecticut River, 59.0 square miles, especially declined compared to the earlier towns; rival land claims, lessening

Towns Incorporated, 1686–1734

* Settled earlier as part of another town

Killingly
1708

Voluntown
1721

Plainfield
1699

Preston
1687
*

Groton
1705
*

Pomfret
1713

Canterbury
1703

Union
1734

Ashford
1714

Windham
1692

Stafford
1719

Willington
1727

Mansfield
1702
*

Lebanon
1700

Tolland
1715

Coventry
1712

Bolton
1720

Hebron
1708

Colchester
1698

East Haddam
1734
*

CONNECTICUT RIVER

Glastonbury
1693
*

Durham
1704

Waterbury
1686

Litchfield
1719

Newtown
1711

New Milford
1712

Danbury
1687

Ridgefield
1708

supplies of land, and the natural barriers imposed by the variegated uplands regions combined to limit the size of towns in period
two. Certainly the size of towns did not decline because Connecti-
cuters no longer wanted land to farm. Much of the land settled in
period two was relatively isolated upland of marginal quality, but if
claims to land were secure it seldom went without settlers; even the
unusually barren land of two of the towns, Willington and Union,
attracted enough residents to allow them to incorporate. All of the
towns created between 1686 and 1734 owed their settlement to
farmers seeking land; not a single town in this period was peopled
by religious dissenters or hopeful merchants. Nor did many of
them owe their original populations to communal movements.
Group migrations founded only six of the twenty-four newly settled towns; acquisitive persons who did not previously know their
fellow townspeople founded the others. The individualistic
piecemeal process by which the towns were settled accounts for the
long average gap, 10.5 years, between first settlement of the towns
and their actual incorporation.

While a desire to farm almost exclusively motivated the first
settlers of these towns, a desire to profit almost exclusively motivated the first purchasers of them. Land speculation, playing an
important role in all of the towns in the east and in four of the
seven in the west, took many forms: individual or group
speculators purchased land directly from the Indians with and
without General Assembly sanction; speculators purchased it from
the General Assembly or had it given to them by the Assembly as a
reward for political or military service; and finally the General
Assembly itself profited from the planting of some towns by selling
land directly to individual settlers instead of deeding it free of
charge as it had done in the earlier period.

The speculative nature of the founding of towns in this period
sometimes engendered controversy and sometimes unduly pro-
longed the settlement of individual towns. At times different
groups of speculators each claimed title to an area and fought with
each other, and at times speculator absentee proprietors and
farmer resident proprietors battled over control of the lands. The
General Assembly several times was faced with the difficult tasks of
deciding between the claims of rival speculators and of judging
whether the guiding principle for which towns were formed was to
provide profits for capitalists or land for settlers. The Assembly

invariably proposed compromise solutions to land disputes and refused to endorse one group of speculators or one principle exclusively. The highly visible nature of the controversies surrounding the founding of several towns, however, should not obscure the fact that most of the towns in this period were settled with a minimum of discord. Even though much of the immediate responsibility for supervising the planting of new towns was transferred from the colony government to speculators, and even though settlement usually lacked the cohesion and social constraints provided by group migration, the process of town formation and settlement proceeded in an orderly fashion for most towns. Those towns that were wracked by dissension occupied such a prominent place in the Assembly's business that the quiet and relatively peaceful normal pattern of town planting in this period has escaped notice and description. Probably the crucial factor that accounts for this stability in a period with the potentiality of being very chaotic was the nature of the new town residents. Unlike speculating in land, moving to a new town offered few opportunities for getting rich quick — profit came only with hard work. Hence, most new settlers were not adventurers but solid family men and women in their early adulthood, anxious to build a community with enduring and stable qualities.[22]

PERIOD 3:

*Speculators, Farmers and Diplomats: Settling
the Northwest and Rounding out the Borders, 1737–1761*

BETWEEN 1737 and 1766 fourteen new towns were founded in the only remaining unsettled area of the colony, Litchfield County in the northwest; eleven of these attracted enough settlers to be incorporated in this period, while the remaining three were too thinly populated to receive township privileges. The colony incorporated five additional towns in this period, all of which had been settled earlier; four had been under Massachusetts' jurisdiction but were within Connecticut's boundaries, and the other, sold and laid out in the first quarter of the eighteenth century, had its incorporation delayed by an insufficiency of settlers.

Speculation played an important role in the founding of the fourteen new towns, but it was speculation of a different kind from that of the preceding period: companies of proprietors ranging in membership from 41 to 182 men planned each of the new towns with a degree of organization unknown among earlier town planters. Towns were carefully surveyed and laid out and divided among settlers by precise formulae. Some of the original proprietors became actual settlers, but more were speculators who sold their shares for profit. The new towns, smaller in land mass than past towns and almost exclusively hilly, rugged terrain of even poorer quality for farming than the towns in the eastern uplands, had little trouble attracting settlers, except in a few cases where the notorious barrenness of the land did discourage buyers and retard settlement. These new towns were typically settled by individuals and not by group migration, but several of them did have large blocks of settlers emigrating from the same town, who undoubtedly shared a feeling of communality.

The lands of Litchfield County on which these new towns were planted were originally part of that giant chunk of land deeded in 1687 to Hartford and Windsor to thwart the Dominion of New England. Few believed, when the crisis caused by the Dominion's creation passed, that Hartford and Windsor would be able to sustain their claims to the land. The question of ownership of the tract was not fully aired until, in the early 1720s, people petitioned the Assembly for grants of land there. Hartford and Windsor, aware that they would not be allowed to monopolize most of the remaining unsettled land in the colony, pressed their claims in hopes of retaining some of the land or being compensated for its loss. Amidst a welter of petitions, counter-petitions, and deep acrimony, a committee named by the Assembly reached a typical compromise decision in 1726, which upheld the validity of the original grant but advised the Assembly to assume ownership of about half of the lands and confirm the two old towns in their ownership of the rest. The General Assembly enacted the committee's compromise and decreed that Hartford and Windsor retained ownership of the lands east of the town of Litchfield, but that the lands west of it reverted to the colony. This boundary line was adjusted eastward when, upon surveying, it was found to give more than the agreement specified to the two old towns. Thus, of the new towns settled in this period, seven were settled under the supervision of Hartford and Windsor and seven under the supervision of the General Assembly.[23]

Hartford and Windsor, upon receiving secure titles to their land, immediately appointed joint committees who divided the land between them; Hartford received 130 square miles that included the future towns of New Hartford, Winchester, and Hartland, and the eastern half of Harwinton; Windsor received 128 square miles that included the future towns of Colebrook, Barkhamsted, and Torrington, and the western half of Harwinton. By a General Assembly enactment each person on the Hartford and Windsor tax lists of 1720 received a share of his town's western lands in proportion to the size of his assessed estate. Companies were formed by the two parent towns for each of the future towns and each taxpayer was designated a proprietor in one of the companies. The companies were then free to lay out their towns as they saw fit.[24]

Harwinton, whose name derives from the two parent towns, was the first town planted under the aegis of Hartford and Windsor; it was close to the two old towns, a cleared road ran from them through it to Litchfield, and it was their joint property. The West Harwinton Company of Windsor, comprised of fifty-four men, made its first division of land in 1732, and the East Harwinton Company of Hartford, comprised of forty men, followed suit the next year. Once the lots and shares were distributed, each recipient was free to occupy or sell his consignment. Most sold their land and rights, but many original owners or their sons did move to the new town, and the two parent towns furnished a substantial portion of Harwinton's early settlers. A large number of people from Branford purchased land from the proprietors; other purchasers came from all over the colony. By 1737, when Harwinton successfully petitioned to be incorporated, it had a population of over thirty families.[25] In similar fashion the New Hartford Company of Hartford and the Torrington Company of Windsor also organized and laid out their new towns in quick order.

Settlement of the other four towns owned by Hartford and Windsor — Hartland, Barkhamsted, Winchester, and Colebrook — was slower because their "rock-ribbed hillsides," in the words of one local historian, "offered little incentive."[26] When Hartford and Windsor originally valued these four towns for the purposes of fairly apportioning land among taxpayers, the land of each of the four was valued substantially lower — in some cases 50 percent lower — than that of the two parts of Harwinton, New Hartford, and Torrington.[27] Hartland, the most successful of the

four in attracting settlers, was not incorporated for over two decades; and the least successful two, Barkhamsted and Colebrook,
did not become towns until 1779, by which time land pressures on
population had become acute and sons of Windsor proprietors
moved to the sites.

None of the other towns in the colony's share of western lands
had as much difficulty in attracting settlers; only in Norfolk, adjacent to Winchester and Colebrook, was securing settlers a problem.
Indeed, the General Assembly experienced the opposite problem.
It first planned to offer the towns for sale by subscription but was
deluged with so many requests that the lands were almost immediately oversubscribed. The Assembly then decided that without
enough land to satisfy all those who wanted it, the best way to
dispose of its western lands was through a series of public auctions
for each town. The Assembly finally agreed in May of 1737, after
great debate, to divide each town site into fifty-three shares, three
of which would be reserved for public purposes and the other fifty
sold by competitive bidding. In a four-month period that started
with the sale of Goshen at New Haven in December, 1737, and
ended with the sale of Kent at Windham in March, 1738, the fifty
shares in all seven towns were put on the block in a series of auctions held in the various county seats; all shares were quickly
snapped up except those of Norfolk. Most were purchased by
speculators, but many were bought by people intent on settling
their new land.[28]

The first four towns created out of the colony lands, Canaan,
Sharon, Goshen, and Kent, were all incorporated in 1739, just one
year after their sale. Soon after Cornwall and Salisbury incorporated, in 1740 and 1741, respectively. The process of division and
settlement was virtually the same in all six cases. The proprietors,
usually numbering about forty because a few men bought two or
three of the fifty rights, met within a month of the auction and
elected a committee to survey the land, plan highways, and divide a
portion of the town into lots, which were "pitched" for by chance
drawing. This process took less than four months, and once it was
completed the proprietors were free to settle their land or try to sell
it for a profit. Approximately 40 percent of the proprietors became
settlers and moved to the new towns, while the remaining 60 percent disposed of their land to others. In the two towns where the
origins of the settlers have been precisely determined, Kent and

Sharon, over three-fourths of the first settlers in each emigrated from just four towns. Thus, even though the land was bought individually and not by companies, there were in the towns discernible groups of people with a shared past.[29]

. Four other towns were formed in the colony when Suffield, Enfield, Somers, and Woodstock were detached from Massachusetts and placed under Connecticut's jurisdiction. All four towns were settled by Massachusetts inhabitants in the 1680s, but there was no doubt in anyone's mind by 1740 that the towns were entirely south of the Bay Colony's border. Massachusetts' legal claim to the four towns was based solely on an agreement negotiated between the two colonies in 1713, which had never received royal confirmation. Upon the requests of a majority of inhabitants in each of the four towns, who thought their communities' economies would benefit from annexation to Connecticut, the Connecticut General Assembly renounced the bargain and sent an agent to England to argue its case in 1749. Massachusetts, not surprisingly, fought the annexation attempt first by sending blustering and threatening letters to Governor Jonathan Law and second by exercising physical force to make the towns pay their colony taxes. In England, Massachusetts argued before the Board of Trade that although Connecticut might have made a bad bargain in 1713, she was now obliged to live with it. Connecticut, in turn, admitted that the agreement explicitly gave the towns to Massachusetts but said that the boundaries agreed upon so clearly violated Connecticut's charter that the agreement should be declared null and void. Connecticut won the decision undoubtedly because the Board of Trade, faced with a difficult choice that could have justifiably gone either way, chose to respect the wishes of the towns.[30]

With the annexation of the four disputed towns, Connecticut's external borders assumed the form they have today. With the settlement of the last of Litchfield County, all the land in the colony had been granted to towns. The period from 1737 to 1766 can best be described as the final phase of forming the colony and settling its lands. All future towns created would have to be carved out of territory already inhabited and already belonging to existing towns.

Once the General Assembly divided the western land between Hartford and Windsor and the colony, the settlement of Litchfield County proceeded in an orderly, controlled manner, free from

contention. In some cases absentee proprietors and resident proprietors did disagree over town policy, but in none of the towns was
the ownership of the land disputed, any boundary contested, or
settlement delayed because of conflicting claims to the land. In nine
of the fourteen Litchfield County towns the process from proprietary formation to incorporation was remarkably quick, taking less
than five years. In the five towns where the development was not as
rapid, it was delayed because of the exceptionally poor quality of
the land. All fourteen communities were inhabited by people want-
ing land to farm, and their settlement is symptomatic of demographic pressures upon the land supply in the older towns. The
land of Litchfield County at its best was of only acceptable or marginal quality when compared to the land of the river valleys, and it
was much more difficult to subdue and cultivate because of its
rugged terrain and lack of significant clearings — at its worst it
verged on total barrenness. Had it not been for the demographic
pressures in the older towns, the settlement of the northwest would
not have occurred when it did. The smaller average land mass of
the newly settled towns in this period, 45.6 square miles, also reflects the pressure of population on land. Instead of creating five or
six towns with large land areas that would take three generations to
be fully utilized, the Assembly and Hartford and Windsor carved
out fourteen small towns whose available lands would almost all be
distributed within a decade of town formation. Although no comprehensive study of town size in Massachusetts has been attempted,
the available work suggests that no such drastic shrinkage in town
land grants occurred in the Bay Colony in the eighteenth century.
This difference undoubtedly reflects the fact that Massachusetts
had more uninhabited land at mid-eighteenth century than Connecticut did and could still afford the luxury of large towns with
significant amounts of undivided acreage. Yet, the difficulty five of
the Litchfield towns had in attracting settlers, compared to the
quickness with which lands of the other nine were snapped up,
shows that although Connecticut farmers may have been willing to
move and endure hardships to acquire farms, they were not sufficiently desperate to have lost the ability to discriminate among
types of land. The relatively slow settlement of the five towns is
indicative of the remarkably accurate assessment of land quality by
Connecticut farmers of the time. With the exception of Winchester, the various towns' settlement rates reflect their good judgment
of farm land quality.

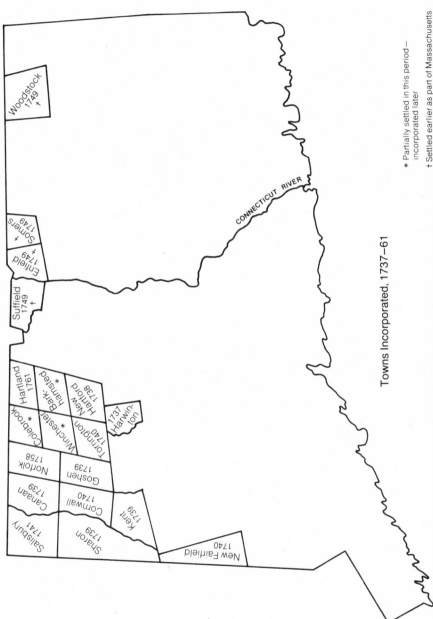

Towns Incorporated, 1737–61

Woodstock 1749 +

Somers 1749 +

Enfield 1749 +

Suffield 1749 +

CONNECTICUT RIVER

Hartland 1761

Bark- hamsted *

New Hartford 1738

Colebrook *

Winchester *

Torrington 1740

1737 Harwin- ton

Norfolk 1758

Goshen 1739

Canaan 1739

Cornwall 1740

Kent 1739

Salisbury 1741

Sharon 1739

New Fairfield 1740

* Partially settled in this period—
   incorporated later

† Settled earlier as part of Massachusetts

While the towns of this period of settlement were physically much smaller than earlier towns, they were much larger in population at date of incorporation, averaging 30.8 families, than the towns of the preceding period. This change also reflects the demographic pressures, and it had the effect of raising the population density and giving more people a chance to own land. None of the new towns in Litchfield County was incorporated with less than twenty-five families, whereas most of the eastern towns settled in the second period had been. Northeastern Connecticut towns had been settled a generation earlier by small numbers of farmers owning mostly undivided rights to large tracts of vaguely defined and unsurveyed lands. Northwestern Connecticut towns, by contrast, were founded by significantly larger numbers of farmers owning specified lots in clearly bounded and precisely laid out communities. The difference between the two patterns reflects the declining availability of land and the increasing population of the colony.*

PERIOD 4:

Revolutionaries: Carving New Towns out of Old Ones, 1767–1789

STARTING in 1767, when Redding was detached from Fairfield and incorporated as a town in its own right, a wave of town formation began that reached a climax in the 1780s in the aftermath of the Revolutionary struggles. Between 1767 and 1790, the year of the first federal census, twenty-nine new towns were carved out of old ones. Prior to Redding's creation only six towns had hived off in this manner in Connecticut's entire colonial history, and none had done so in the thirty-three years since 1734, when East Haddam separated from Haddam; in sharp contrast, in Massachusetts fifty-nine towns had separated from preexisting ones by 1770.[31] The six towns in Connecticut that did result from town divisions before the Revolutionary struggles were all unusual cases. Lyme, Glastonbury, Groton, and East Haddam were separated from their parent towns by the colony's widest rivers, the Connecticut and the

---

* This discussion will be expanded and made much more specific in chapter two in an analysis of population growth and density.

Thames; Mansfield, although founded as a part of Windham, had been settled as a distinct and separate village from its start; Canterbury was split from Plainfield to settle the conflicting claims of the Fitch and Winthrop proprietors. No group opposed the creation of any of these six towns; the separation of Lyme from Saybrook was called "the loving parting" by participants, and the parent towns in each case unanimously approved of the division.[32] Neither did many outlying parishes aspire to township status. Only five parts of established towns, the parishes of Mortlake, Thompson, Redding, East Windsor, and East Haven, unsuccessfully petitioned the General Assembly for incorporation as towns, and in each case there was opposition from some interested party that the Assembly chose to honor.[33] While new parish creation within old towns reached epidemic levels in the eighteenth century, few parts of established communities sought to go all the way and seek an entirely distinct local identity.* This was undoubtedly because problems were much more severe and vexatious in travel to worship than in getting to town business. Religious services with required attendance were performed at least once and often twice a week, whereas town meetings were seldom held more than twice a year and the freemen, by statute, met only twice a year. Frequently, as a concession to the hardships of travel, town meetings and freemen's meetings would be scheduled on the same day. It did not seem oppressive to most reasonable men to travel a couple of hours a few times yearly.

Although hiving off is a universal way of starting new communities and is a familiar phenomenon to anthropologists and geographers,[34] the creation of twenty-nine new towns out of old towns in just a twenty-two-year period was clearly related to the Revolutionary struggles in three important ways: (1) widespread discussion of the English constitution made Connecticut inhabitants more aware of their rights and privileges and more determined not to be deprived of them, and moreover, the pervasive nature of the Revolutionary spirit made the inhabitants more assertive in demanding these rights and privileges; (2) the necessity of debating the English connection and then of fighting a war dramatically increased the number of town meetings in every town and hence directly exacerbated the hardship of travel over long

* See chapter four below for a discussion of parish creation.

distances to meetings; and (3) the Revolution provided a chance to
reshape the local polity of Connecticut in response to demographic
and economic changes in the past century.

The petitions for new towns in each of the sixty-two cases (the
number was higher than the number of new towns because most
aspiring towns were required to submit several petitions) stressed
as the primary factor that inhabitants in remote areas of the town
were deprived of their opportunity to take part in the decision-
making procedures of the town because they lived at prohibitive
distances from the place of the meeting. The petitioners desiring
township status for Hamden complained that "not a twentieth part
of them" could attend meetings, and the rest were "deprived of any
vote or agency in the management of the affairs of the town, the
choice of town officers, the levying of town taxes."[35] Similarly,
because of their average distance of thirteen miles from the
meetinghouse, the inhabitants of North Fairfield could not "attend
. . . meetings or use the privilege of freemen to elect rulers, to enact
laws, to pay taxes, and transact the business of this state, tho [sic]
they are citizens of this state and their persons and properties are
bound by the laws thereof."[36] Even more explicitly making the link
between the Revolutionary experience and their own, the petitioners for the new town of Woodbridge "heartily embrace[d] the doctrine . . . that *the people* [italics theirs] of every community ought to
have a place either personally or by representation in all regula-
tions made respecting their persons or properties."[37] It was no
fortuitous coincidence that made virtually every aspirant town
stress the need to be directly represented in the election of its rulers
and the levying of its taxes. Nor did it seem farfetched to most to
assert that the distance from home to the meetinghouse, usually
eight to twenty-two miles, made their representation in town government as difficult as American representation in Parliament
would have been.

Not only did Connecticut men develop a heightened sense of the
need for participation in town government, they also developed a
more aggressive style to get their way; before 1767 petitions for
town status *asked* for the privileges in order to bring law and order
to their communities; after 1767, with increasing assertiveness,
they *demanded* their rights and liberties.[38] As one might imagine, a
government willing to fight a war against England for the same
reasons and with equal bumptiousness could oppose these demands only with good cause and even then with difficulty.

The increased activity of the town meeting and its increased importance in decision making contributed significantly to the town-formation process. Town meetings increased in number by at least 300 percent in most towns during the Revolutionary years, and what previously seemed like a perfunctory body became an action-charged forum.* Town meetings not only were held occasionally as often as fourteen times a year, but the meetings frequently lasted two days or were adjourned and reconvened in a week. The petitioners of Amity and Bethany societies in New Haven and Woodbury articulated the problem and argued that the very fact that there were so many town meetings prevented them from attending the meetings; they could travel the great distance a few times a year but not as often as meetings were now being held.[39] The townspeople and the General Assembly were facing the same circumstances — frequent meetings — that led to the proliferation of ecclesiastical societies and the response was the same — bring the meeting closer to the homes of the citizens.

Everywhere in the American colonies the Revolution engendered a questioning spirit that led citizens of the new nation to debate the nature of their government and reshape their institutions in response to newly perceived needs. With so much coming apart it was natural to put Humpty Dumpty back together again in at least partly altered form. No one in Connecticut suggested changing the nature of town government, but over and over again the petitions for new towns stressed that the old community had grown so much in population that it was too unwieldy to be governed as one unit by one town meeting, that the population had so dispersed from the center that many parts of the community no longer were oriented to the original village, and that the outlying parts, previously too small to sustain themselves as towns, had grown to the point where town government for them was not only desirable but eminently feasible. As part of the litany of town formation, all the petitioners listed, as well as long distance from the meetinghouse, the number of their inhabitants, their grand list, and the difficulty large towns had in conducting their business. Referring to the physical size of Farmington, Southington Parish complained that its large extent made "the public business . . . very difficult, troublesome, and inconvenient"; and citing the popula-

* See below, chapter three, for an extended discussion of the increase in meeting activity.

tion size it argued that not only could Farmington get along well
without Southington, but "indeed they are too large to transact . . .
business with ease and advantage."[40] The West Society of Norwich
told the General Assembly that, "by reason of the extent of the
boundaries of said town, the number of inhabitants, magnitude of
the list, it is impossible to conduct the prudential affairs of said
town with that care, prudence and economy which is necessary in
this time of distress."[41] Several of the parishes were not above
pointing out to the Assembly that their square mileage, population,
and grand list were substantially higher than those of the towns
incorporated in Litchfield County in the previous three decades.[42]
One hopeful town included a list of twelve towns with smaller or
similar-sized grand lists.

At their inception, the towns founded in the period prior to 1675
had been easily governable by town-meeting government despite
their large physical size, because they had consisted of small numbers of families clustered together. The great increase in population and its dispersal made town government increasingly difficult,
and the Revolutionary shake-up provided a natural occasion to
rearrange the local political units and reduce them to a size more
manageable by town-meeting government. The original twenty-
five towns of the colony had been large because their founders
were anxious to own as much land as possible and there were few
restraints on the amount of territory the towns could garner. Their
fourth-generation descendants, however, who were now spread
over the vast extent of those towns, realized that the economic
aspirations of the town founders had unforeseen political consequences and were subverting the ideal of participatory town meeting government. Twenty-two of the twenty-nine new towns separated from the large towns founded prior to 1675. New Haven, the
most populous town in the colony, spawned four new towns; Norwich, the second most populous, and Farmington, with the largest
land mass, each parented three.

The failure of town founders to site original villages in central
locations was a crucial factor that increased the distance outlying
farmers had to travel for access to town services and exacerbated
the tensions between sections of communities. New Haven, Norwich, and Farmington, the three leading parents of new communities, for example, each had its original settlement on the edge
of the town's boundaries; New Haven village was sited on the coast,

Norwich village at the southern extreme of the town to take advantage of the confluence of two rivers, and Farmington at an eastern point in the town in order to be closer to the original River Towns and the Connecticut River. Four other new towns were the northern sections of coastal towns with original villages sited on the southern shoreline. Waterbury, Windham, Windsor, and Woodbury, four other communities that spawned Revolutionary towns, had each located its village at a noncentral site to have the best access possible to rivers. In a sense, then, the decisions of the town founders in siting settlements militated against the continued corporate integrity of their communities as much as did their original quest for large amounts of land. Central locations for original villages would undoubtedly have preserved more towns intact, but it would have been unrealistic for town founders to forego the advantage of a site that promised great economic benefits in order to head off a problem in the distant future; and there is no evidence indicating that the founders envisioned the problem surfacing. Moreover, given the large amounts of land early towns contained, centrally located villages would not have completely solved the problem and outlying settlers frequently would still have had distances of seven or eight miles to travel, which they might have regarded as prohibitive. One would assume, however, that since village services would have been more available in central locations had the siting patterns been different, fewer outlying areas would have developed their own villages, and townspeople disgruntled over their distances from central villages would have had less cohesion and less of an alternative to turn to.

Local political life was also rearranged to match the economic and social realities that had altered the Connecticut landscape since the founding generation of towns. Not only did the Revolutionary period occasion the formation of twenty-nine new towns, it also witnessed the incorporation of five cities. Hartford, Middletown, New London, New Haven, and Norwich had emerged as economic central places by the mid-eighteenth century and had become nucleated business districts with appended outlying countrysides. Conflict between the merchants clustered in the center and the farmers in the outlying areas surfaced regularly and caused many business leaders to become dissatisfied with town government. Tensions between villagers and outlying residents seem endemic to the human experience; they surfaced everywhere in the American colonies where there was a significant nucleation of population and were among the most disruptive forces in Massachusetts, Connecticut's Puritan neighbor to the north. Merchants in Connecticut complained that the farmers who constituted a majority of the towns had interests antithetical to those of the towns' centers and blocked programs needed to promote commerce. As early as 1771 New Haven appointed a committee to investigate the possibility of incorporating the business district as a legally separate city.[43] The Revolutionary experience, while originally producing unity, ultimately intensified the conflict between merchants and farmers and also intensified the movement for city incorporation. The centers of New Haven and New London, exposed by their shoreline locations to the devastation of British raids, lost much of their commerce to the three protected interior urban towns of Hartford, Middletown, and Norwich and were looking for ways to marshall all their resources in efforts to regain their previous status. Incorporation as separate cities, the merchants argued, would help gain the power to rebuild themselves as major trade centers. Logically, the three interior cities, Hartford, Middletown, and Norwich, jealous of their recently won trade eminence, envisioned incorporation as a device to maintain it. Largely as a result of these motivations, the five cities were incorporated in 1784, effectively separating farmers in outlying areas from urban merchant centers.[44] Freeing the urban centers from the outlying farmers also meant, of course, freeing the outlying farmers from the urban centers, and eight of the twenty-nine new towns were created from the five urban towns in the two years following the five cities' incorporation. Several petitions from aspiring new towns articulated the split between city and country and some even suggested a quid pro quo; farmers would not oppose city incorporation if merchants would not oppose new town formation. Hamden petitioners flatly stated that "merchants, professional men . . . have notions . . . and modes of conducting business very different from those which are your petitioners who are all farmers."[45] The North Haven parish told the Assembly that "your petitioners are far from complaining of the privileges granted to said city [New Haven]." However, "your petitioners have no concern in trade and navigation but wholly subsist themselves by agriculture."[46]

One of the consequences of the proliferation of acts of incorporation in the Revolutionary era was to reduce greatly the square mileage of the average town. In 1789 the average town size in the colony still was substantially larger than the 36-square-mile tract of folk culture, but it had dropped from the 106.3 square miles of 1675 to 49.6 in 1789. This reduction dramatically brought the locus of town government closer to home for many and was in keeping with the participatory ideology of the Revolution. Of the towns founded before 1675, only Stonington remained intact; and the largest towns of the founding years, Farmington and Windsor, were reduced in size by over two-thirds. The twenty-nine new Revolutionary towns averaged only 39.4 square miles. The Revolution created a geographical democratization of sorts by dismembering the larger old towns and promoting a rough equality of size. Of course, some extremes still existed; Stonington possessed ninety-nine square miles, compared to the 12.6 of tiny East Haven.

While the increase in towns in the Revolutionary era is striking, it must be placed in its proper perspective; most parishes in the state did not seek to achieve town status and the Assembly did not grant every request for incorporation that came before it. Over one hundred parishes did not apply for town status; several parishes applying were unsuccessful; seventeen of the twenty-nine new towns were forced to apply more than once; and only three new towns were created over any formal opposition. Every request for an act of incorporation was carefully reviewed by the Assembly, which was determined to see (1) that the difficulties cited were real physical problems of distance and not masks for political jealousies, (2) that the grand list and number of inhabitants were capable of sustaining a town, and (3) that separation did not seriously injure anyone. The Assembly always sent a writ to the parent town asking if its town meeting approved the separation or if there was any opposition to it. Even if the proposed town had sufficient resources and all concerned people approved the separation, the Assembly would not issue an act of incorporation until all the details of the separation had been fully worked out. Huntington had its incorporation delayed three times because its proposed border with the parent town, Stratford, could not be fully agreed upon in advance to everyone's satisfaction.[47] Brookfield was forced to petition to five separate Assemblies over a sixteen-year period because New Milford, one of three parents of the hopeful new town, opposed the separation. Not until all three old towns sent their town meetings' approval to the Assembly was the new town created.[48] When the

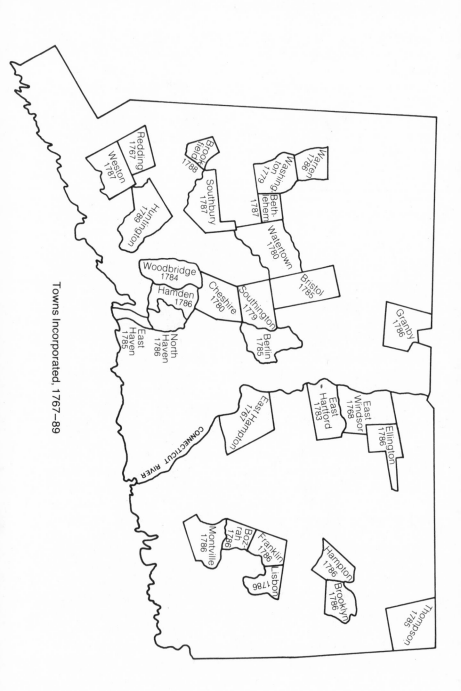

Towns Incorporated, 1767–89

second society of Preston applied for an act of incorporation, the rest of the town opposed it, saying that the town was "by no means enormous in size or in numbers of inhabitants, neither is the amount of polls and estate great in the list." The opposition petitioners charged that the seventeen-mile distance the dissidents alleged they had to walk to meetings "is made by measuring in a very crooked road far from being the most direct" and that "the conduct of some of the leading men for division has been rather more conspicuous for craft and intrigue than for honesty."[49] The act of incorporation was not issued. Opponents, from within the parish, to creating a town out of Andover society charged that the complained distance was not oppressive and that the grand list was too small to sustain a town. The two parent towns, Hebron and Coventry, agreed; in concurrence, the Assembly rejected the original petition.[50] While the spirit of the Revolutionary era gave the climate and occasion to redraw the local political map, this was done under the watchful supervision of the General Assembly and not in a frenzy of unthinking or uncontrolled secession.

THE first generation of English towns planted in Connecticut was fashioned out of the wilderness with a spirit of community enterprise. First settlers generally knew each other and moved to the town sites in groups. While they were anxious to amass all the land they could, settlers within the first generation did not seek land for immediate profit but for long-range security for their progeny; accordingly, they wanted more land than they could possibly farm but they were not land speculators in the strictest sense of the term. Although traces of this communalism can be found in the settling of the last of Connecticut's lands in Litchfield County, by and large that spirit had been replaced by one of individualism. Residents bought their lands separately and were usually strangers to one another when they formed their towns. Large and small tracts of lands were bought by speculators uninterested in settling what they purchased. Perhaps the best symbol of this erosion of the communal spirit and the growth of competitive individualism can be seen in the differing methods by which lands were acquired: in the first generation, land was assigned in one large tract at no cost to the recipients, who applied as a group to the General Court for it; in the settling of the last area of Connecticut unpeopled by Englishmen, land was sold in individual shares by an auctioneer to whoever could pay the highest price.

The towns formed in the Revolutionary era are further indications of this rise of independence and individualism. No longer content to submerge themselves in the larger body, the residents of many outlying areas wanted to redefine their communities to include only their immediate neighborhoods. They were not groups of people banding together *to join* larger communities in a spirit of commonwealth; they were *leaving* the larger communities in a spirit of independence. Of course, the rebelliousness of the residents of these new communities could also be overstated; they petitioned for separation in a lawful manner and the Assembly carefully considered and debated the merits of each petition. Yet, there was an assertiveness in the petitions that did bespeak a new spirit of independence; and the assembly did grant most of the petitions, rejecting only those that were obviously based on contrived grievances or that worked great hardships on the parent towns.

[II]

THE GROWTH AND DISTRIBUTION
OF POPULATION

SURPRISINGLY, given the primary importance of people to the study of history, historians have not thoroughly explored the implications for society of patterns of population growth and distribution. Sociologists, geographers, and economists have developed mines of theory on the basic relationships between population and almost every aspect of life, psychological and physical, but only recently have early American historians begun to exploit the rich potential inherent in the social science literature. Beginning with Charles Grant's study of Kent published in 1961, pioneering work by Grant, Richard Bushman, Philip Greven, Jr., and Kenneth Lockridge, among others, has shown that farming, character, family relationships, and migration patterns were profoundly affected in early New England by the rapid rate of population growth; farmers produced more crops for a commercial market, the drive towards individualistic aspirations was enhanced, parent-child relationships became more strained, and people moved more readily. All of this scholarly work is predicated on the premise, stated with pith by Lockridge, that eighteenth-century New England was becoming an "overcrowded" society. None of this work, however, attempts to analyze how wide a variety of population experience characterized a region or a colony in the seventeenth and eighteenth centuries and to what varying degrees the "overcrowded" model can be applied to various places. Connecticut's example suggests that although common population trends and resulting reactions can be identified, significant variations developed that can be correlated with several variables and that, if analyzed, lead to a fuller understanding of the range of community life.[1]

Precise population figures exist for Connecticut for the latter part of the colonial period, but there are few hard data antedating the 1750s. The colony had accurate censuses taken in 1756, 1774, 1782, and 1790; the earlier years, however, are not similarly blessed and no reliable direct information is available.[2] Estimates for Connecticut's population at various points during its first 120 years must be based on backward projections from the censuses and on scattered pieces of indirect evidence. Fortunately, our demographic knowledge is now sufficient to allow us to make these estimates with some sophistication.

Two twentieth-century historians, W. S. Rossiter and Stella Sutherland, in independent studies, developed a series of decadal growth rates for New England's population beginning in 1670 and ending with the federal census of 1790. Though differing widely in their estimates for a few decades, their overall estimated rate of growth is remarkably similar — Rossiter estimates a 28.6 percent mean growth rate per decade and Sutherland estimates 27.4 percent. Corroborating these figures, a recent study estimates from another type of evidence, fertility rates among women, an average *annual* increase in population of approximately 2.5 percent. The clustering at the same point of these three estimates arrived at by different scholars with different methodologies and sources imparts a strong degree of confidence to them.[3]

General growth coefficients for a region, however, are not in themselves necessarily trustworthy for one part of that region; the coefficients must be tested against the particular data. From the first federal census we know that Connecticut's total population in 1790 was 238,127. If one projects backward from this figure, using the decadal growth rates provided by a midpoint between Rossiter's and Sutherland's figures, the population for 1780 should be 187,427 — it was not; from the data in the 1782 census it was clearly well over 200,000. Similarly, if one projects backward using Rossiter's and Sutherland's figures for the previous decade, the population should have been 154,007 in 1770. The census of 1774 shows that this figure is grossly wrong — Connecticut's population was nearer 181,000 in 1770. Based on the actual censuses, Connecticut's decadal growth rates for 1760–70, 1770–80, and 1780–90 were 25 percent, 13.7 percent, and 15.3 percent, compared with the 31.6 percent, 21.7 percent, and 27 percent estimates of Rossiter and Sutherland.

That Connecticut was growing after 1760 at a slower rate than its neighbors should not be surprising. In all of New England a sizable out-migration from the older towns occurred in the third quarter of the seventeenth century as the available land shrank in relation to the population. However, in Massachusetts and particularly in

New Hampshire, uninhabited land was available for new town sites and out-migrants from older towns could settle on new land in the same colony and hence not be a net loss to the population figures. Both of these colonies had a population density significantly lower than Connecticut's. Connecticut, as we have seen, had planted towns in the last of its uninhabited regions by 1760 and had no frontier lands available for new settlement.

It appears, then, as we pursue our analysis, that Connecticut's land supply directly affected its rate of population growth. As one moves backwards from 1790, the state and colony's decadal population growth rates in each of the three decades move closer to the New England norm; in 1780–90 it was 56.6 percent of the norm, in 1770–80 it was 63.1 percent of it, and in 1760–70 it was 79.1 percent of it. Given this trend, given that Connecticut had land available for out-migrants before 1760, and given that the qualitative sources for Connecticut history usually date the beginning of the exodus of Connecticut's young men to 1760, it may be accurate to assume that Connecticut, prior to 1760, did not differ sharply from the New England norm. The best way to test this assumption is to make backward projections from the 1756 census using Rossiter's and Sutherland's figures and see if the results agree reasonably with the other available evidence. These projections yield the population figures of table 1.

TABLE 1
Population of Connecticut by Decade

1790[a]	238,127	1720	51,166
1780[b]	206,447	1710	38,339
1770[b]	181,583	1700	31,502
1760[b]	145,217	1690	27,464
1750	112,921	1680	21,013
1740	90,120	1670	15,799
1730	68,169	1660	11,276

[a]Based on census.
[b]Based on interpolations from censuses.

These decadal estimates do indeed accord well with the bulk of other evidence. Three New England colonists, all seemingly in good positions to know, made estimates of Connecticut's population that have received widespread credence; two of them approximate closely the projected figures, one does not. In 1700 an Anglican minister doing a study of the number of Church of England communicants in New England estimated Connecticut's population to be 30,999 in that year — the projected figure was 30,431; in 1715, a Massachusetts royal official estimated Connecticut's population at 46,750 — the projected figure was 43,424.* Only the colony's estimate of 38,000 in 1730, in an answer to a Board of Trade inquiry, markedly differs from the projected figures.[4] Almost certainly, however, the figure of 38,000 provided by Colony Secretary Hezekiah Wyllys is drastically wrong and has been the source of much distortion in assessing Connecticut's past. If it were accurate, Connecticut would have had to experience a decadal growth rate higher than 56 percent between 1730 and 1760 — an utterly improbable figure by any standard.

Why the colony's response to England was so grossly in error will probably always be a mystery. Perhaps it was carelessly prepared; more likely, however, it was a deliberate ploy to lull England into the belief that Connecticut was a thinly populated colony of mostly farmers. The reports of the colony always understated the amount of commerce and manufacturing in an attempt to keep England's interest in the colony low and to minimize outside interference with the colony's self-government.[5]

Another source suggests that the figures projected backwards from the 1756 census are accurate. For two dates, 1762 and 1774, the precise number of men in the colony's militia is known. When the number of militia is divided into the population derived from the censuses for these dates, it yields in both cases a ratio of 1 militiaman for every 7.6 inhabitants.[6] The precise agreement in both cases indicates that the ratio is accurate — at least for the late colonial period. In 1674 and 1730 exact figures for the militia are also available, and if they are multiplied by 7.6 they give populations for those respective dates of 15,732 and 64,000. These results correspond closely to the figures for those dates derived from the backward projection, 16,500 and 65,852;† the militia projections

---

*The projected figures used here are lower than those of table 1 because the populations of Enfield, Somers, Suffield, and Woodstock must be deleted, inasmuch as they were part of Massachusetts in 1700 and 1715, when the contemporary estimates were made.

†This figure is lower than the one in table 1 because Enfield, Somers, Suffield, and Woodstock are deleted.

and the census projections differ by only 4.7 percent in 1674 and 1 percent in 1730.

Two other independent sources provide additional corroboration. In 1675 the number of dwellings in the colony was estimated at 3,120. From the 1790 census we know that families averaged 5.7 persons. If we assume a higher birth rate for the seventeenth century, which from all recent demographic studies is a safe assumption, and if we assume that houses in 1675 contained servants and non-family members, a minimal figure for the number of persons per dwelling would be six. This figure multiplied by the number of dwellings yields a population for 1675 of 18,720, which corresponds closely to the 18,406 of the projected figures. In one of the few other contemporary estimates of the colony's population, a New York minister wrote in 1696 that Connecticut possessed 5,000 families. Applying the same conversion figure of 6 to 1 to this number yields a population of 30,000; the number for 1696 from the projected population figures is 29,886.[7]

The only primary evidence, besides the 1730 report to the Board of Trade, suggesting that the backward projections are in error is the tax records, which have been used extensively by historians to estimate Connecticut's colonial population. An examination of these tax records and how they have been used suggests that they have misled historians and caused them mistakenly to accept the colony's gross understatement of its population in the 1730 report. There is no empirical evidence that the conversion figure generally used to translate tax polls into inhabitants, 1 to 4, is accurate; the polls themselves contain many omissions; and the reporting of polls was erratic, suggesting that no consistent policy on enumeration existed.[8]

The figures arrived at by the backward projections are at present, then, the most reliable ones yet produced, and nearly all available evidence indicates that they are accurate. Many scholars, misled by the tax lists and the 1730 report to the Board of Trade, have substantially underestimated Connecticut's population prior to the census. Benjamin Trumbull, for example, the colony's first comprehensive historian, wrote in 1818 that Connecticut's population in 1713 was 17,000 inhabitants. This was at least 100 percent beneath the actual figure; a quick calculation of the growth rate required to increase 17,000 inhabitants in 1713 to 132,799 in 1756 shows Trumbull's guess to be entirely improbable. J. G. Palfrey, in his comprehensive history of New England written in the 1890s, and Franklin B. Dexter, in an article on colonial population written in 1887, both perceived that the Trumbull guess and the 1730 report seriously understated the population. Dexter, in the first systematic analysis of population in the colonies, had the clearest idea of the magnitude of Trumbull's and the report's error. He wrote that Trumbull's estimate was wrong by nearly 100 percent and that the 1730 estimate was about two-thirds of the actual total. Richard Bushman, however, in the finest recent study to appear on colonial Connecticut, accepted the figures of some earlier historians based on tax polls, which indicate wildly fluctuating growth rates that are highly improbable; the growth rate Bushman accepts for the period 1670–1700, 58 percent, is inconsistent with known demographic data on the seventeenth century.[9]

One of the fortunate results of having a decadal population series about which we can feel some certitude is that it permits accurate calculation of the density of population in a decadal series (see table 2). From this density series it is apparent that the amount

TABLE 2
Population Density by Decade

Year	Persons per square mile	Year	Persons per square mile
1670	6.39	1730	15.91
1680	7.91	1740	18.43
1690	9.27	1750	23.10
1700	9.52	1760	29.22
1710	9.67	1770	36.26
1720	12.22	1780	41.23

of new land being opened up for settlement between 1670 and 1770 did not match the increase in population. Only for the 20-year period 1690 to 1710, when the population rate of growth temporarily slowed and many new towns were settled in the east, did the density remain relatively stable. It grew quickly after 1710 and after 1740, when most of Litchfield County was settled, and took quantum leaps for the next five decades; over the 120-year period 1670–1790 the density of the colony's population increased sixfold.

Connecticut's inhabitants reacted in several ways to this dramatic increase in the density of population and the resultant pressures it put upon the resources of the colony. As the settlement of Litchfield County shows, they scrambled for more land even if it was of dubious quality and settled the land in a pattern of small towns in order to utilize all the resources within the present generation. Old towns that had husbanded their common lands carefully divided up their land in increasingly frequent allotments, until almost none of them had any remaining undivided lands after 1750.[10] The penultimate result of this scramble to find land for younger sons was the formation of the Susquehannah Company, which sought to colonize the Wyoming Valley in Pennsylvania under the authority of the sea-to-sea clause in the Charter of 1662. All of these devices to gain more land were stopgaps at best, and the other side of the density equation received serious attention — the rate of population growth was substantially reduced, as we have seen from the censuses. Out-migration to New Hampshire, Vermont, western Massachusetts, and New York accounted for most of the reduced population growth, but indirect and direct birth control undoubtedly accounted for some. Marriage ages were rising in New England, as young men did not feel economically qualified to support a family; this was an indirect way of controlling family size. More directly limiting population growth, colonists faced with economic hardships practiced *coitus interruptus*.[11]

With the exception of Litchfield County, the population was spread with a remarkable degree of consistency over the various counties in the colony in 1756 (see table 3). The county with the highest concentration of population, New London, was 24 percent more densely populated than the county with the lowest, Hartford. However, prior to the Revolution, the three counties with coastlines, New Haven, New London, and Fairfield, were growing at a more rapid rate than the two inland counties, Hartford and Windham, and by 1774 the gap between most densely and least densely populated counties had grown to 29 percent. As Connecticut's trade grew in the mid-eighteenth century those areas able to take best advantage of it offered more economic opportunity to young men and attracted more immigrants. The advantage in peace turned into a liability in war, and during the Revolutionary years the two coastline counties, New Haven and New London, both attacked by the British, experienced net losses in population, while Hartford County grew 10 percent; Fairfield County grew only 2.3 percent during the war and Windham County, even though protected by its interior location, grew only 1.9 percent. After the Revolutionary dislocation, New Haven and New London counties resumed their prewar growth rates, and between 1782 and 1790, Hartford, New Haven, New London, and Fairfield counties grew at rates of 13.5 percent, 18.7 percent, 16.8 percent, and 17.5 percent. Their density rates ranged from 55.06 persons per square mile in New London County to 45.35 in New Haven, a difference of 21 percent. Only Windham County failed to keep pace with the growth of the rest of the new state. Despite its protected position it failed to grow as rapidly as Hartford County during the Revolution, and after the Revolution, between 1782 and 1790, it grew only 2.2 percent. Qualitative sources that discuss the out-migration of Connecticut men in the late eighteenth century always list Windham as the leader in the exodus of young men, but few have realized the extremity of the imbalance of out-migrants and how widely Windham County led the out-migration.[12]

TABLE 3
Population Growth by County

County	1756	1774	1782	1790
Hartford				
Density	26.28	37.29	40.94	46.48
Percent increase		+ 41.9	+ 9.8	+13.5
New Haven				
Density	26.74	39.45	38.21	45.35
Percent increase		+ 47.5	− 3.1	+18.7
New London				
Density	32.60	47.91	47.16	55.06
Percent increase		+ 47.0	− 1.6	+16.8
Fairfield				
Density	29.48	43.23	44.24	51.98
Percent increase		+ 46.6	+ 2.3	+17.5
Windham				
Density	27.6	38.81	39.56	40.43
Percent increase		+ 40.5	+ 1.9	+ 2.2
Litchfield				
Density	15.11	34.95	43.01	49.53
Percent increase		+131.0	+23.0	+15.2

Nor does the traditional reason given for this population flow hold up under scrutiny; Windham's out-migration was not occasioned because of a high population density, as is commonly thought. It was less densely populated than the four older counties of the colony and by 1790 had 36 percent fewer people per square mile than New London County. One might suspect that Windham County led the out-migration because its soils were less fertile than those of Hartford, New Haven, New London, and Fairfield counties, and because, unlike those four counties, Windham was landlocked and had no access to oceangoing vessels. The experience of Litchfield County, however, suggests causes other than, or in addition to, intrinsic soil infertility and poor location. Litchfield County had poorer quality land than Windham County and was equally isolated from the sea but was growing at a rapid rate and by 1790 had become 23 percent more densely populated than Windham. While there is no doubt that land hunger motivated Windham County's young men to leave the state, it remains to be explained why their counterparts in Litchfield County were not equally dissatisfied and impelled by the hunger for new land. Two variables differ between the two counties — their methods and dates of settlement. It is doubtful if the method of settlement affected the land supply once all the available land was brought under cultivation, but the settlement dates could be of importance. Windham County, settled a half century before Litchfield County, would have exhausted its soils much more quickly and by the 1780s would have required significantly more land per capita than the newer areas in Litchfield County. Unlike the areas settled prior to 1675, which also had much-farmed soils, Windham County did not have a location favorable to trade and could not put as much of its population to work in nonagricultural pursuits. This would suggest that it was not intrinsic soil quality and isolation from the seacoast alone that accounted for its land desperation but that these factors, when combined with early settlement, resulted in an economy that could not sustain a growing population. As further evidence for this theory, Litchfield County experienced its greatest out-migration in the early nineteenth century, the period in its chronological development that corresponded to the 1780s in Windham County's. There is no way to *prove* that this intersection of variables caused the high Windham County out-migration, but the correlation suggests that in the absence of other evidence this is the best explanation.[13]

Another measurement supports this conclusion. In general it was the communities settled in the second period of town formation that had the lowest density of population in the colony; in 1790 they averaged 40.6 persons per square mile, compared with the 52.5 persons per square mile of towns settled before 1675 and the 49.5 persons per square mile of those settled in period three. This is not just because of the heavy number of Windham County towns in the sample of period two towns; the seven towns founded in the west and the six towns founded in Hartford County in this period also had the same low density. Consistently, the young men of period two towns were more inclined to leave their places of birth than their counterparts in towns settled on major waterways in period one and in the Litchfield hills in period three.

Surprisingly, the density of population when measured by regions does not correlate with land quality. New London County, for example, had poorer land for farming than Fairfield, Hartford, New Haven, and Windham counties; yet it was the most densely populated county and was still growing at a rapid rate in 1790. Fairfield County had by far the most productive land in the colony but it was growing at approximately the same rate as the other counties, if one excludes Windham. This absence of a correlation by region between land quality and population growth adds further evidence to the conclusion that the ability of an area to support a population is related to the location and age of the settlement as well as to intrinsic land quality.

Within the individual towns of a county, population densities and growth rates varied widely. In 1756, among the fifty-three towns established for over two generations, Norwich, with 55 persons per square mile, was the most densely populated, while New Milford, with 11 persons per square mile, was the least. Each county had a share of densely populated and lightly populated towns; among the seventeen most densely populated ones, four were in Hartford County, four were in New London County, four were in Windham County, three were in Fairfield County, and two were in New Haven County. Among the sixteen least densely populated towns, four were in Hartford County, three were in Fairfield County, three were in Windham County, three were in Litchfield County, two were in New Haven County, and one was in New London County. This heterogeneity suggests that in each county there were highly developed towns serving as central places and less developed towns that depended on the central places for services. However, it is clear that density is not a precise guide to the commercial development of an area or to its role as a central place. Hartford, for example, had a substantially lower population density than Wethersfield, even though other incontrovertible evidence shows that Hartford was far more of an economic center. This difference points out a problem with these density figures; they are accurate for the town as a whole but they give no indication of what geographers call residential density. Hartford's 38 persons per square mile is the result of densities that in the business district may have approached 80 persons per square mile and that in outlying areas may have been as low as 15 persons per square mile. Most towns were amalgams of villages and countryside, and the population density figures merge the two.

One would assume that the quality of land affected population density, but mere assumption cannot tell us the degree of influence land exerted. Modern soil maps enable us to estimate the quality of lands in the past with convenience and reasonable accuracy. Although soil maps are seldom used by historians, geographers use them routinely to indicate past growing conditions and potential. Soil profiles change in intrinsic quality only over many hundreds or thousands of years and then only slightly. Flooding, erosion, and the depletion of nutrients through over-farming change the soil's immediate utility to man in the short run rather dramatically, but because the soil-forming processes remain the same, estimated intrinsic values in modern maps would closely approximate intrinsic values in the seventeenth and eighteenth centuries, and these maps can be used with reasonable confidence by historians as a guide to earlier land quality — indeed, they are the only guide of any precision.[14]

These soil maps help us considerably to refine our population analysis. When measured by town instead of by region, a strong correlation can be established between land type and population density; the highly dense towns in the colony had a 6.6 rating on the land quality scale, the dense had a 4.4, the moderate a 3.7, and the light a 3.3 (see table 4). The only exception to this correlation is in the sparsely populated towns, which had a 4.2 rating for land quality; this can be explained by the smallness of the sample — there were only four towns in the sparse category — and the high quality of land in one of them, Waterbury. Waterbury's population

TABLE 4
Population Density and Land Quality in 1756
(All Towns but Litchfield County)

Population density	No. of towns in sample	Land quality
Highly dense	5	6.5
Dense	12	4.4
Moderate	24	3.7
Light	12	3.3
Sparse[a]	3	3.3
Selected sample of twenty inland towns of similar size and location		
Most Dense	10	4.4
Least Dense	10	3.7

[a]Excludes Waterbury.

density did not correlate with its land quality because it experienced frequent devastating floods, which discouraged settlers. Excluding Waterbury, the towns in the sparse category averaged 3.3. These figures tend to overstate the impact of land quality on population density, inasmuch as the towns with the best land also had the best locations and it is not clear which of the two variables was the more operable. When the land quality ratings of twenty inland towns of similar size and locations were compared, the ten most dense of the group had a land quality rating of 4.4 and the ten least dense had a rating of 3.7. This ratio more accurately reflects the effect of land quality on population densities than do ratios that do not program out the variables of location and size. Individual examples abound of the importance of land quality; Norwich, the most densely populated town in the colony, had the best-quality land in New London County, and this factor, when combined with Norwich's advantageous location, explains its attractiveness to immigrants. The second most densely populated town, Wethersfield, had the best farming land in the colony. Fairfield, which contained a better harbor than Norwalk or Stamford but had less fertile land, was less densely populated than either. However, the relationship between land quality and population permits exceptions: Coventry and Plainfield, two very hilly, rugged towns, were among the most densely populated communities in the colony; both were more densely populated than Pomfret or Canterbury, two towns with better land. Preston had much better land than its neighbors to the south, Groton and Stonington, but did not have access to the sea as they did and had a significantly lower density.

At first glance it appears that a positive correlation can be established between early settlement and high density; the five most densely settled towns in the colony were all founded before 1675, as were twelve of the seventeen most dense. However, among the sixteen least dense were four towns settled before 1675. Three of these four early-settled towns with thin populations were removed from navigable waterways. This would suggest that it was neither early settlement per se nor the land division policies of the first communities that inclined a town towards a high population density but that a location for trade was the operative variable. Norwich, for example, was over 300 percent more densely populated than Farmington but was founded fifteen years later. The major difference between the two was that Norwich was accessible to seagoing vessels and Farmington was not. Among the seventeen most densely populated towns only five of them, clustered together in eastern Hartford County and the neighboring section of Windham County, were not on major waterways. Among the seventeen least populated towns, only Derby was on navigable water.

A final factor that influenced the population density of a town was its physical size; not surprisingly, towns with large areas were significantly less densely populated than towns with small areas (see table 5). The five towns with the largest square mileage in the colony all were substantially below the population density median. Land tended to be used more intensively in towns with little of it and less so in towns with a large supply. The average size of the ten most densely populated towns in the colony, 73.7 square miles, was significantly smaller than the average size, 113 square miles, of the

TABLE 5
Population Growth by Town Size,
1756–74

Area of town	No. in sample	% growth in population
Over 90 square miles	16	60.1
65–90 square miles	17	49.4
Less than 65 square miles	21	38.8

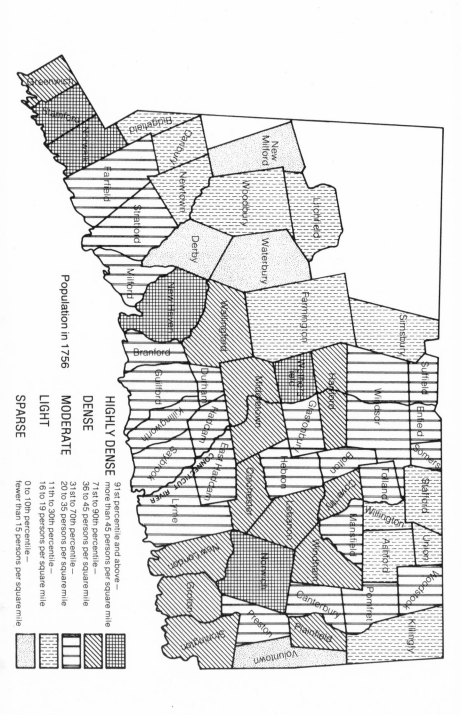

ten least densely populated. Also not surprisingly, the population growth rate was a function of physical size — the fastest-growing towns were the ones with the largest land areas. Between 1756 and 1774, when the rate of population growth was relatively similar for each county, towns with over 90 square miles grew 60.1 percent, towns with between 65 and 90 square miles grew 49.4 percent, and towns with less than 65 square miles grew 38.8 percent. Inhabitants of small towns, feeling restricted by their community's land shortage, moved in great numbers to the large towns where the shortage had not yet become acute.

When one compares the relative densities of towns in 1756 with the corresponding figures for 1774, it is apparent that the rising commercialization of Connecticut and the increase in external trade had a heavy influence on local social structures. All ten of Connecticut's most densely populated towns in 1774 were located on navigable waterways. The three eastern hill towns that had been among the ten most dense in 1756 grew more slowly than the towns with advantageously situated mercantile communities. Norwich and New Haven, the two major entrepôts of the West Indian trade, and Wethersfield, a river port, were nearly 50 percent more densely populated than the densest towns not accessible to ocean-going ships. Hartford and New London, two other major commercial centers, increased their densities by nearly 80 percent, while the three eastern hill towns with high densities in 1756 increased by less than 20 percent and by 1774 lagged significantly behind the towns on navigable water.

At the lower end of the spectrum little relative change occurred in rank between 1756 and 1774; the light and sparsely populated communities of 1774 were essentially the same ones as in 1756. However, although the least dense towns of 1756 remained so as of 1774, their population was growing more rapidly than that of the rest of the colony. The fifteen least dense towns in 1756 grew at a rate of 72 percent between 1756 and 1774, while the rest of the colony grew at a rate of 40 percent. This figure suggests that while these towns remained lightly and sparsely populated compared with the rest of the colony, their scrubby or rugged terrain was able to attract immigrants simply because it was available. The fastest-growing towns between 1756 and 1774 were those of commercial nature and the thinly populated farming towns; the slowest growing were the already well-populated farming towns.

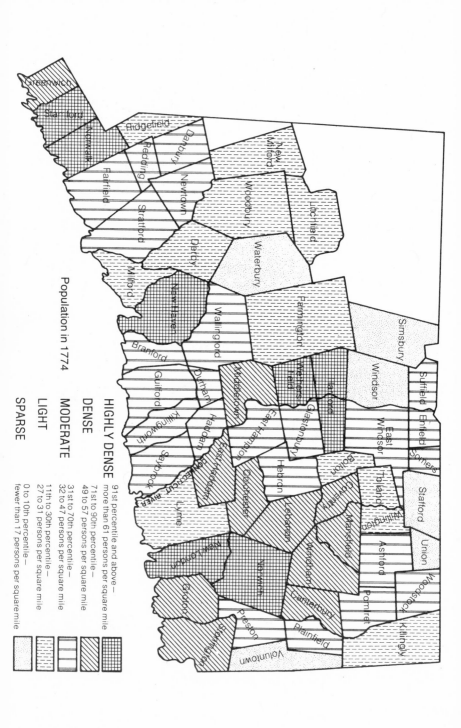

Population in 1774

HIGHLY DENSE   91st percentile and above—
                more than 61 persons per square mile

DENSE   71st to 90th percentile—
                49 to 57 persons per square mile

MODERATE   31st to 70th percentile—
                32 to 47 persons per square mile

LIGHT   11th to 30th percentile—
                27 to 31 persons per square mile

SPARSE   0 to 10th percentile—
                fewer than 17 persons per square mile

Trends established on the eve of the Revolution were not altered in the period immediately following. The 1790 census shows little change in relative densities from that of 1774; once again the ten most densely populated towns were located on navigable water; once again towns removed from waterways failed to grow as fast as those on them; once again the least densely populated towns were those with the poorest lands, although they continued to grow at a more rapid rate than the others. The 1790 census, however, occurring after the great spate of town divisions in the Revolutionary years, enables us to assay some more finely tuned statements about residential density. New Haven and Hartford, which were, as previously noted, amalgams of business districts and outlying farming areas, now were partially shorn of their countrysides. New Haven's density shot up to 142 persons per square mile, while Hamden, formerly part of New Haven, had a density of only 43 persons per square mile. Hartford, which still possessed a sizable amount of outlying area, nevertheless increased its density to 112 persons per square mile when it was separated from its eastern half. These density figures provide deeper insight into how the living patterns of Connecticut's inhabitants were changing in the eighteenth century in response to commercialization than do the more crude figures of the census of 1774. New Haven, for instance, was 700 percent more densely populated than Union, but Hamden, formerly a part of New Haven and now contiguous to it, was only 200 percent more dense than Union. Most of the new towns that were formerly parts of the major centers and by 1790 were their suburbs had only moderate densities. The early censuses that had lumped the suburbs together with the centers had partially disguised the growing concentration of population in central places and had made the differences in population density between trading centers and rural towns seem smaller than they actually were.[15]

POPULATION growth as rapid as Connecticut experienced invariably places strains on society and creates tensions.[16] In addition, the effects of this rapid growth on the economy and the uneven distribution of the growth could be expected to exacerbate these strains and tensions. The economy was threatened by a land:man ratio that was becoming critically low in the third and fourth generations and must have been particularly frustrating to a society

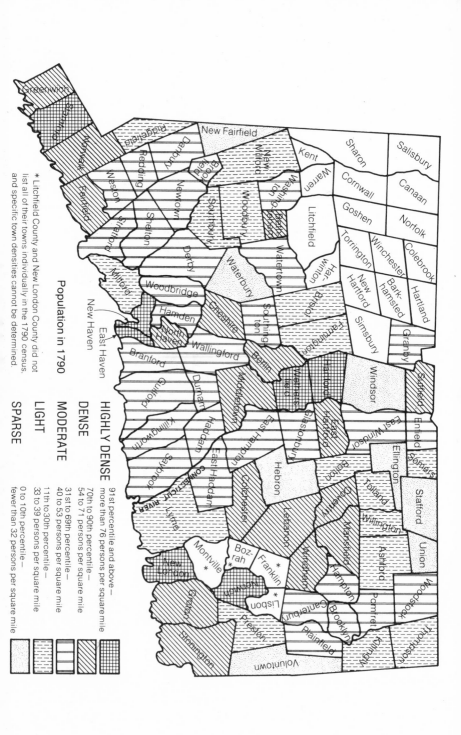

HIGHLY DENSE
91st percentile and above—
more than 76 persons per square mile

DENSE
70th to 90th percentile—
54 to 71 persons per square mile

Population in 1790

MODERATE
31st to 69th percentile—
40 to 53 persons per square mile

LIGHT
11th to 30th percentile—
33 to 39 persons per square mile

SPARSE
0 to 10th percentile—
fewer than 32 persons per square mile

* Litchfield County and New London County did not list all of their towns individually in the 1790 census, and specific town densities cannot be determined.

that could contrast it to the highly favorable conditions of a generation earlier. The population density among towns and parishes was becoming increasingly differentiated, creating communities that imparted fundamentally differing socialization experiences and offered differing levels of economic opportunity. Thus, these three factors — the rate of population growth itself, the effects of the growth on the economy, and the distribution of the growth — could all be expected to militate against feelings of harmony and contentment and to promote feelings of contention and frustration.

[III]

THE EVOLUTION OF
TOWN-MEETING GOVERNMENT

ALTHOUGH New England town-meeting government has several unique features and much new nomenclature, few present historians would argue, as the Frontier School of historians did for the first half of the twentieth century, that it was a New World original creation. Nor would today's historians claim, as the nineteenth-century Anglo-Saxonphiles did, that New England local institutions could be traced back to the folkmoot of the German forests. The painstaking transatlantic research of the past scholarly generation has rooted town-meeting government firmly in the soil of late medieval and early modern England — specifically in the manorial courts and parish meetings. Through a process that can best be described as "selective borrowing," the New England colonists winnowed out those parts of the English institutional past that were not congenial to the New World conditions and adopted and adapted those that were.[1]

The selective borrowing process, however, did not mean that Connecticut's local polity was fixed for all time at its inception; town government grew in size and complexity and underwent a differentiation within its internal structure. Change was gradual and never abrupt, but the end product in the late eighteenth century probably would have amazed the first settlers if they could have seen it. Moreover, even those parts of local government that stayed approximately the same in structure, such as the town meeting, changed demonstrably in their method of operation, and the relationship of town government to colony government underwent a transformation; the process of adopting and adapting thus continued throughout the colonial period. Surprisingly, although the activities and numbers of town officers increased in the Revolutionary years, little dramatic change in structure occurred; the organic method of slow adaptation was maintained amidst the turbulence occasioned by the creation of many new towns and the redrawing of local boundaries.

The governments of the settlements around Boston Harbor in

the Massachusetts Bay Colony unquestionably served as the basic model for the rest of New England, excluding Rhode Island. Connecticut's early town-meeting governments, however, differed in degrees from Massachusetts Bay because of two factors. First, as Charles Andrews wrote ninety years ago, Connecticut's local institutions were "twice purified." If the Puritans of the Bay Colony purified English antecedents through their selective borrowing, the Puritans of Connecticut purified them again by winnowing the grain once more. Second, and more importantly, the early local institutions of Connecticut were created to a much greater extent by the General Court of the colony than were those of Massachusetts. These two factors imparted a fundamental uniformity in early Connecticut town government that did not exist to the same degree in Massachusetts. The purification of the Massachusetts example enabled the Connecticut colonists to avoid what they regarded as wasteful experimentation; and the close control of the central government enabled them to prevent the divergent patterns of institutions that develop when the institutions are built from the bottom up.[2]

The three River Towns of Hartford, Windsor, and Wethersfield preceded the colony of Connecticut; local government in the three prior to 1639 had little formal structure and has left few traces. Each of the towns elected a constable and apparently no other secular officials. The church meeting was the crucial decision-making body in each, and the dominant religious figures were undoubtedly the leaders in political affairs as well as religious ones. Had this situation continued, the amorphous decision-making procedures would have hardened into custom and would have led to divergent institutions. It did not. After covenanting together and creating the colony of Connecticut, the River Towns surrendered their local autonomy to the newly created General Court, which proceeded to take control of the three settlements, hammered out institutions for them, and fashioned them into functioning political bodies. The colony adopted the Fundamental Order of 1639, often called the first constitution written in the New World, which established the supremacy of the central government over the towns and defined the methods by which the towns would relate to the General Court. Later that year, in October of 1639, the Court passed a number of laws creating and prescribing town government, and it added to them substantially over the course of the next decade. In

1650, the General Court commissioned Roger Ludlow, a distinguished lawyer and probably the most prominent man in the River Towns, to draft a body of law that would codify in one coherent whole the constitutional arrangements of the colony and towns. The result of Ludlow's work, the Code of 1650, was a sweeping corpus of law that described the duties and powers of every colony and town official. It became the local constitution of each town in Connecticut.[3]

The polity of each town was unified at first in the town meeting; it was the only local deliberative body and dealt with religion, defense, economics, morality, and all other aspects of governance. This unity did not last long and, beginning in 1650, when the militia was detached from the town meeting's control, other local bodies were created by the colony to perform specific local functions. From 1639 onwards, the freemen in a town, the voters who elected colony-wide officers and the towns' deputies to the General Court, had no connection with the town meetings; however, inasmuch as only the Court could admit freemen, their meeting was more an extension of the colony government than a unit of local government. Technically, the men designated as proprietors in each town by the General Court owned the town's lands but, since most adult white male inhabitants were proprietors, early towns saw no reason to distinguish between the proprietary and the town meetings and the one acted for both. Similarly, the town meeting acted as the church society meeting, since parish and town were coterminous in the early towns. Hence, the town meeting and the officers the colony told it to elect comprised the government of the early towns.[4]

Until 1679 the town meeting embraced all adult white men in town, but in that year the General Court enacted a statute requiring town-meeting voters to have fifty shillings of assessed property; as towns grew in population the colony's leaders wanted to stop newcomers or chronic paupers, who, they thought, might be irresponsible, from taking part in the decision-making processes. Another way of ensuring the sobriety of the town meeting was to regulate carefully who was and who was not admitted to the town as an inhabitant. Without written affidavits from outside authorities or oral testimonials from local residents, a stranger would be "warned off" and not allowed to settle. Few town residents were disenfranchised from local voting by the property requirement, and, although it stayed on the books throughout the colonial and Revolutionary periods, it was never enforced after the 1720s and became a dead letter.[5]

Generally, the first five to ten years of a town's existence saw frequent and lengthy town meetings, where questions of real importance were debated, but subsequent years witnessed a decline in activity. In Hartford in 1639 there were thirteen town meetings and in 1640 there were sixteen, but by 1644 the number dwindled to five and generally continued at four or five a year until the late 1670s; then it further declined to two or three a year and remained at that level for the rest of the century. In Norwalk, founded in 1654, the town averaged seven meetings a year until 1675, but the average reflects a steadily declining number in each succeeding year after 1660, even though Norwalk never held as few meetings as Hartford. In Norwich, founded in 1650, the records are not complete for the first years, but by 1675 the town was meeting an average of four or five times a year. Windsor had an undeterminable but apparently high number of meetings in its first five years, but by 1642 it had settled into a pattern of holding an average of four a year. It underscores the importance of town meetings to note that in their early years some towns fined inhabitants for missing them.[6]

Not only the frequency of the town meeting changed after the first few years of a town's existence; the nature of the meeting changed also. In Hartford the meeting declined constantly in activity until it reached a low point in the late 1670s, which remained constant throughout the rest of the century. In 1638 the town meeting of Hartford passed seven detailed restrictions on the townsmen (selectmen) that carefully circumscribed and limited their activities. The town meeting also in that year acted on such seemingly petty affairs as ordering a specific man to mend certain fences. Similarly, the townsmen of Norwalk and Fairfield were always subordinated to the town meeting in the first few years of the towns' existence. However, by the 1670s, the typical town meeting in Hartford was much shorter and, instead of limiting the townsmen's authority and acting on small affairs, merely ratified decisions made by the townsmen. In Norwich and Windsor by the 1670s, the town meeting was doing little beyond electing the town's officers, appointing special ad hoc committees, and ratifying decisions made by the townsmen.[7] Of course, the meeting in all towns retained its theoretical power over town affairs. But in actual practice the meeting sought only to choose the people who would actually govern the town, acting on its own only occasionally in exceptional cases. In Hartford the dormant nature of the meeting is reflected by the fact that in the 1670s most of the meetings were held in the winter months, between late November and early March. The town could do without a meeting for as long as eight months during the time of the year when the townspeople were actively engaged in agriculture.

The townsmen, who were not called selectmen until the 1690s, were the key figures in each town's political life. The towns were instructed by the General Court to choose yearly three, five, or seven of their "chief inhabitants" as townsmen, one of whom was to be moderator of the town meeting. The office of moderator was not set apart from that of townsman until the eighteenth century. The townsmen's powers comprised all three functions of government: executive, legislative, and judicial. Accordingly, because of their wide range of powers and because there were few other town officers elected in the founding years, the townsmen functioned as all-around political handymen. In many ways they were jacks-of-all-trades. They were empowered to act as an original court and to hear all controversies criminal and civil which involved less than forty shillings in potential fines and in which all parties lived in the town. They were also empowered to issue a summons to anyone in their town and compel him to appear before either the town meeting or the townsmen's meeting. As part of their judicial duties the townsmen were required to make up a complete inventory of all the personal and real estate of any deceased person and forward it to the probate court.[8]

Originally, in each town the townsmen assessed all the wealth of each man for tax purposes and also set a "rate," or a town tax, which was always a percentage of each individual's assessed wealth. The General Court, in the Code of 1650, outlined the duties of a town treasurer, but one of the townsmen invariably assumed the job. Among their other financial duties, townsmen were allowed to determine what parents of schoolchildren should pay for the school's support. While they did not personally collect the taxes, before the last quarter of the century one of the townsmen did always act as the financial agent of the town, and most towns did not elect treasurers until the eighteenth century.

Puritan control of morality is a well-known story to historians of

Connecticut; in the towns during the founding years it was the townsmen who enforced this tight control. The townsmen, instructed by the General Court to keep a vigilant eye on their fellow townspeople, were given the power to search any home in town without a search warrant if they suspected its occupants were breaking the law. They also enforced the colony laws regarding taverns and made sure that no one was tippling (which was defined as drinking more than one half-pint of wine or remaining more than one half hour in the tavern at a single time). Even what modern people would consider the sanctity of parent-children relations was breached by the instructions of the General Court to the townsmen, who were told that it was their duty to make sure that every child was taught how to read and to know all capital laws. Townsmen were encouraged by the Court to question children on the basics of religion to ensure that parents were properly teaching the catechism. Further, the townsmen were required to see that every child in town was taught "an honest lawful calling in labour, employment, or husbandry." If parents did not give their children this training, the townsmen could take the children away from them. The laws passed about morality were meant to be enforced, and there is ample evidence that they were.[9]

Moreover, the townsmen administered a program of general welfare in each town. We tend to think of the welfare state as a twentieth-century phenomenon, but townsmen were given broad powers to provide for the general welfare of their towns. They could administer an idiot's estate in order to support him, abate taxes on the estate of a widow, refund the taxes of an injured or sick man, put a person to work if he threatened to become a charge to the town, grant sums of money to indigent people, and place any minor orphan in a home. All of this, of course, was subject to appeal first to the town meeting and then to the General Court, but appeals of townsmen's orders were rare.

The New London town meeting in 1659 provided its townsmen with a detailed list of twelve obligations after the townsmen inquired "to know of the town what their duties were." The list shows that the community shared the General Court's vast expectations of the townsmen and also shows the extraordinarily wide-ranging and detailed nature of their chores:

1. "Keep up" town bounds and supervise the fence viewers;

2. See that children are educated and servants well ordered, and that there is no living in idleness;

3. Maintain town and colony laws and provide the town magazine with arms and ammunition;

4. Maintain the streets, lanes, highways, and common lands and provide some method of calling forth individuals to work on them;

5. Take care of the meetinghouse;

6. "Consider of some absolute and perfect way and course to be taken for a perfect platform of settling and maintaining of records respecting the towns, that they be fully clearly and fairly kept, for the use, benefit and peaceful state of the town and after posterity";

7. Control the agenda of town meetings and prevent needless discussion;

8. Regulate matters concerning Indians;

9. Regulate the felling, sawing, and transportation of all timber, boards, masts, and pipestaves;

10. Oversee the ferries;

11. Determine all complaints regarding land grants except "difficult" cases that had to be referred to the meeting;

12. Hold regular meetings of their own and give an advance notice of their times and locations.

Some of these duties for which New London held its townsmen responsible had been assigned by the General Court to lesser town officers, such as the town clerk or constable; the townsmen, however, bore the ultimate responsibility for the actions of all the lesser town officers.[10]

The constable, the second most important officer in these towns, was the first town office created by the General Court in 1636 and was originally intended to deal with Indians and other threats to the peace. The early military structure of the town was under his control; he was ordered to enforce the law that required each man over sixteen to have a ready gun. Told by the General Court to maintain a night watch in town, the constable was given the authority to order men to take part in it. A town's relations with the Indians were regulated by the Court and townsmen, but if any Indian broke a town law the constable was empowered to bring him before the local magistrate. The constable shared with the townsmen the duty of seeing that people obeyed the plethora of behavior-controlling laws. Directives to the townsmen to watch out for "tavern haunters" and "tobacco takers" always included the proviso that the constable should also make sure that these laws were obeyed. If the townsmen wanted someone brought before their court, it was the constable who executed their orders. The constable alone was empowered to raise the "hue and cry" that would warn all other towns about a lawbreaking person. In a statement reminiscent of the medieval *posse,* the General Court empowered the constable to swear in as many men as he needed to assist in dealing with lawbreakers. The constable was charged to arrest people promptly for vagrancy, sabbath breaking, and lying, and he was required personally to supervise the tavern in his town.[11]

The constable was more than merely the peace-keeping figure and the arm of the townsmen. He had an important constitutional place in the structure of Connecticut government. He had some power over the freemen's meeting, since he was required to supervise the elections for deputies, assistants, and governor. He was empowered to appoint a jury to investigate any possible crime in town. Once a year at a town meeting the constable was required to read all the laws passed by the General Court in that year. Later, when the Court printed up copies of all Connecticut laws, the constable was required to make sure that every family in town had one. The colony government also placed the constable in charge of presenting all financial accounts of the town to the General Court when the Court asked for them and made him collect the colony rate in each town and present it to the Court. Usually, when the colony government wanted any specific action taken in a particular town, it would issue a directive to the town constable. If the Court fined a man or wanted to collect a debt from him, it would order the constable to carry out its order. The constable was elected by the town meeting but served as the local arm of the General Court: he was the key administrative figure connecting the two levels of government in the founding years. Not infrequently, constables were fined by the General Court for not performing their duties to the Court's satisfaction.[12]

Town clerks, like many secretaries of organizations, bore a great deal of the work of each town but received relatively little attention from either the town meeting or the General Court. In the first eight years of Hartford, Wethersfield, and Windsor, one of the townsmen served as a record keeper, but the Court in 1644 ordered each town to elect a clerk. He was required to keep a ledger book of all town meetings and a record of all land transactions. For each land transaction he recorded, the clerk charged sixpence, of which he kept fourpence and sent twopence to the secretary of the General Court. The law Code of 1650 further amplified the clerk's duties by requiring him to keep a record of all deaths, marriages, and births in his town and to forward these figures once a year to the Court. The massive detail of all this record keeping was acknowledged when the Court in the Code of 1650 ordered the clerk to keep an index to the land record books.[13] The town clerk did not have any policy-making role and was not required to attend meetings other than the town meetings. He did not keep records of the townsmen's meetings.

The other important positions in the early towns were the special ad hoc committees appointed by the town to deal with specific problems. There were few of these in the first ten years, but as the town meeting grew more inactive it appointed more of them. By the 1650s, the town meeting was appointing an average or two of three ad hoc committees a year, and they played a crucial role in town decision making. In exceptional years Fairfield named as many as ten such committees per year. Usually, these committees in all of the towns consisted of three or four men, all of whom were prominent and one of whom sometimes was a townsman. They were often designated by names like "the committee for the new school," "the committee for the boundaries," or "the committee for the meetinghouse." Often specific problems between individuals in town were settled by ad hoc committee arbitration instead of by recourse to courts. Usually, if the town wanted to petition the General Court for something, it would designate a committee to draw up the petition. Invariably, the committee's actions were ratified by the town meeting.[14]

There were no major town officers other than the townsmen, constable, clerk, and special committees, but there were several lesser ones. Two of the most active groups of officers were the surveyors of highways and the fence viewers. Surveyors were not chosen in the first seven years of the River Towns' existence, but in 1643 the General Court created the position and defined its duties. Surveyors were responsible for maintaining existing roads and building new roads when needed. They were empowered to commandeer every able-bodied man in town to work on the roads, if the work required it. The surveyors were also warned by the Court that if the roads were not built and maintained properly, the Court would fine them. The position of fence viewer was created in the next session of the General Court. These important officers were required to maintain fences along the common lands, observe and bring to order those who neglected animals there, and note whose animals got loose from private land and caused damages to others' lands. Both the surveyors and the fence viewers had their duties reiterated and spelled out even more specifically by the Code of 1650. The number of men to be elected to both positions was not stated by the General Court; prior to 1675 usually two to four surveyors and four to six fence viewers were elected per town.[15]

Other officers elected at the town meeting in this period were the packers and the sealers. These were men who inspected certain goods in a town, usually barrels of pork and beef and tanned hides, and then stamped them to show that the goods conformed to existing colony standards. These positions also were created in 1644.[16] All towns were required to elect a meat packer and a leather sealer, and some towns separated the post of meat packer into the two positions of beef packer and pork packer. Towns were also required to elect a sealer of weights and measures, whose job was to inspect and certify all the scales used in business transactions.

The only other town officers created after 1643 and before 1675 were the ratesmen, whose positions were established and defined in the Code of 1650. The ratesmen were created probably to ease the townsmen's work; they were required to list and assess all the town goods of any male in town above the age of sixteen. The General Court detailed to the ratesmen the prices at which most types of goods must be assessed. Thus, a cow was to be assessed at five pounds if it was four years old and four pounds if it was between three and four years old. The ratesmen were instructed to assess year-old goats at eight shillings and year-old swine at twenty shillings.[17] Every second or third year the General Court would establish a new assessment rate schedule and pass it on to the ratesmen. While their duties were specific and their discretionary powers were limited, the ratesmen could be considered mid-level officers between the high-level townsmen, constable, and clerk, and the low-level fence viewers, surveyors, packers, and sealers.

A few lesser town officers whose duties were not specified by the General Court were created individually by towns. Hartford elected four chimney viewers, who were, as their name suggests, to inspect all chimneys in town for fire hazards. Norwalk in some years elected a treasurer apart from the townsmen, though in most years a townsman performed the treasurer's duties. Fairfield elected sheepmasters to assist the fence viewers and also elected a man "to beat the drum for town meetings." Other towns occasionally elaborated on General Court intentions. Windsor, for instance, in 1641 established a hayward, who inspected all grains that were sold and certified them to be of acceptable quality. Thirty-one years after Windsor elected its first hayward, the General Court ordered all towns to follow suit.

However, the normal procedure was for towns to elect officers after the positions had been created and defined by the General Court. There was never any doubt who initiated the action. It was also clear that the General Court would intervene in the actions of officers in each town if the officers questioned the authority of the Court or if the town's peace was threatened. The Charter of 1662, which gave royal sanction to Connecticut's de facto government, empowered the Court to make any laws that were "wholesome and reasonable" and to set forth "the several duties, powers, and limits of every officer within the towns."[18] The General Court took this power seriously, and the towns, while obviously not closely supervised in mundane affairs, always operated within the bounds established by the Court. Thus, the oath for each town officer was prescribed by the Court and not by the town, implying that the officer's greatest loyalty should be to the colony government. The Court, through the constables and through arbitration committees, issued instructions to towns that appear trivial by today's standards. For example, when the town of Wethersfield in 1640 elected an officer who was unacceptable to the Court, the Court stipulated that "he and the town who chose him to that place are to have notice to appear at . . . the next court." When anything threatened local peace, the colony intervened to settle the controversy whether the town requested colony aid or not. "The Court being acquainted of a difficulty" between Guilford and Killingworth, over a bridge across the Hammonasset River, ordered each town to help finish the bridge by December and to pay half the cost. Nor would the colony allow the towns to pervert General Court legislation or circumvent its intent. When New London undervalued its estates for tax purposes in 1663, the Court rebuked it severely, saying, "They have not attended any rule of righteousness in their work, but have acted very corruptly therein." Constitutionally, the towns had no power other than that delegated to them by the colony government — they were not legally incorporated self-governing boroughs — and by English seventeenth-century theory, the delegation of authority carried no implied powers with it and had to be closely supervised. The colony government was as vitally concerned with local affairs as its creations, the town governments, were, and the two levels practiced a "dual localism," in the words of one recent scholar.[19]

When one compares the relationship between the colony government and the towns of Connecticut with the same relationship in Rhode Island, the carefully defined power flow in Connecticut and the General Court's interference in local government become more apparent. In Rhode Island the towns were practically self-governing republics in the seventeenth century; at one time, individual towns could actually nullify a statute of the General Court.[20]

A comparison with Massachusetts is not as clear-cut, because historians disagree over colony-town relations in Massachusetts, and the definitive analysis of the power arrangements between the two levels has yet to be written. The preponderance of recent evidence suggests, however, that while the Massachusetts towns were not autonomous Puritan villages of collective Adams in new Gardens of Eden, they were not as closely supervised and controlled as Connecticut towns. The General Court of Massachusetts insisted in theory that the towns acknowledge its hegemony, but in practice Massachusetts towns seem to have been at a midpoint between the loose supervision given towns in Rhode Island and the close supervision practiced in Connecticut. The most probable explanation is that Massachusetts was larger and control was administratively more difficult than in its Puritan neighbor to the south. As Connecticut towns grew in number, central control over them declined because, among other things, it was not administratively feasible. In both Massachusetts and Connecticut, the Puritan desire for order and the trend towards centralization of Tudor-Stuart England inclined the General Court to curtail local freedom sharply. Juxtaposed to this influence, however, were the decentralizing impact of the Congregational church polity and the tradition of localism that was nurtured in the English past and transported to New England. The "persistent localism" that T. H. Breen has recently identified in Massachusetts was also present in somewhat lessened form in Connecticut and could lead to tensions between the two levels. Yet, despite some local jealousy of the central government and an occasional outburst of defiance (usually short-lived), early Connecticut towns were the most closely supervised in New England, and especially so in the New Haven Colony. For example, the rationalization and standardization that Connecticut imposed upon its towns in the Fundamental Orders, the legislation of the 1640s, and the Code of 1650 did not occur in Massachusetts until after 1660.[21]

All parts of the mature colony of Connecticut were not, of course, fashioned at their inception by the General Court. New Haven Colony, prior to its amalgamation with Connecticut, contained towns with functioning local governments. New Haven Colony even more than Connecticut tried to maintain a tight control over towns under its jurisdiction. In particular it used traveling magistrates to ride circuit and hold court in the towns in an effort to require the towns to adhere to a uniform standard of justice and morality. The magistracy, far more important in New Haven's towns than in Connecticut's, was the bulwark of local government. The "free burgesses" of each town elected deputies and magistrates for the General Court in New Haven; these deputies and magistrates together comprised the "plantation court" of each town, which was required to meet monthly to hear cases, promulgate bylaws, and issue executive orders. Thus town and colony government in New Haven were indissolubly tied together, since colony officials constituted the most important organ of local government. The judges of the plantation courts exercised their magisterial powers in many ways, like the justices of peace in England and the colonial South. The free burgesses of each town did assemble in a meeting to deliberate local problems; by 1656 the meeting of the burgesses had been transformed into a town meeting similar to that of the Connecticut towns. In their meeting, the burgesses for each town elected a law enforcement officer called "the marshall" and a recorder of deeds and records called "the secretary."[22]

When forced by imperial fiat in 1662 to join Connecticut Colony, New Haven tried to protect and perpetuate its magisterial form of town government. As part of its terms for submitting, New Haven asked to be constituted into a separate county within the larger colony; Connecticut agreed, and the county system was created four years after the formal amalgamation. Mindful of New Haven's fears, Connecticut also agreed not to question any past judicial decisions of New Haven, to admit all New Haven burgesses as freemen of Connecticut, and to respect all the church societies of New Haven. These minor concessions, however, did not obscure the fact that New Haven was forced into the union on Connecticut's terms and had to alter her institutional arrangements. The laws regulating local government in the future were Connecticut laws, not New Haven's past ones, and the New Haven towns were to "order the[ir] civil, prudential affairs" with selectmen chosen annually by a majority of the local inhabitants. With this fiat, town government replaced magisterial government as the dominant force in the towns formerly under the jurisdiction of New Haven Colony. After a few years, town government in the old New Haven Colony was indistinguishable from that in the rest of Connecticut. Estelle Feinstein's careful case study of a New Haven Colony town in this transition period concludes, on a basis of examining the town records and not the colony ones, that the transfer from New Haven to Connecticut greatly enhanced local decision making.[23]

Not only did union with Connecticut lessen the tight control over town government in the communities of New Haven Colony, the amalgamation of the two colonies also had the effect of lessening central control over towns in the rest of Connecticut. As the colony increased from the three proximate River Towns to numerous and often distant towns, it became increasingly difficult to maintain close supervision of the localities. The Code of 1650 in many ways represents the high point of centralization, which was followed by a gradual but perceptible decline in control. Union with New Haven increased the number of towns by nearly 50 percent and added to the growing administrative difficulties. In addition to this practical problem, the zeal and urgency of the original Puritans, which produced the commonwealth spirit of the first generation of Connecticut settlers, was waning; the acquisitive Yankee spirit replacing it enhanced the latent feelings of localism that the Puritan drive for order had temporarily overcome. The proliferation of local bodies, particularly the development of separate proprietary and church society governments, which was virtually inevitable given the growth of population, splintered local government and added an additional impediment to central control. Like the much-vaunted social transition "from Puritan to Yankee," the political transition from central control to local power can be seen most graphically in the eighteenth century, but both transitions were ongoing processes starting with the end of the first generation of colonists.[24]

A quantitative analysis of the business of the General Assembly over the course of the colonial and Revolutionary periods tends to support the hypothesis of growing town autonomy. The colony government issued the largest number of direct orders to specific towns in the 1640s, 1650s, and 1660s; thereafter, the number of specific directives per town generally declined. Moreover, town matters comprised an increasingly smaller percentage of the General Assembly's business as time passed. The decline was slight, and one might be led to believe that the lessening of central control was slight; however, the Assembly always became involved in intertown disputes, and since intertown economic activity grew massively in the eighteenth century, it is an indication of substantially lessened control that the number of directives per town went down slightly instead of up massively. When reading the records of the General Court in the 1640s and those of the General Assembly in the 1780s, one is struck by how many more appeals of local decisions there were in the latter decade than in the former; but this is no indication of increased central control. Appeals, by themselves, do not mean that local government was not the crucial decision-making level in the colony. Appeals simply mean that Connecticut's inhabitants protested local decisions and were more inclined to question authority and control of any kind. The Assembly was the place a quarrelsome Yankee could question a decision already made by the town. Moreover, although the Assembly was deluged by private business and the processing of it became a serious problem because of the time it consumed, almost never after 1680 did the Assembly initiate any of these cases. Most of the private business was requests relating to military matters, such as training exemptions or compensation for injuries; appeals in civil suits; and appeals from probate courts. It is a measure of the colony's sense of ultimate authority that the Assembly entertained so many appeals and private petitions, but it is not a measure of its desire to make local decisions. Although the colony government changed its name from General Court to General Assembly in 1698, it maintained an increasingly important relationship to the towns as an appeals court.

As an *assembly* it passed general legislation giving the towns broad powers to make decisions; as a *court* it heard numerous appeals from these decisions; as an *executive* it seldom acted in local affairs (see table 6).[25]

TABLE 6

General Court and General Assembly Business,
1640–1790

Items of business[a]	1640s	1650s	1660s	1670s	1680s	1690s	1700s	1710s
External and colony-level business items	14	9	20	18	13	11	15	16
Statutes applying to town officers in general	7	3	5	1	3	2	0	2
Directives to specific towns (no. per town)	1.1	.8	1.0	.8	.5	.5	.5	.5
Directives to individuals	7	16	22	16	25	24	27	31
Other	0	0	0	0	0	0	0	0

Items of business[a]	1720s	1730s	1740s	1750s	1760s	1770s	1780s
External and colony-level business items	16	20	28	37	22	45	52
Statutes applying to town officers in general	2	3	2	1	2	1	9
Directives to specific towns (no. per town)	.8	.6	.5	.4	.4	.5	.5
Directives to individuals	48	29	59	79	118	95	142
Other	2	2	0	1	1	3	19

[a]Represents the average number in a year. Compiled by sampling two years per decade.

Although the towns gained increased power from the Assembly's enlarged conception of delegated authority, the town meeting itself did not increase in activity in the first two-thirds of the eighteenth century but instead declined. Connecticut's pattern of town meetings contrasts sharply with the picture of heightened meeting activity in Massachusetts painted by Kenneth Lockridge and Alan

Kreider (and widely cited as indicative of the New England experience); either Connecticut and Massachusetts differed markedly, or the two towns used as evidence by Lockridge and Kreider are not a good sample of the whole.

The easiest way of seeing this decrease in activity is by examining the frequency of meetings.[26] In a sample of sixteen Connecticut towns, all of them, though varying slightly in time and degree, tended to show a declining frequency of meetings in the early eighteenth century. Generally, in either the 1730s or 1740s each town reached a new low level of average frequency that lasted from then until after 1765. Every town at some time between 1765 and 1775 underwent a sharp increase in the frequency of the meeting, as events in the Revolutionary years brought out a response in the meeting that reversed its pattern of declining or stagnant activity. The years of actual prosecution of the military aspects of the war brought the highest town-meeting frequency of the Revolutionary years. In some towns the Revolutionary rate of activity equaled or exceeded the rate of the beginning of the century in 1701–10; in other towns the Revolutionary rate was higher than the lowest rates in the middle of the century but still lower than the 1701–10 rate. But one can easily see in the decadal averages for each town a significant increase in the activity of the meetings during the Revolutionary years. Generally, the increased activity enlivened the meeting beyond the Revolutionary years and lasted until at least 1790. Tables 7 and 8 show that this increase was not caused just by the inclusion of the years 1781, 1782, and 1783 in this decade averaging, but that the meeting was often active even after all immediate problems with the war were past. The Revolution activated the meeting, and so did the Revolution's political and economic consequences.

From table 7 it is obvious that in some towns the drop from 1701–10 to the middle of the century was drastic and abrupt and that in others it was mild but steady. In all towns, however, there was a decline. Derby dropped from an average of 4.4 in 1701–10 to one of 1.1 in 1761–70. Groton steadily declined from an average of 3.2 in 1701–10 to an average of 1.8 in 1751–60. Every meeting, barring those of towns newly founded in the middle of the eighteenth century, experienced mid-century doldrums. Every town had at least one decade between 1731 and 1770 that averaged fewer than two meetings per year.

TABLE 7

Yearly Frequency of Town Meetings in Towns Settled
before 1720, Averaged by Decades

Town	1701–10	1711–21	1721–30	1731–40	1741–50	1751–60	1761–70	1771–80	1781–90
Branford	3.2	2.0	2.1	1.4	1.8	1.5	1.2	3.5	3.7
Derby	4.4	2.2	2.0	3.0	1.9	1.4	1.1	1.6	2.7
Groton	3.2	3.0	2.6	2.2	2.2	1.8	2.7	4.9	4.1
Hartford	1.6	1.6	2.5	1.8	1.4	2.8	3.4	5.2	4.0
Lebanon	3.7	2.4	2.4	2.4	1.4	2.2	2.0	3.0	2.4
Mansfield	a	2.2	2.1	1.5	1.7	1.9	2.4	5.3	4.8
Newtown	b	b	b	b	1.6	1.5	2.2	2.5	3.7
Norwalk	2.3	2.2	2.0	1.1	1.1	1.5	1.9	2.9	2.4
Norwich	3.9	4.3	b	2.6	1.9	2.5	4.7	6.7	7.1
Ridgefield	a	a	1.5	1.9	2.3	1.4	1.3	2.5	2.6
Windham	2.1	1.4	1.4	1.6	1.4	1.5	2.6	3.8	3.7
Total	3.05	2.37	2.07	1.95	1.70	1.81	2.32	3.81	3.75

Note: I would have separated these towns into two groups, those founded in the early period of town settlement, prior to 1675, and those founded in a later period, except that the two groups showed no significant differences for the frequency of meeting. Figures for each town are not based on a sample but include meetings in all years.

a Not in existence as a town in these years.
b Missing data.

The only town meetings that were active in the middle years of the century were those of the newly founded towns. A sample of five Litchfield County towns, all founded between 1738 and 1741, shows them to have had averages in 1741–50 of 5.0, 4.0, 3.6, 4.6, and 2.2, when the highest average of any of the eleven earlier-settled towns was 2.3. The Litchfield County towns followed the same cycle the other towns had followed in the seventeenth century: frequent meetings in the founding years and then declining frequency of meetings. For the Litchfield County towns, however, with the model all around them of inactive meetings, the decline was abrupt instead of gradual. All five towns declined drastically in frequency of meeting between 1741–50 and 1751–60. Salisbury declined from an average of 5.0 to 1.9 and Sharon from 4.6 to 2.5.

The years between 1721 and 1765 were the most inactive of Connecticut's town meetings. Table 9 measures the percentage of times in this forty-five-year period that each town had just one or two meetings. Unlike Massachusetts, where two meetings a year

TABLE 8

Yearly Frequency of Town Meetings in Litchfield County Towns
Settled 1738–41, Averaged by Decades

Town	1741–50	1751–60	1761–70	1771–80	1781–90
Canaan	3.6	a	1.5	3.5	2.0
Goshen	4.0	2.9	2.1	3.0	2.9
New Hartford	2.2	2.1	1.5	2.3	2.7
Salisbury	5.0	1.9	2.0	3.4	3.3
Sharon	4.6	2.5	3.2	4.2	3.6
Total	4.0	2.4	2.1	3.3	3.0

a Missing data.

TABLE 9

Years between 1721 and 1765 with Only
One or Two Meetings in Towns Founded before 1720

Town	Total years available	Years with one or two meetings only	% of total
Branford	45	37	82
Derby	44	35	80
Groton	45	32	71
Hartford	45	32	71
Lebanon	45	31	69
Mansfield	45	34	76
Newtown	25	21	84
Norwalk	45	41	91
Norwich	38	23	61
Ridgefield	45	39	87
Windham	45	43	96
Total average			79

TABLE 10

Years between 1751 and 1765 with Only
One or Two Meetings in Towns Founded 1738–41

Town	Total years available	Years with one or two meetings only	% of total
Canaan	8	7	88
Goshen	15	8	53
New Hartford	15	9	60
Salisbury	15	12	80
Sharon	15	9	60
Total average			66

were required by law, Connecticut required only one.[27] Norwich, with the most active meetings, had only one or two meetings 61 percent of the time during this period, while Windham had only one or two meetings 96 percent of the time. The towns founded before 1720 had one or two meetings 79 percent of the time. The lack of any exception makes the norm all the more meaningful. The five Litchfield County towns all conform to this pattern in the years after the higher activity of their founding years (see table 10).

All of this analysis shows a massive reduction in the activity of the meeting in mature eighteenth-century towns; it seems to indicate that perhaps the meeting had become a lesser part of each town's decision-making apparatus and that the balance of power between the meeting and its elected officials had tipped in favor of the officials. In years when there was just one meeting, it was held in December and usually just elected the town officers, and perhaps an ad hoc committee, and ratified the town rate. In years in which two meetings were held, the second was usually on freemen's day in April or September and merely replaced a few deceased officers. This all suggests quiescence and lack of involvement beyond elections. However, the data for all the towns reveal occasional spurts to high levels of activity for one, two, or three years. Lebanon proceeded for seventeen years with one or two meetings a year and then suddenly jumped to three (for two years) and four (for one), before going back to two. Derby jumped from one meeting a year for two years to six and five meetings each for two years and then again subsided to one or two meetings a year. Generally, all years with one or two meetings were years in which the meetings were pro forma and lacked issues aside from elections, but in years where there were three or more meetings some issues had become exceptionally controversial. The meeting was inactive during times of tranquility and presumably allowed the elected officials to govern the town. However, the meeting could become politicized by a controversy and assert its latent power as the ultimate political body within the town. Thus, while it is accurate to talk about a generally inactive meeting in the middle of the eighteenth century, it is not accurate to discount totally the role of the town meeting in town affairs. In normal times the townspeople seemed willing to allow the selectmen to make the decisions for them, often year after year, but the meeting's power was always there and could be and occasionally was asserted. This latent power certainly must have affected the selectmen's perception of their own jobs. There is no doubt that the selectmen were the prime movers in each town, but they must always have known that storms could come.

The leading reason for holding extra town meetings (extra being defined as more than two) was a crisis requiring the town to deal with the General Assembly. Usually these meetings either elected a committee to petition the General Assembly, ratified the petition itself, or in some other way discussed a matter relative to the town in which the General Assembly was involved. The General Assembly was almost always involved because a dispute had already erupted in town. The second leading cause of extra meetings concerned the physical aspects of running a town: controversies or emergencies about highways, bridges, or ferries. The third leading reason concerned the meetinghouse — locating, building, and repairing it. Hiring a minister, extra elections, and financial problems round out the list of frequent causes of extra meetings. Few extra meetings dealt with many issues at the same meeting (many being defined as three or more separate issues discussed at the same meeting). Usually, if an exceptional meeting was called, there was one overriding issue or emergency that precipitated it. Specific reasons for holding extra meetings range from controlling the harvesting of oysters in a seacoast town to importing a doctor to remove a kidney stone from a local woman in a Litchfield County frontier town.[28]

The temper of the town meeting depended on whether it was held under normal circumstances or had become politicized by local controversy. Under normal circumstances lack of attendance was often a problem. The Hartford annual meeting of 1769 adjourned for a week after merely selecting a moderator, who then declared attendance too low to conduct any further elections. Waterbury, plagued by poor turnouts at town meetings during the 1740s and frequently forced to adjourn for that reason, tried to solve its problem by starting the meeting at ten instead of nine in the morning. In Sharon, where inhabitants frequently refused to attend meetings on cold winter days, meetings were postponed "considering the extremity of the weather and the fewness of the people," and "on account of the great coldness of the season." Pomfret, worried over the legitimacy of bylaws passed at meetings in which "the inhabitants . . . have wholly failed in attendance," declared that its statutes were as binding "as if all were present."

When the Norwich meeting of August, 1715, voted on a previously unannounced issue, 25 votes constituted a majority. The attendance must have been less than 50 in a town that had at least 2,500 inhabitants. In a petition to the next meeting 32 men complained that the calling for this vote was a "surprise" and stated that while they normally did not attend meetings, they would have done so had they known the vote was to be taken. Similarly, in Windham, a portion of the town, counting on the customary poor attendance, "packed" the meeting and forced through an unpopular decision by a vote of 38 to 34; a good turnout at the next meeting reversed the vote. Meetings also could become large; New Haven and Wallingford meetings in 1761 were attended by 234 and 120 inhabitants, respectively. This attendance was substantially less than 25 percent of those eligible; yet they were sizable gatherings for effective deliberative bodies. The size of the meeting, as might be expected, correlated with the importance of the business under consideration. In 1726, 150 inhabitants attended a New London meeting when the town was involved in a bitter controversy; this was regarded as an unparalleled turnout. In Woodstock, in the same year, over 90 percent of the town attended the meeting deliberating the fate of the minister. In the new towns of Litchfield County, which had more frequent town meetings, attendance was much higher than in the rest of the colony and at times exceeded 90 percent; these towns also were more zealous in maintaining elaborate "warning" systems for meetings.[29]

Meetings ranged from small, quiet affairs with little debate to highly charged sessions almost impossible to control. In 1729, apparently in response to rowdy meetings, the Assembly passed a law forbidding tumults and riotous behavior at them. After one such meeting in Middletown the town voted that no one should "interrupt the meeting by disorderly speaking." In a 1709 election meeting in Farmington a committee was named to "keep the youth in order during the meeting." Most communities recorded votes with the succinct expression "the town votes," but occasionally they would preface this statement with "after much deliberation" or "after great discourse," indicating a more than usually heated debate. Middletown recorded tallies "by unanimous vote" often for periods as long as ten years and then would distinguish a rare instance as "by majority vote." During the 1720s and 1750s Ridgefield usually recorded votes as unanimous — "yea universally" one clerk wrote — but during the 1730s and 1740s the town had a long series of tallies that were "by major vote," indicating that town consensus, while desired, could break down for protracted periods. Voting on issues was frequently oral, but towns could go to great lengths to protect the anonymity of voters on sensitive questions. Norwich, in a secret ballot tailored so that even illiterates could vote, specified that marks on a ballot meant that a minister should be let go, while a blank ballot meant that he should be kept.[30]

The election of town officers was the main business of the annual meeting after the founding years. Election procedures were never codified either by the General Assembly or by any town in its written records. From indirect and occasional evidence in the records we can surmise that procedures varied both from town to town and within towns. In 1712 Middletown proposed that the three selectmen be chosen "by nomination and then voting upon nomination." This proposal was defeated, and instead the town voted by "papers." Five years later, Middletown chose officers by "nomination and by lifting the hand." The moderator instructed the meeting to "shout to nominate." Still a third method in Middletown was used for the election of selectmen in 1720: the voters queued up and each gave a name orally to the clerk, who declared a man elected when he had a majority of the meeting. Other towns employed this oral system — Sharon called it "going round" the meetinghouse — but if someone requested it, the vote would be by "proxies" (written ballots). Although discussion of voting procedures was only occasionally recorded, and discussion of qualifications of candidates was never recorded, elections must have involved some debate. Election meetings lasted from nine or ten in the morning to four in the afternoon and usually took at least two days. By unwritten but scrupulously followed custom, town meetings could not go past dark. As Litchfield stated during a controversy, "No act of the town should stand in force that was passed after daylight."[31]

An election system known to have been utilized by several towns may have been widespread and could explain how the meeting handled the election of large numbers of officers. In 1765 the Farmington moderator told the selectmen "to bring in their nominations of town officers to the meeting as usual." The selectmen must have prepared a slate of officers in advance. The meeting could add or subtract nominations, but the consistency of Farmington's officeholding patterns supports the view that a small group of men constantly controlled them. The Newtown meeting voted that the "selectmen shall nominate the selectmen" for the following year; Guilford "desired the selectmen to make a nomination of town officers and lay it before the town"; Ridgefield "disapproved of the nominations published"; and Norwalk "brought in nominations" — all suggesting that a small group of men, usually the selectmen, nominated officeholders in advance. As further evidence supporting this hypothesis, elections were smooth and seldom contested after the fact. In five of seven towns examined — Fairfield, Hartford, Kent, Lebanon, and Middletown — there were no controverted elections during the eighteenth century; the other two towns in the sample, Farmington and Norwich, each had but one.[32]

As the towns grew in size and complexity, the kinds and numbers of officers needed to administer their affairs increased correspondingly. Much of the increase resulted from additions to the numbers of such officers as fence viewers and surveyors of highways, required by expansion of settlement to the outer geographic limits of the towns. In addition, several new offices were created. Their functions were outlined by town practice and by the Assembly.

The position of grand juryman offers an interesting example of the evolution of a local office. In 1666 the General Court created four counties — Fairfield, Hartford, New Haven, and New London — each of which was a judicial unit presided over by a county court. In 1667 the General Court ordered each county court to appoint a "grand jury of twelve able men at least" from among the towns. These grand jurymen were to meet once a year with their county court and "make presentments of the breaches of any law." They could also at any time make a presentment of a breach of law to a local justice of the peace, a magistrate appointed by the colony government. Most towns had at least one justice, who assumed the local judicial duties exercised earlier by the selectmen; large towns sometimes had two or more. Over the next forty-five years the General Court added to the grand juryman's duties, making him a social constable in each town. Grand jurymen were required to assist the selectmen and constables in maintaining order and assuring high standards of moral conduct. At sessions between

1667 and 1712 the Assembly frequently enjoined the selectmen, constables, and grand jurymen to watch out for unacceptable social or moral behavior. These injunctions were issued in Connecticut at the time that Massachusetts took similar action. This is, of course, the period in which historians have seen the falling away of many people from strict Puritan codes of behavior. In 1679 Massachusetts created the local office of tithingman for each town to help combat this moral decay. Grand jurymen were the Connecticut General Court's answer to the same problem. But unlike the Massachusetts tithingman, who was elected by the town meeting, the Connecticut grand juryman was appointed by the county court. In 1712, however, the Assembly ordered all towns to elect at least two grand jurymen a year, and at the December 1712 annual meetings all the towns complied. Grand jurymen were thus incorporated into the operating structure of every town.[33]

Similarly, the office of tithingman, borrowed from Massachusetts, was created by the General Assembly in 1721 to combat moral laxity. Hartford began electing tithingmen in that year, and many towns did the same in 1722 and 1723. From then on, the Assembly always included tithingmen when it issued annual pronouncements about social control to town officers. It instructed the tithingmen to "carefully inspect the behavior of all persons on the Sabbath or Lord's Day" and to make "due presentment of any prophanation." By 1732 all the towns were electing tithingmen, who assumed the constabulary functions that grand jurymen had originally performed. Neither the tithingmen nor the grand jurymen were given additional duties (although the grand jurymen's duties at the county courts were elaborated) until 1761, when they were instructed by the Assembly to meet with the constables once a year in June to discuss provisions for the effective enforcement of local morality.[34] This was a last and anachronistic institutional attempt to preserve the old moral facade of the Puritan village.

The town offices of lister and rater, although originally created by the Assembly, developed their functions in response to local needs, and in a variety of ways. In the early seventeenth century the towns were ordered to elect ratemakers, who assessed all townspeople's wealth for tax purposes. Originally, the selectmen, not the ratemakers, set the tax rates. Between 1675 and 1700, however, ratemakers took over that function in most towns. In some, they kept the name of ratemakers, and in others they were newly designated "listers and raters" or "list makers and rate makers." Between 1700 and 1720 some towns began to elect separate "listers" and "raters," while others still kept the functions combined. These changes took place without any interference by the General Assembly. Although the Assembly did finally decree in 1724 that each town must elect between four and nine listers, the towns still took various approaches to the creation of financial officers. A few towns elected financial auditors, such as the inspectors of Hartford and the auditors of Middletown, to whom the listers and raters were directed to report. The Assembly was responsive to local needs concerning finance; when several towns complained that they were prohibited by colony statute from electing more than nine listers and more were needed, the Assembly passed a law authorizing the towns to elect as many "as they shall judge necessary and convenient."[35]

The offices of moderator and treasurer were both shaped more by local needs than by enactments of the General Assembly. In the early years of the seventeenth century a selectman performed the functions of each position. Gradually, with no prodding by the legislature, the towns began to elect treasurers. Hartford chose its first treasurer in 1706, and by 1749, when Fairfield elected its first, the practice had become general. The moderator's office evolved similarly. In the founding years most towns did not designate a moderator, although Windsor did so as early as 1642. Instead, one of the selectmen usually presided over the meeting. Between 1680 and 1720, however, virtually every town began electing moderators, who might or might not be selectmen. Practice varied because the central government never prescribed rules concerning moderators. For instance, while in most towns the moderator was elected for a single meeting, Fairfield named its moderator to serve for a number of meetings in a year. Theoretically, the moderator was not presiding over two meetings but over two parts of an adjourned meeting. However, the two sessions were often months apart and might consider totally different business. Middletown elected its first moderator in 1708, stopped electing the officer in 1712, and started again in 1720; Derby and Lyme each elected one man to serve continually as moderator during the town's pleasure.[36]

As grand jurymen, tithingmen, raters and listers, moderators, and treasurers were added to the roster of town officers, the number grew to sometimes staggering proportions, further increased by the addition of branders, key keepers, rate collectors, and sealers. Occasionally a town carried the electoral process to extremes; Guilford elected "makers of coffins" and "gravediggers," and Middletown elected "hog watchers." Not only were new officers added, but each multiple office had its numbers expanded. Towns averaged 50 to 60 officers in 1725, 60 to 70 in 1750, and 75 to 100 in 1775. Both large land size and large populations inclined a town to have a large administration; of the two, land size was the more crucial. In a sample of twenty towns, for example, Farmington, with by far the largest land mass in the colony and with the third largest population, had the most elected officials, 206; New Hartford, with the smallest land mass and smallest population, had the fewest, 41. The bulk of the officeholders were minor officers; the huge number of officers in Farmington included 22 grand jurymen, 22 listers, 10 constables, 25 tithingmen, 50 surveyors of highways, 7 leather sealers, 7 weight sealers, 9 measures sealers, 16 fence viewers, 8 key keepers, 7 branders, 9 collectors of rates, 4 ratemakers, and 1 packer. It was necessary to have many of the town-meeting officers — grand jurymen, tithingmen, listers, and raters — because expansion to the outer edges of the town and the growth in population made it impossible for the selectmen to perform all of these functions personally. Other town officers, such as the largest group, the surveyors of highways, and the fence viewers, became much more numerous because growth placed new demands on the services they provided.[37]

As local government grew, the selectmen exercised increased authority. The Assembly passed more and more general enabling acts delegating greater discretionary powers to the selectmen. As noted above, in 1690 the selectmen were given supervisory power over all other town officers and were told "to take cognizance of such as do neglect the duties of surveyor, hayward, fenceviewer," and so forth. In 1703 the Assembly passed an act providing the selectmen with broad military power "to order what houses shall be fortified and what they do order shall be done forthwith." In 1708 they were delegated the extremely important power to levy a tax whenever the town's finances required it. An act of 1719 gave the selectmen virtual carte blanche power over the administration of local welfare. An unusual grant of authority in 1715 permitted them to reduce or eliminate an individual's colony rate if, in their judgment, it constituted a hardship. Acts of the Assembly passed in 1775 and 1776 enhanced the ability of the selectmen to deal with the problems of civil strife. They could issue warrants against suspected loyalists and confiscate the estate of anyone deemed a partisan of Britain. All persons who traveled between towns had to carry letters from their selectmen. Charles Grant's study of Kent led him to conclude that much of the local war effort in that town was directed by the selectmen.[38]

The authority of the selectmen was expanded not only by enabling acts from above but also by delegations from the town meeting. When Hartford elected new officers in 1706, the meeting directed them to report to the selectmen. In Farmington the meeting in 1708 gave the selectmen total control of town finances, in a sweeping delegation of power, and later it empowered them to act as the town's agents in such external matters as relations with the Assembly or with other towns. The Norwalk meeting in 1702 and again in 1704 put its weight behind the selectmen in all their decisions between meetings. As we have seen, in several towns, perhaps in most, the selectmen nominated all town officers, and in some they prepared an agenda for the town meeting. In Norwich, in the 1740s and 1750s, the many problems for which the town usually named ad hoc committees were turned over to the selectmen, and the number of such committees steadily declined. As the town meeting decreased in activity and frequency during the first seven decades of the eighteenth century, the selectmen took up the slack and became the key decision makers in the towns.[39]

Connecticut ratified its charter and existing common law as its new constitution during the Revolutionary years, and the *structure* of town government was not altered; two important changes did occur, however. First, the operation of government increased at all levels and Connecticut became a much more "governed" society than it had been previously in the eighteenth century. The General Assembly met more often and transacted more business at each session; the governor and his council were in almost constant meetings and acted in many ways like a ministry; the courts held more and longer sessions; and the towns, similarly galvanized by the emergency, became much more active.[40] The selectmen supervised most of the towns' efforts to support the war but were aided by both the town meeting, which was activated by the emergency, and by the committees of inspection, often numbering as many as

twenty-five men, which the Assembly ordered every town to elect.
The committees of inspection were disbanded after the war, but
throughout the 1780s the selectmen and town meetings remained
more active than they had been before the Revolutionary years.
The war's end on the battlefield did not end its effects on the
towns, and selectmen and meetings labored throughout the rest of
the decade to solve the many problems occasioned by independence. Secondly, by providing the impetus to create twenty-seven
new towns, the Revolution indirectly expanded the number of local
officials and brought town government closer to the homes of
many people. Although this gain in local offices was not as large as
one might assume — most of the parent towns losing a portion of
their land cut down on their number of officers — approximately
five-hundred more local officers were elected because of the newly
created towns. Even more significantly, many Connecticut inhabitants after the Revolution lived much closer to their local officials
and town meetings.

Neither the growth in governance nor the increase· in the
number of towns and town officers indicates any unhappiness with
the structure of town-meeting government by the Revolutionaries
in Connecticut. Indeed, the desire for "more of the same" and the
lack of any attempt to alter town government in this era of reform
and change suggests that the town meeting and its officers were
serving their communities well and were perceived by the citizenry
of the new state of Connecticut as institutions too basic to be tam-
pered with.[41]

THE expansion and differentiation that occurred in Connecticut's
town government are consistent with two principles advanced by
scholars who have studied government and authority in a wide
context. First, the differentiation of a governing structure invariably accompanies an increase in population and economic complexity. More people and new methods of producing and distributing goods require more governing officers and new types of
officers.* Second, government expands and tends to become more
frankly coercive when authority is being questioned. In a closed
communal peasant society, government structure can be simple

*See chapter six below for a discussion of economic growth.

and governing officials few because the voluntary submission of the inhabitants and the moral sanctions of the community are sufficient to give it the needed scope and power. Undifferentiated governments exist, then, in communities that are in fundamental agreement on the nature of society and the good life. The enjoinders issued by governing figures in communities like this are somewhat less than commands and somewhat more than mere advice. The weight of communal agreement gives these enjoinders their power; seldom are local decisions appealed to higher authorities. However, when a society becomes more pluralistic, less in agreement, and more individualistic, its moral sanctions lose their power and coercion is required to enforce decisions; this process invariably involves the expansion of the governing structure; more officers give government a greater scope and provide it with some legitimacy for its decisions to replace the legitimacy formerly provided by agreed-upon community standards. Also, of course, with the decline of the voluntary submission of the individual and the decline of the power of moral sanctions goes an increase in the number of appeals from the local governing structure.[42]

The Western world in general in the eighteenth century was in a transition from community authority to government officials as the ultimate source of power in society.[43] As in Connecticut, the questioning of authority that resulted in this widespread transition can be attributed to the growth of toleration and pluralism, the mobility and growth of population, and the development of the economy, all of which strained the community's ability to order its affairs through a few officers and an informal structure. Growth and differentiation in governments was the political response to the modernization process.

[IV]

THE GROWTH AND GOVERNMENT
OF CHURCH SOCIETIES

THE economic reasons behind the founding of Connecticut towns and the settlement of their lands should not obscure the fact that godliness and salvation, although not necessarily the immediate goals of all persons, were central concerns of society in general. Reflecting this concern, the most basic institution in the colony, apart from the family, which in itself had important religious functions, was the ecclesiastical society; Connecticut's Puritans grounded their orthodoxy upon it. The ecclesiastical society was the corporate body created when the General Assembly gave a group of petitioners permission to "embody in church estate." It encompassed one parish and hired a minister, levied and collected taxes for his support, elected governing officers, conducted local schools, and enforced the moral code of the colony. Because of the Puritans' unwillingness to tolerate other religions, all of the seventeenth-century societies were based on the Congregational church parish. Every bona fide Congregational church parish was granted society status and, until dissenting parishes made their appearance in Connecticut, society and parish were synonymous. In a very real sense, the colony's history as a corporate polity started with the formation of the Windsor church society, which antedated the settlement of the River Towns; in 1790 the society, though weakened, still was a core institution of the new state.

Added to the Congregational societies of 1790, however, were the societies of the dissenting churches, Anglicans, Baptists, Separatists, and Quakers. Although Connecticut had never been religiously homogeneous, even in its earliest years, the relative agreement of its inhabitants enabled them to prevent the establishment of any dissenting parishes until the eighteenth century. Starting with the creation of a Baptist parish in Groton in 1705 and an Anglican parish in Stratford in 1707, dissenters gained an institutional foothold in the colony; and after a century of agitation for toleration and a series of concessions by the Standing Order, the dissenting parishes composed about 33 percent of the colony's total in 1790. Not until 1784, however, were dissenting parishes legally recognized as religious societies equal to Congregational ones in all important respects. Prior to that, dissenting parishes were groups of people who worshipped together but were not granted the self-governing privileges of legally constituted societies. Thus, with the growth of dissenting parishes in the early eighteenth century, it was possible to distinguish between parish and society; after 1784 parish and society again became synonymous, as they had been before the rise of dissent.

The first Congregational society in each community was originally coterminous with the town, as the parish in England had always been with the village until the rise of dissent. However, town and society were not always incorporated in the same year.[1] In the first eleven towns incorporated in the colony the two bodies were created within a year of each other, but beginning with Saybrook, the incorporation of the society usually lagged significantly behind that of the town. The twenty-nine newly settled towns created between 1650 and 1734 averaged 6.3 years between the creation of the town and its first ecclesiastical society. In the settlement of Litchfield County after 1734 the colony reverted to the earlier pattern and town and society were constituted in the same year. In the long period 1650–1734, new towns lagged behind in their applications to the General Assembly to be incorporated as societies because they could not afford the cost. In most cases, the middle-period town had fewer inhabitants at its inception than did the first towns and the Litchfield County towns and did not have the tax base to pay a minister's salary. Not until an increase in population made a minister's position economically feasible was a petition for society status usually forthcoming. In the interim, the religious needs and duties of a community were not neglected; until a church was formed, inhabitants met regularly in private houses and prayed together in religious services; yet they could not enjoy the ordinances of the church until they were fully organized and had acquired a minister.[2]

Until the rise of dissenting churches, an ecclesiastical society was usually created by the colony government upon the petition of members of a newly created church; hence, society formation until the eighteenth century invariably and almost immediately followed the formation of a church. Creation of a church, however, was not an activity undertaken lightly. Besides the heavy financial obliga-

tions it imposed upon its members, it required a community to
articulate its Christian ideals and to identify and seek out its most
pious men. Once it was generally agreed that the time was right to
establish a church, the town chose seven men of "blameless conversation" from the community to be the seven pillars who sponsored
it. This practice was based on the Biblical admonition in the Book
of Proverbs, "Wisdom hath builded her house, she hath hewn out
her seven pillars." Being chosen a pillar conveyed great honor, and
choosing them was a serious business; a meeting of those interested
in forming the church nominated candidates, who would be
screened intensively. Once chosen, the pillars drew up a covenant,
applied to the General Assembly for an act of incorporation, and
announced a date for the gathering of the church. The day of the
gathering was a momentous one in a town's life; the seven pillars
read the covenant aloud and signed it in the presence of the
townspeople and guests from the neighboring churches. After the
formal gathering, the seven pillars usually met once a week for a
period of up to a year to screen applicants for membership, permitting acceptable ones to "own the covenant." After a sufficient
number of people joined the new church, it then hired a minister
and perhaps a teacher. Not until the minister was ordained with
the laying on of hands by the ruling elder, the most pious man in
the parish, who was usually chosen from among the seven pillars,
was the entire process of church formation regarded as completed.[3]

Until the 1660s no town in the colony had more than one society, and society and town were coextensive. In 1669, however,
Hartford and Windsor were each divided into two separate
ecclesiastical societies, and a process began that would see almost
every town in the colony subdivided into several societies. The
large land areas of the towns and the dispersal of population from
the center of the towns caused real hardship on many inhabitants,
which only smaller societies could remedy. The churches required
attendance at services at least twice a week, and this frequency of
traveling long distances and crossing rivers created extraordinary
difficulties, wasted enormous amounts of time, and posed serious
dangers. Almost all towns on rivers, for example, had experienced
some tragedy in river crossings. Moreover, besides the frequency
of religious meetings, which sharply distinguished them from town
meetings, church meetings were also distinguished by the fact that

women and children as well as men were required to attend. Thus the physical size of the towns precluded maintaining coterminous societies and towns. Distance from the meetinghouse was a prime reason for the creation of virtually every new society, with only a very few splits caused by doctrinal reasons. As an example of the crucial nature of geography, property values varied proportionately with the distance of a dwelling to the meetinghouse. The General Assembly was sympathetic to the problem. The early leaders were keenly interested in giving each individual in the colony regular access to religious services and almost always responded favorably to a petition for a new society, despite frequent opposition from the original one. The only basic question the Assembly would raise was whether the town could afford to maintain two societies. Unless there was overwhelming proof that dividing a town's religious structure was economically not feasible, the act of incorporation would be issued.[4]

Although the first division of a town into two societies occurred in 1669, not until the first decade of the eighteenth century did the practice of society division become widespread. Between 1700 and 1780 an average of seventeen societies a decade were divided, the peak occurring in 1721–30, when twenty-three new ones were created by division. Except for the 1680s, when only one new society was created, the growth in Congregational societies kept pace with the population growth or exceeded it until 1730; from that year onwards population growth steadily exceeded society growth and the average number of inhabitants per society grew from 695 in 1730 to 1,173 in 1790 (see tables 11 and 12).

By 1790 there were 203 Congregational societies in the colony. Their size had been reduced to an average of twenty-five square

TABLE 11
Society Growth by Decade

1630s	1640s	1650s	1660s	1670s	1680s	1690s	1700s
8	4	2	5	6	1	12	11

1710s	1720s	1730s	1740s	1750s	1760s	1770s	1780s[a]
21	28	28	21	17	21	17	1

Note: Includes both first societies in new towns and divided societies in old towns.
[a] Includes only Congregational church societies.

TABLE 12
Mean Population per Society

Year	1660	1670	1680	1690	1700	1710	1720	1730
No. of persons	805	831	840	1056	829	782	736	695
Year	1740	1750	1760	1770	1780	1790[a]		
No. of persons	715	768	885	981	1022	1173		

[a] Includes only Congregational church societies.

miles, a manageable area that worked little hardship; few people would be more than three miles from a society meetinghouse, and established religion was readily available to most. The inhabitants of the colony seemed satisfied with the accessibility to them of church services; only one division of a Congregational society occurred in the 1780s. The new societies created in the eighteenth century often formed around population clusters that disregarded existing political boundaries. It was commonplace for societies to be formed that were comprised of outlying parishioners in two or three separate towns who grouped together in intertown villages; prior to the proliferation of towns in the Revolutionary aftermath, thirty-seven of Connecticut's sixty-eight towns contained societies that encompassed land in two or more towns. This reflects the desire of the inhabitants and the Assembly to provide easy access to worship for all people and also reflects a willingness to ignore the artificial boundaries of towns in favor of natural boundaries based on population distribution.

On the eve of the Revolution four towns each contained nine societies or parts of societies; at the other extreme, only nine towns contained but one, and six of these were recently settled Litchfield County towns. As one would expect, the towns with the largest land areas and the largest populations had the largest number of societies; the two factors were of equal importance. The twelve most populous towns averaged 6.6 societies per town and the twelve with the largest land area averaged 6.5. Long distances created a need for a new society and population numbers enabled the need to be translated into reality.

A breakdown of Congregational society growth by counties in 1790 reveals that there were substantial regional variations in the creation of new societies. Several hypotheses, consistent with one another, can be supported by the data and may explain the re-

gional differences. The newest county, Litchfield, possessed both
the largest number of inhabitants and the largest square mileage
per society. There was no significant difference between the eastern and western parts of the state, but there was a significant difference between the two inland counties, Hartford and Windham,
and the three on the coast, Fairfield, New Haven, and New London. The coastal counties averaged 14 percent more population
per Congregational society than the inland ones. This difference
cannot be explained by per capita wealth and the amount of the tax
base. If it could, one would assume that the less wealthy areas
would require more persons per society to support the society economically; Litchfield County, however, with more persons per
Congregational society, had more per capita wealth than New
London County. New Haven and New London counties, the highest and lowest in per capita wealth, had approximately the same
number of persons per society. The difference between the inland
and coastal counties was that dissenting parishes had grown more
numerous in the latter than in the former. Thus, it may not be
meaningful to note the difference in population per *Congregational*
society between the two groups of counties. There were more
people per Congregational society in Fairfield, New Haven, and
New London counties because more people in these counties were
attending the religious services of other denominations. By an Assembly enactment of 1728, dissenters could have their society taxes
delivered to the minister of the church they attended and hence,
with a sizable portion of their taxes being siphoned off to Anglican
and Baptist ministers, societies in the three coastal counties needed
a larger population base to support themselves. When the dissenting societies are added to the total of each county, Windham had
more people per society than any of the three coastal counties and
Hartford had approximately the same as Fairfield and New London (see table 13). With dissenting societies included, however,
there still is no clear correlation between per capita wealth and the
population per society; New Haven, the wealthiest county, did have
the smallest population per parish, but New London, with a
significantly lesser amount of per capita wealth than Hartford and
Fairfield counties, had approximately the same number of persons
per society as those counties.

There is a correlation, however, between the founding and location of a county and the number of persons per society, including

dissenting societies. The two last-settled counties, Windham and
Litchfield, both of which were removed from commercial waterways, had significantly more persons per society than the other
four, earlier-settled, counties, each of which had much of its land
situated on navigable waterways. The conclusion seems inescapable

TABLE 13
Ecclesiastical Societies by County in 1790

	Hartford	New Haven	New London	Fairfield	Windham	Litchfield
No. of Congregational societies	60	26	32	28	27	28
Average square mileage per Congregational society	23	26	22	25	27	28
Average no. of persons per Congregational society	1,078	1,186	1,206	1,295	1,085	1,384
No. of dissenting societies	20	19	16	17	4	12
Average no. of persons for all societies	808	685	804	806	945	968
Per capita tax assessment	$10.1	$11.0	$8.6	$10.5	$9.6	$9.9

Sources: Figures for Anglican parishes are derived from E. Edwards Beardsley, *The
History of the Episcopal Church in Connecticut* (Boston, 1883), 397; and Bruce E.
Steiner, "Anglican Officeholding in Pre-Revolutionary Connecticut: The Parameters of New England Community," *William and Mary Quarterly*, 31 (July, 1974), 370,
374, 375. For Baptists see David Benedict, *A General History of the Baptist Denomination in America* (New York, 1848), 365, 478–84; John Ledyard Denison, *Some Items of
Baptist History in Connecticut from 1674 to 1900* (Philadelphia, 1900), 8; and A. H.
Newman, *A History of the Baptist Church in the United States* (Philadelphia, 1898), 244,
245. For Quakers see Nelson R. Burr, "The Quakers in Connecticut: A Neglected
Phase of History," *Bulletin of the Friends Historical Association*, 32 (Spring, 1942),
11–24. For Separatists see C. C. Goen *Revivalism and Separatism in New England,
1740–1800: Strict Congregationalists and Separate Baptists in the Great Awakening* (New
Haven, 1962), 302–30; and James P. Walsh, "The Pure Church in Eighteenth-
Century Connecticut" (Ph.D. diss., Columbia University, 1967), 88. The per capita
assessed wealth is obtained by dividing the population of a county into its total
assessment.

that the older, more commercial counties had more heterogeneous and pluralistic social structures that inclined them more towards a fragmented religious structure. Litchfield and Windham counties maintained more religious unity within their more homogeneous communities.

Connecticut's Puritans did not welcome dissent but had toleration forced upon them; the Toleration Act of 1708, and other acts of 1727, 1777, and 1784, which enlarged the privileges of dissenters, were passed grudgingly and were the minimal responses permissible under the circumstances.[5] This reluctance to accept the legitimacy of worship outside the established church indicates Connecticut's desire for a monolithic religious structure, but it should not deceive us into believing that uniformity and agreement characterized the established church prior to the toleration acts. As Paul R. Lucas has shown in his recent analysis of the churches of the Connecticut River Valley, at the colony's inception discord surfaced over doctrinal differences, and with the death of the awe-inspiring ministers of the first generation, the debate over the Halfway Covenant, the growth of non-church members, and the increasing power of the laity, this discord grew in intensity.[6] However, dissent from within a structure is fundamentally different from dissent from without a structure, and until 1708, if Connecticut did not maintain harmonious congregations, it did maintain just one church, no matter how rife it was with doctrinal differences; all local congregations did come under the purview of the General Court, and outside intervention was possible and indeed practiced when the peace was threatened.

The first Anglican parish was formed in Stratford in 1707, the first Baptist parish in Groton in 1705. From these original centers of dissent, the two churches grew to fifty-eight and thirty parishes, respectively, in 1790. The Great Awakening acted as a catalyst to quicken the growth of dissent. When the Awakening split the Congregational church into contending parties, many extremists left the fold; many of the most conservative members became Anglicans and many of the most radical became Baptists. Congregationalists upset with the "enthusiasm" of the evangelical New Light brand of religion and its "most astonishing effects . . . screechings, faintings, visions, apparent death for twenty or thirty hours," frequently turned to the Church of England because it was "sound" and resisted what these conservatives thought to be the vulgarization of religion. On the other hand, awakened Congregationalists who felt that they were losing the fight within the church to institutionalize what they regarded as the purity of the evangelical reforms frequently left the church and set up illegal Separatist parishes, most of which eventually became Baptist. Between 1745 and 1750 thirty groups of these Separatists, or, as they preferred to be called, "Strict Congregationalists," left the established church and formed their own churches.[7]

Aside from Anglicans, Baptists, and Separatists, little other significant dissent appeared in Connecticut before 1790. Quakerism, so deeply feared by the established church, made few inroads and managed to start only two meetings, one in New Milford in 1735 and one in Hartford in 1788. The New Milford outpost was started by emigrants from New York, and the Hartford meeting was an offshoot of it. As another aspect of minority religion, while one could hardly say it constituted a parish, private Jewish worship was held in New Haven by some merchants. Although some Catholics lived in the largest trading centers, no evidence indicates that Catholic worship was ever practiced. Two additional groups of dissenters, Rogerenes and Sandemanians, both regarded as wildly heretical by the established church, held meetings and services in several towns, but neither group survived as a sect or grew into a denomination.[8]

Attempts by historians to characterize dissenters as misfits, the economically dispossessed, or substantial inhabitants "on the outs" with the power structure, have floundered under the minute scrutiny of specialized and local researchers who show that both Anglicans and Baptists drew their members from a broad stratum of the community.[9] Because one cannot show with any degree of certitude that dissenters tended to be the dispossessed, however, it does not necessarily follow that the religious ferment in the colony was unrelated to economic or social circumstances. Religious fragmentation in all societies can be correlated to perceived deprivation. If people feel deprived politically, socially, economically, ethically, or psychically, they frequently protest by religious rebellion. New churches are not always founded by the economically disinherited, but societies where many people feel that in some sense they are disinherited give rise to new churches. Similarly, economic stratification, while not producing churches of solely poor men and wealthy men, does lead to an increase in denominationalism. The fact that dissent *in some form* was epidemic everywhere in the colony at the middle of the eighteenth century would indicate an alienated population who felt a need to express anger. The rise of Anglicanism, Baptism, and Separatism and the fratricidal fighting within the established church are indicative of a frustrated society containing a high level of blunted aspirations.[10]

The presence of dissenting churches raises a difficult question for historians — were dissenting parishes considered societies? Legally, the answer to this question until 1784 was no. Societies encompassed a distinct territorial area and were a form of neighborhood government. However, dissenting parishes encompassed no distinct and unique territory but overlapped one, two, or several societies. While sober dissenters were given the right to worship as they pleased by a colony law of 1708, dissenting parishes were never incorporated by the colonial Assembly. Neither, until 1784, were they ever given the right to levy and collect taxes, elect officers, and perform the other governmental functions of a society. From the Toleration Act of 1708 until 1727, dissenters were taxed by the Congregational society in which they lived and supported their own parish by voluntary contributions; thus, they were forced to pay for their dissent by supporting two churches. In 1727, under extreme pressure, the Assembly gave dissenters some tax relief but still did not give their parishes the powers of a society. Henceforth, a dissenter who furnished the Congregational society clerk with a certificate attesting to membership in a dissenting church could require the society clerk to deliver his taxes to the dissenting minister. The dissenter was then relieved of the burden of double taxation, but his parish was not empowered to levy and collect its own taxes and had to rely on the officers of the established societies. Not until 1784, after the Revolutionary agitation against the Congregational church's establishment, was the dissenting parish granted the full rights of an ecclesiastical society. Previously, dissenting parishes often petitioned for society status but always were denied. However, despite their lack of success with the General Assembly, by informal local agreements dissenting parishes sometimes acted like societies, electing their own officers and levying and collecting taxes; if the local Congregational societies acquiesced, dissenting parishes frequently operated as de facto societies.[11]

After 1784, dissenting Christian parishes could and always did

apply to the General Assembly to be embodied in church estate as
ecclesiastical societies; when the Congregational parishes ceased to
be the only societies and when Anglicans, Baptists, and Strict Congregationalist parishes attained the status, the society itself was
transformed from a geographical unit that embraced all people
within it to a religious unit composed of people who attended its
worship. It was no longer possible to know which society a person
belonged to merely by knowing the location of his residence. Most
people lived in areas that allowed them the choice of a Congregational society or a dissenting society, and in some places one could
opt for any of four societies. The only residue of establishment was
the privilege of the Congregational society to receive the taxes of all
inhabitants who did not declare for one of the dissenting churches;
and the Christian religion in general was established: everyone had
to pay a society tax and the societies were still regarded by the
General Assembly as units of government.[12]

In 1790 there were 307 societies in the colony: 203 Congregationalist, 58 Anglican, 30 Baptist, 14 Strict Congregationalist,
and 2 Quaker. While dissenting societies comprised about one-
third of the total number, they were only about 20 percent of the
population.[13] Yet the presence of over 100 dissenting societies had
powerful effects on the colony. It injected the colony's social structure with a pluralism that destroyed the old Puritan ideal of one
corporate people uniform in belief. It also changed the function of
the church society from that of a unit of government embracing a
specific territory to that of a church parish with governmental
functions embracing members not always resident in that territory.
Finally, the growth of dissenting societies contributed to the separation of church and state, since it made the church society a less
reliable and less easily controlled political unit. In 1795 the General
Assembly transferred the supervision of schools from the societies
to newly created school districts and thus stripped much secular
power from the church; and in 1818, when religious taxation was
abolished and the Congregational church was disestablished, the
role of the ecclesiastical society as a form of local government
ended.

SOCIETY GOVERNMENT

SOCIETY government came into existence when a town became
subdivided into two or more Congregational church parishes. Al-

though general agreement could be found throughout the colony on the functions of a society, its duties, obligations, and powers were not codified by the General Assembly until 1728. In October of that year the colony empowered societies to raise taxes, elect officers, erect meetinghouses, and regulate primary schools. Law followed custom, for the societies were already performing all of these functions. The 1728 legislation did, however, stipulate that to be a society voter one must have forty pounds of assessed property; this was a new requirement. In addition, society voters had to be either freemen or full communicants of the church.[14]

A function of crucial importance that the societies always had performed and continued to perform was the selection of a minister. Technically, the church meeting, as distinct from the society meeting, chose a new minister; but because the two meetings had similar memberships and because the church meeting was seldom convened, the society usually arranged for the hiring (or firing) of a minister. On a few rare occasions in colonial Connecticut the two meetings came into conflict over who should occupy the pulpit. In the most publicized of these disputes, the Windham Consociation stated "that it belongs to ye church to call ye pastor to office," but the two meetings had "mutual interests . . . blended together [and] ought always . . . to . . . act in concord." Indeed, while conceding the ultimate power of choice to the church meeting, the consociation argued that the society can "conscientiously negative ye choice of candidate." For most practical purposes, however, it is safe to say that the society hired ministers. The society was basically the *political* arm of the parish and the church meeting was the *religious* arm; the church meeting, composed of members of the church in communion, handled matters concerning doctrine, the covenant, and church membership and discipline, while leaving secular matters and matters that involved any expenditure of funds to the larger group, the society meeting, composed of all men who were subject to society taxes and were either freemen or full church communicants.[15] Because hiring and firing a minister involved the use of society funds, it would have been difficult to remove the process entirely from the society meeting's control. As the wishy-washy verdict of the Windham Consociation shows, the selection of a minister was one of those gray areas of confused jurisdiction that the Standing Order of Connecticut chose to leave legally unclear, rather than endorsing either the principle that a majority comprised of some non-church members could choose a minister or the principle that control of a portion of the public expenditures could be removed from the taxpayers.

The General Assembly never specified what officers a society should elect; in practice, most societies set up positions similar to those of the first towns. Once established, society government grew but moderately, unlike the rapidly expanding government of the town meeting. Instead of greatly expanding the governmental operations within a society, new societies with their own governments were created to deal with the problems caused by a growing population. Societies always elected a three-man "society committee" charged with, as it was invariably put, "taking care of ye prudentials of ye parish." It constituted the executive arm of the society, controlled the agenda for society meetings, and supervised the ongoing business between meetings. Clerks were elected for all societies and treasurers were eventually elected for all of them, although until the 1750s one of the society committee sometimes acted as the treasurer. Two sets of collectors, one for the "society rate" and one for the "minister's rate," were usually elected; occasionally as many as five collectors of each type were elected, but more normally one or two of each were chosen. Frequently the society committee supervised school affairs, but as school districts proliferated, most societies began electing "school committees." School committees could have large memberships, which in one case went as high as thirteen — one member for each school in the society. By the 1750s most societies elected two to four ratemakers to assist the society committee in setting tax rates.[16]

Besides these usual society offices, a number of societies elected an officer or two to serve particular local needs. Hadlyme Society chose a man to "tune the psalms," and Guilford First Society elected "choiristers." Several societies elected men "to keep the boys in order." Glastonbury First Society elected a "sexton" to look after the meetinghouse; Mansfield Second Society, not as given to titles, elected one man "to sweep the meetinghouse" and another "to take care of ye doors." In addition to these offices, the societies, like the towns, utilized a large number of special committees. Any decision, such as seating the meetinghouse or building a new one or hiring a minister, that was not made annually was the occasion for electing an ad hoc committee, which would report to the society meeting. These committees added a great deal of participatory involvement to society affairs; seldom did a society elect more than twenty annual officers — fifteen was more the norm — but the special committees frequently had as many as ten members and gave a large number of men an entry into decision making in a role other than as a member of the society meeting.

Every society, like the towns, held an annual meeting, but unlike the town meeting it was not held in any month specified by colony law. More societies held their annual meeting in December than in any other month, but every month between September and April was utilized by some society for its annual meeting. Frequently, individual societies themselves would change the month for the annual meeting every few years. The annual meeting usually took at least two days and occasionally would last as many as four. One of the reasons for meetings of several days' duration was that they were generally held in the afternoon, once in a while as late as five o'clock, though one and two in the afternoon were the norm. Undoubtedly they held afternoon meetings after attending morning church services.

In almost all cases, if no business out of the ordinary had to be dealt with and if no controversy erupted, a society held just one meeting per year, the annual election meeting; this was the case 48.7 percent of the time in a sample of twenty societies. However, like town meetings, society meetings could become activated by extraordinary circumstances and be convened as many as thirteen times in a year. Financial problems, hiring a minister, and building and repairing the meetinghouse ranked nearly equally as the three leading causes of extra meetings, followed by another grouping of nearly equal causes: schools, business with the General Assembly, and seating the meetinghouse. The minister's salary, disputes with neighboring societies, arguments over the type of music employed in church services, wrangles with the minister over matters other than salary, and special elections also were the occasions for extra meetings.

Unlike the town meetings, the society meetings did not evolve through a pattern of several meetings in the first years of their existence, followed by a decline in frequency. The society meeting had no life cycle and was irregular throughout the eighteenth century (see table 14). Nor were the society meetings in any way activated by the Revolutionary experience; towns did not use society government for help in mobilizing for war, and one would never know by reading the society records that a war was being fought.

The business most frequently discussed at the annual meeting, besides the election of officers, concerned the schools the society ran. It is hardly surprising that the societies spent a great deal of time on school affairs, inasmuch as Connecticut's Puritans were vitally concerned with the education of their children; and operating the schools was the societies' second greatest expense, running a close second to supporting the minister. By colony statute every town with more than thirty families was required to maintain a "writing" school, and in 1712, at the time when most of the large towns were being subdivided into several societies, the General Assembly transferred the responsibility for these schools to the societies. The colony government after 1700 financially aided the societies by remitting annual funds to them to be used for the schools. These "school funds," based on the amount of assessed wealth on the local grand list, were augmented by large sums of

TABLE 14
The Frequency of Society Meetings in the Eighteenth Century

Society	Average per year	Most in one year	% of years with just one meeting
Greenfield Hills (Fairfield)	2.9	13	11
Hartford First	1.5	6	71
Hartford West	1.7	6	69
Glastonbury First	1.8	6	60
Guilford First	1.6	4	56
Killingworth Second	1.6	6	71
Litchfield First	1.3	3	70
Hadlyme (Haddam-Lyme)	2.4	7	37
Mansfield Second	2.4	5	33
Middletown First	1.4	6	69
New Roxbury (Woodstock)	2.6	5	0
North Fairfield	1.6	5	59
North Killingly	2.4	11	32
Norfield (Weston)	2.1	9	47
Preston Second	1.6	5	62
Ripton (Stratford)	1.9	5	38
Stamford First	1.3	5	84
Stonington First	3.1	9	16
Winchester First	3.6	9	35
Windsor First	1.7	5	54
Total	2.02	6.5	48.7

money in the 1730s, 1740s, and 1750s, derived from the colony's sale of the western lands.[17]

The society meeting each year had to decide where the schools would be held, who would teach at them, how long they would be in session, and how much of the cost would be borne by the society and how much by the scholars. In the first few decades of the eighteenth century, many societies had just one or two schools and almost all of the school locations were rotated. Pomfret First Society voted to have its schools in session "eight weeks at the north, seven at the west, seven at the south, and four at Wappaquasset."[18] In the Greenfield Hills Society and Glastonbury First Society the details of school rotation frequently were responsible for lengthy society meetings that required an additional session to meet by adjournment. A common device used to decide the length of time each area had a school in session was to make the time proportional to the wealth of the area on the grand list. Students, or "scholars," as they were invariably called, usually attended school only when it was in their area, but they were free to follow the school around if they wished. The total amount of time schools were in session at some location in the society ranged from a low of six months to a high of twelve in a few societies. Glastonbury First Society, for example, operated two schools in the 1730s, one for eight months and one for four, the sessions to run consecutively.

As the population of the colony increased, the number of schools per society increased accordingly, and by mid-eighteenth century all but the lightly populated societies stopped rotating their schools and instead established many permanent ones to serve the various areas. As the Middletown First Society stated, "Considering the number of scholars being very much increased," some major reorganization of their school system was required. Five to seven schools per society was the norm in the latter part of the eighteenth century. Several societies with large populations, however, had many more; Preston Second Society, for example, had twelve and Litchfield First Society had thirteen.[19]

It is usually unclear whom the society engaged to teach in its schools. Schoolmasters were more prized as teachers than schoolmistresses but were also more expensive and probably were fewer in number, although it is certain that both men and women taught. Which sex to employ could be a matter of concern to a society, and in one known case a society compromised by hiring masters for four months and mistresses for six.[20] Although teachers' salaries and school expenses were a source of anxiety for societies, the list of fees for scholars covered only a fraction of the costs and exempted "the poor and indigent."

As schools increased in number, the elected officers of the society who comprised the school committee did also. Usually, the first school committee a society elected contained three members, as did the society committee itself. It became common, however, to elect a number of school committeemen equal to the number of schools in the society and to designate each committeeman a representative for a particular school. Occasionally a society elected no school committee; in all cases the amount of time the meeting spent on school business shows that while a committee might guide and inform the society voters, the meeting kept a close watch on its actions and was closely involved in school supervision.

Although hiring and paying a minister was potentially a more explosive problem than running schools, the ministry occupied less of the time of a society meeting in normal years. If the minister was popular and in good health and able to preach regularly, the only ongoing business the society had to discuss concerning him was his salary. The minister's importance was shown, however, when one died, retired, or was fired, and a new one had to be hired. The meeting's attention would be riveted on the ministry until a new pastor was ordained. Hiring a minister was a decision not taken lightly. The first step taken was to name a special committee; after much deliberation it would recommend a likely candidate to the meeting, who would then issue an invitation to the prospective minister to preach in the parish "on probation" for a period of from three to six months. Being asked to serve on probation was no insult to any divine; it was part of the normal selection process through which all ministers went. Societies usually sought out young men, of whom many were recent Yale graduates. Neither was being asked to preach on probation a guarantee of being offered a permanent job.[21] If a society had a quarrelsome congregation or one that was simply hard to please, it might go through four or five probationary ministers before asking one to "settle among them" (that being the phrase that designated permanency). In an extreme case, a Colchester society engaged fifteen probationary ministers before one was finally ordained. One of the maxims agreed upon by prospective ministers was that a prudent man should not accept a call from a society that was divided over his ministry. Unanimity or near unanimity was desired if a minister did not wish to borrow future trouble. As one said in accepting a call to the Second Society of Mansfield, "What most induces me to comply with your invitation is the great degree of unanimity."[22] Societies usually stressed in the records that *all* voted for a candidate, and even a vote as one-sidedly in favor of a man as ninety-four to twenty-one contained enough opposition to persuade the trial minister to turn down the offer.[23] A popular probationary candidate in Durham First Society, desired by a "great majority" of the people, declined the offer, giving as his reason "that there are several people against his settlement."[24]

Less prosperous or less attractive societies, or ones known for their contentiousness, had a hard time attracting able men as ministers. Voluntown First Society could pay so little that several candidates refused its offers until a group of local men made a "gesture of love" towards one and pledged him substantial contributions above and beyond their normal tax obligations. A society in Pomfret, becoming desperate after a few years with an empty pulpit, "voted to invite Mr. Abel Stiles to preach with them by way of probation; and if he can't be obtained to send for Mr. Swift; and if he can't be obtained to send for Mr. Brown." Often attractive young candidates would be wooed by several societies, and those with small tax bases or poor locations could not meet the competition. Farmington First Society, bogged down in wrangling that with good reason frightened away several candidates, requested help from the General Assembly in order "that we may have the word of God preached among us."[25]

The importance societies attached to the quality of their ministers ironically caused many of them to be without an ordained preacher for long periods. It was rare to fill a vacant pulpit in less than a year; two or three was more normal, and at times it remained vacant for more than a decade. Colchester's parade of fifteen probationary ministers, mentioned above, took twenty years to march by. One of Branford's societies conducted a ten-year search for a minister, and Farmington's problems kept them without one for nine years. Even the usual two- or three-year transition from one minister's tenure to another's, which may sound short to historians accustomed to dealing with centuries, was long enough to cause trauma to the society.[26]

Once a call to settlement was agreed upon, issued, and accepted, the anxiety still was not over. The terms of settlement had to be hammered out, and again an ad hoc committee would be named by the society to frame an offer, subject, of course, to the meeting's approval. The most crucial details to be worked out were the financial ones. Besides their salaries, ministers received a "settlement" payment to defray the expenses of moving and setting up a new household; this usually consisted of outright specie and amounted to about two or three (or as high as four) times the amount of the annual salary. The settlement payment was a major expense to a society and was one of the reasons it exercised such caution in making a permanent offer to a candidate. Settlement payments were nonrefundable, and few societies could afford to make them very often. The new minister always received land in the society, the amount and terms of ownership of which had to be worked out. Frequently, he received land under two kinds of tenure: some given to him in fee simple, which conveyed full title and was his to assign to his heirs or dispose of should he leave; and some termed "the parsonage," which reverted to the society at the minister's death or departure. Unique conditions would sometimes be stipulated in the agreement between society and minister. When John Goodsoll agreed to minister to Greenfield Hills Society, he negotiated a retirement plan whereby, if "thru age or other inability" he was unable to perform the work of the ministry, he would still be paid 100 Current Money, "provided he does not neglect the services by his own faith." Matters of religious doctrine were occasionally negotiated. The Hadlyme Society, for example, required Grindal Rawson to state "upon what platform and way of church discipline he would set up with us." Usually, however, a society knew its new minister's views because of his period of probationary preaching. There is overwhelming evidence that the whole settlement process was characterized by some hard bargaining, and it was not unknown for an impasse to result, although usually after some negotiation an accord was reached. The agreement was always entered into the society's records, along with a formal acceptance signed by the new minister.[27]

Once ordained, most ministers served for life, although they may have been involved in some dispute along the way. The average tenure of New London County ministers, for example, was 43.4 years, and 74 percent of them were lifelong pastors who died in office. Although ministers and congregations did sometimes disagree on religious doctrine, the disputes that surfaced most frequently were over salaries. The salary had to be set annually, and with an erratic but high rate of inflation it could be the source of friction between minister and society. No less revered a minister than Gershom Bulkeley of New London, probably the most esteemed divine in the colony, bickered with the society meeting over his salary. Seldom would salary disputes lead to a parting of the ways, but many ministers must have felt a lack of Christianity in the way the society meeting treated them financially, and many parishioners must have felt that their pastor was more interested in their tax lists than in their souls. Even if the minister's salary did not cause controversy, it always was an important point of business discussed at the annual society meeting.[28]

As the religious and secular worlds met and intertwined in the hiring and paying of a minister, they also met in the locating, building, and maintaining of a meetinghouse. The meetinghouse was both the religious center of the community, where all divine services were held, and the political center, where society meetings were held. Paying for the meetinghouse was a major financial burden to the society, and locating it was one of the most vexatious problems in colonial Connecticut.

To modern sensibilities the colonial meetinghouse was so small and singularly unimpressive (New Haven's initial one, known as the largest in the colony, was fifty feet square) that one might be tempted to dismiss its propensity to generate division and controversy as much ado about nothing. The meetinghouses, however, if not edifices of grandeur, were the largest buildings in most communities and the only public ones. Building a meetinghouse was like hiring a minister; it took much planning and a variety of special committees, occasioned extra society meetings, frequently caused controversy, and could take as long as a dozen years. Usually, before a new structure was authorized, the society meeting responded to population pressure by building additions to the existing meetinghouse in the form of galleries, which were second floor balconies; this extension, in itself, could double the seating capacity. More pews were also added and the existing ones rearranged to accommodate greater numbers. However, within each generation, the time invariably came when the growth in population or the creation of a new society made it impossible to avoid constructing a new building.[29]

Locating the meetinghouse had been no problem for the first

generation of colonists because the towns had been nucleated; the meetinghouse was built on the most visible central hill and faced south "to be square with the sun at noon." But as Connecticut's population dispersed, the center of a community was no longer as easily determined and the meetinghouse's religious and political importance made its geographic centrality necessary; the meetinghouse had to serve the largest number of people in the least inconvenient location. Bitter fights erupted so frequently over establishing sites and proved so disruptive to the local peace that the colony government in a 1731 statute required every society planning on building a meetinghouse to apply for a committee from the General Assembly to specify the location. The Assembly committee, composed of deputies and assistants from other parts of the colony, would travel to the society in question and, after surveying the land and the house locations, drive a stake in the grounds that the sills of the new meetinghouse had to enclose. This method, poetic and precise, had two serious drawbacks: (1) unless the site pleased the vast majority of local residents, its legitimacy was not accepted, and (2) it placed a heavy burden on an already overworked Assembly. Societies opposed the external decisions most frequently by appealing back to the Assembly that the location specified by the committee "does discommode" the majority or was "placed out of the center and to the disadvantage of the inhabitants in general." Occasionally a society simply ignored the committee's decision and started construction somewhere else; usually this decision was to the disadvantage of some minority, who would cry foul and appeal. Stakes mysteriously disappeared in a few societies and reappeared a few miles distant. The Assembly, unable to solve the problem and unwilling to continue trying, passed the burden to the county courts in 1748, but they had even less authority and could not compel local compliance any more satisfactorily. The problem of meetinghouse locations was never solved in the eighteenth century. At times the fights were spectacular; in the most celebrated, the Simsbury First Society split into four societies after ten years of contention over a site.[30]

Building meetinghouses was never as difficult as locating them. The construction usually took four or five years, not because it engendered controversy but because it was expensive. The society contracted out part of the work to local artisans, who of course were paid, and had part of the work performed by society inhabitants, who worked free of charge. Every step in the construction was discussed at society meetings. In Ashford, the First Society voted "to have gin [for liquid refreshment] to raise the frame with," but later held a meeting to rescind this vote and opt for rum because it could get rum at a lower cost. In a Newtown society, a meeting discussed the price of nails that were going into the new meeting-house.[31] When construction was finished, the meetinghouse still was the subject of much business. Roofs needed repairs, windows were broken, bells were added, each instance of which was the occasion for naming a committee and authorizing an expenditure. It was a rare society that did not mention the meetinghouse in its minutes for two consecutive years.

"Seating the meetinghouse," or "dignifying it," as contemporaries sometimes said, was a problem that surfaced regularly and could be troublesome. Each family in town was assigned a pew in which to sit during religious services; deaths, population growth, and changes in the social structure usually necessitated a new seating plan at least once every decade. Three criteria were widely employed: estate, age, and usefulness to the community, each of which reflected deeply held Puritan values. The "seating committee" named by the society was often unsure how to mix the ingredients, however, and measuring a man's usefulness involved making a judgment that could provoke jealousy or wound feelings. Pew assignments recommended by the committee were usually debated and sent back to the committee for at least minor alterations and sometimes major ones. Only the Puritan penchant for frankness could allow a meeting of neighbors and friends to debate publicly where each man stood in status in his community. Some changes occurred in seating over the course of the eighteenth century. Whereas in the seventeenth century men and women sat separately, gradually, between 1700 and 1740, men and women started sitting in the same pews. By the 1760s the winds of change were sufficiently strong that some radicals could suggest doing away with ranking and instead selling the pews; Norfield Society "bid them [the pews] off." In another case some "indecent and unbecoming" inhabitants tried to bring a black into a pew that by "custom and usage [was] appropriated to the use of . . . white people." Glastonbury First Society did away with specific assignments and divided the town into seven ranks or "powers," each of which sat in a specified section of the meetinghouse. Greenfield Hills Society did not actually sell its pews, but it "dignified according to what they have paid" and turned to the tax lists as its sole criterion. The custom of seating the meetinghouse on social as well as economic criteria, however, if under attack, generally survived throughout the era of the Revolution.[32]

Societies zealously guarded the measure of autonomy imparted to them by the Congregational nature of their polity. They were, of course, as the towns were, the creatures of the General Assembly; yet societies expected a fairly large amount of freedom from colony control and they were quick to denounce what they regarded as unwarranted intrusions into their affairs. As the frequent meetinghouse controversies show, the Assembly's help in solving local problems was of limited value; the response of a Killingly society to a General Assembly set of recommendations — "we regard them not" — was not uncommon. Guilford, for example, did not ask for arbitration of a controversy concerning the selection of a minister, and when the Assembly appointed a committee the society indignantly refused to acquiesce on the grounds that the Assembly had no jurisdiction. The Congregational spirit proved difficult to curb and, while the independence of the societies worried the colony government, it remained unchecked. The Saybrook Platform of 1705, which was designed to enforce uniformity on the societies and bring them under the control of consociations of ministers, never was successfully implemented, and the consociations were defied with impunity. Adherence to the platform was voluntary, societies had to consent to be governed by it, and they respected it only when convenient. The religious controversies of the 1740s not only shook the colony and splintered many societies but intensified society independence. There is strong evidence, for instance, that the famous General Assembly law of 1742 that banned itinerant preachers was disobeyed in mass by the societies. One of the clearest examples of the Congregational spirit that was at the heart of the societies' fierce independence was the requirement that every new minister be ordained by his new flock no matter how many times he had been ordained previously. Societies were an effective unit of local government, but they lacked the deferential attitude towards higher levels of government that strong central authorities would have liked.[33]

The lines by which the society related to the town government were never clearly drawn and depended upon local custom, the personalities of local politicians, and probably most importantly the number of societies in a town. The selectmen, though officers of the town, were given some authority to deal with societies if they became embroiled in controversies. The towns also made a deliberate attempt to apportion town officers by societies; frequently towns would designate some of their officers as "surveyors for the second society" or "selectmen for the first society," and in some towns the societies presented the selectmen with nominations for offices. Not uncommonly, a town would increase its complement of officers when a new society was created.[34]

After 1784, when the dissenting congregations were allowed to petition for society status, they borrowed the model of the Congregationalists, elected similar officers and committees, and were as suspicious of outside authority. The leading historian of the Anglicans argues that they were Episcopalians in worship but Congregationalists in government. This behavior of dissenters attests eloquently to the ability of society government to satisfy local needs and to the spirit of independence that pervaded local government.[35]

UNITY, a crucial goal of the established church in Connecticut, was being eroded throughout the colonial period. The colony at its inception was never uniform in faith nor without discord; however, each town at its inception had but one church coextensive with the local community. Geography and economic, social, and political tensions militated against the coincidence of church and town and by 1790 had eliminated it in virtually every town. Not only did the creation of new Congregational churches and dissenting churches fragment the religious structure, within individual churches controversy could not be contained and surfaced persistently when major decisions had to be made. Whereas in the early seventeenth century contention usually arose over doctrinal differences, as the colonial period progressed it arose as frequently over political or other secular matters. Peace within a congregation was so precariously maintained that it was seriously threatened each time a minister had to be hired or a meetinghouse built. The goals of unity, concord, and harmony never were achieved in early Connecticut, but neither were they ever lost, and amidst the contention that pervaded the religious structure everyone professed a belief in them.[36] The reality, however, speaks louder than the rhetoric, and it was the sad fate of Connecticut's inhabitants not to realize the ideals in which they believed.

A unified church is in many ways similar to a large family; it provides parental guidance and discipline and is a primary focus of one's loyalty. Concord and harmony are important to maintain in a church for the same sociological reasons they are important to maintain in a family — their absence will destroy the church community as it would destroy the family community. When the unity of a religious community is destroyed by contention, it frees the members of an element of parental control and makes them more independent; they can ignore church strictures because moral and social sanctions cannot be enforced against them. Moreover, when there are competing churches, they have alternative objects of loyalty. A plurality of religious structures within a society results from tensions within that society, but it also exacerbates those tensions by institutionalizing them. And it promotes the individualism inherent in the right and obligation of choosing where to place one's loyalty.[37] Connecticut children reaching adulthood in 1660 had no alternatives for their religious needs — the community provided a church that, however dissension-ridden, they had to attend, give their allegiance to, and sustain with their tax money. Decision making was communal, not individual. In 1790 young adults had a wide range of religious options, none of which was coextensive with the town or neighborhood — the choice was theirs, not the local community's. If they chose a church and then disagreed with it later in life, they were free to withdraw their loyalty and place it elsewhere.

[V]

THE PROLIFERATION
OF LOCAL INSTITUTIONS

ACCORDING to the folk-cultural view of American history, the town meeting was the only major governing body in the communities of colonial New England and handled all matters beneath the colony level. This was never true in theory, and although the town meeting did in practice exercise all governance in the early towns of seventeenth-century Connecticut, institutional differentiation began within the first generation of colonists. As we have seen, church-society government was a crucial device at the local level. The growth of still other local instruments of government accelerated in the fourth quarter of the seventeenth century and the first quarter of the eighteenth; by 1733, when the proprietors were formally organized by the General Assembly, all towns were holding proprietary, freemen's, and militia meetings that were separate from the town meeting.

PROPRIETORS

THE General Court conferred the ownership of all lands within a town upon the proprietors; they and not the towns exercised all control over the land and determined all land allotments. However, the legal distinction between town and proprietors was blurred by practice, since in all of the towns settled before 1686 virtually all the adult white males who were first settlers and heads of families were proprietors. Several towns even made young unmarried men proprietors and designated their holdings as "bachelor lots." The town meeting acted for the proprietors and assumed the responsibility for land policy. The town meeting's chief officers, the selectmen, served also as the executives of the proprietors and not only made policy recommendations to the meeting but also handled most of the ongoing regulation and distribution of land.[1]

The amount of land distributed by the proprietors in the towns founded prior to 1686 varied greatly, but the general policies of

[V]

THE PROLIFERATION
OF LOCAL INSTITUTIONS

ACCORDING to the folk-cultural view of American history, the town meeting was the only major governing body in the communities of colonial New England and handled all matters beneath the colony level. This was never true in theory, and although the town meeting did in practice exercise all governance in the early towns of seventeenth-century Connecticut, institutional differentiation began within the first generation of colonists. As we have seen, church-society government was a crucial device at the local level. The growth of still other local instruments of government accelerated in the fourth quarter of the seventeenth century and the first quarter of the eighteenth; by 1733, when the proprietors were formally organized by the General Assembly, all towns were holding proprietary, freemen's, and militia meetings that were separate from the town meeting.

PROPRIETORS

THE General Court conferred the ownership of all lands within a town upon the proprietors; they and not the towns exercised all control over the land and determined all land allotments. However, the legal distinction between town and proprietors was blurred by practice, since in all of the towns settled before 1686 virtually all the adult white males who were first settlers and heads of families were proprietors. Several towns even made young unmarried men proprietors and designated their holdings as "bachelor lots." The town meeting acted for the proprietors and assumed the responsibility for land policy. The town meeting's chief officers, the selectmen, served also as the executives of the proprietors and not only made policy recommendations to the meeting but also handled most of the ongoing regulation and distribution of land.[1]

The amount of land distributed by the proprietors in the towns founded prior to 1686 varied greatly, but the general policies of actual acreage a person was entitled to receive, depending upon both the distance the land lay from the town center and its quality. Inequities that were not perceived in the original division but became immediately apparent in the farming of the land were remedied by individual grants at the discretion of the selectmen.[3]

One of the first problems faced by proprietors was how to deal with newcomers to the town who arrived after the original distribution. Usually, men "admitted" to the town in the first five years after the original distribution were given enough land to enable them to be self-supporting, but they were not always designated proprietors and hence did not always have "rights" in future divisions. In Hartford, for example, some newcomers were given land "at the town's courtesy." Derby, with a small number of original proprietors, agreed at a town meeting that it would admit the first thirty inhabitants as proprietors and after that give only parcels of land without proprietary rights associated with them. As time passed, towns differed widely in their approach to the problem. Branford always conferred proprietary status on new settlers throughout the seventeenth century; Norwalk, hungry for new settlers, did the same. Fairfield, however, discriminated among new inhabitants, extending proprietary status to those who married into Fairfield families or who came from nearby towns but denying it to new residents who were less well known to the original proprietors. Milford similarly gave proprietary status only to newcomers who had some special claims to the town's good wishes.[4]

The proprietors' role as a separate local governing body evolved because many new inhabitants were not admitted as proprietors; these newcomers were qualified to vote at a town meeting but, not being proprietors, were not legally entitled to be involved in decision making affecting land policy and divisions. The first recorded proprietors' meeting took place in Hartford in 1665. There was, however, such confusion over who was and who was not a proprietor that the town finally declared that all inhabitants who paid town rates would be considered legal proprietors. Two years later Stamford tried to sort out who was a proprietor and declared that a "true" one was "capable in respect of right." This failed to clear the air and, after a decade of unsatisfactory attempts to solve the problem, Stamford followed Hartford's example of inclusiveness and gave proprietary status to everyone who had eight pounds' worth of real estate. Guilford also wrangled over the problem and in

1691, when a major land division was made, decided that everyone who had been living in the town since 1686 was a proprietor. Distinctions between proprietors and nonproprietors were more than academic; lacking a right in land divisions worked a real hardship. A spirited fight in Milford between first settlers and newcomers lasted until 1713, when the town compromised by declaring that those newcomers who had arrived before 1688 would be considered proprietors. Generally, by the end of the seventeenth century or in the first two decades of the eighteenth century, most of the people who had arrived in the second generation of settlers were accorded proprietary status. However, a few towns were able successfully to thwart the aspirations of newcomers; the New London proprietors, for example, in 1704 numbered substantially less than 50 percent of the population.[5]

The proprietors, unaided by the colony government, groped towards a separate identity from the town meeting. The Lyme proprietors organized as a separate group officially in 1698 but softened the distinction between town and proprietary meetings by making almost all of the permanent residents proprietors. By 1700 the Branford proprietors had established a meeting and government completely separate from the town meeting. In Middletown the first mention of them as a separate group appears in 1686, about thirty-five years after the town had been settled. At that time the town meeting substituted the phrase "the proprietors grant" for the usual "the town grants" in a land distribution. In 1696 use of the qualifying phrase "the town meeting also a meeting of the proprietors" shows that, although one meeting acted for both, a need was felt to legitimize its functions by giving it both titles. In 1715 a Middletown town meeting listed the names of 176 men who were proprietors, a number probably half of the total of the eligible town-meeting voters. Two years later a town meeting divided the proprietors into four geographic groups and gave each some authority in settling land problems, although major questions regarding land divisions were to be decided by all four groups together. Even though divided, the proprietors still did not meet separately from the town meeting; each fourth would be polled during a town meeting for a proprietary decision relating to its section. Between 1717 and 1733 the town members would shift hats and deal with proprietary matters at the same meeting, prefacing the action by "the proprietors vote" or "the town votes," according to the nature of the business. In 1733 the town meeting ceased to act on proprietors' business, and thereafter separate proprietors' meetings were held and separate records maintained.[6]

Norwich's and Farmington's proprietors evolved into separate bodies later than Middletown's. In Norwich, although the town meeting performed proprietary functions, not until 1717 did it feel the need to legitimize them by using the phrase "the proprietors and inhabitants." In 1718 Norwich, like Middletown, divided its proprietors into four groups: East Side, West Side, Crotch of River, and Southwest. However, Norwich's town meetings continued to perform proprietary functions until 1733, when the proprietors began to meet separately and to maintain their own records. Farmington had separate proprietary meetings in the seventeenth century, but still the town meeting frequently acted in land matters. In 1727 the town meeting appointed a committee to find out "who are ye proprietors of commons." In 1733 this had apparently been ascertained, and the proprietors started meeting independently and keeping separate records. By 1736 the separate identities of the two groups were so clearly established that the town meeting records mention negotiations with the proprietors. The General Assembly gave little direction to the proprietors, though it was almost certainly responsible for the sudden and complete separation of town and proprietors everywhere in 1733. The Assembly in 1723 had order the proprietors of each town to meet, but most towns ignored the order. In 1732 the Assembly repeated this order, and the towns, probably perceiving that the statute was meant to be enforced, all obeyed. Stamford and Hartford, with little previous reason for separating the town and proprietary meetings, inasmuch as they had declared the membership of the two nearly identical, then did separate the two into different meetings.[7]

The 1732 act also repeated and expanded a statute of 1727 that gave the proprietors the power to "make Rates to defray the necessary Charges" arising from their new responsibilities. Most proprietors elected a clerk, a treasurer, a surveyor, and a proprietors' committee of three to seven members. These elections, unlike those of the towns, were not annual; rather, the officers served either until they died or, more rarely, until someone expressed dissatisfaction with their performance and asked for a new election.[8]

As we have seen when discussing settlement patterns, a fundamental difference existed between the town proprietors of the seventeenth century and those of the eighteenth. In general, early seventeenth-century proprietors were residents who received their land free from the General Court, while those of the late seventeenth and early eighteenth centuries were speculators who bought the land from the Assembly and frequently did not reside in the new towns. The Narragansett War in 1675 divides the two periods. During the war much of the land east of the Connecticut River came into the possession of a small but influential number of speculators who persuaded the Assembly that the planting of towns would furnish an investment opportunity for private citizens as well as income for the colony.[9]

The proprietary and town meetings of the towns founded after the Narragansett War were distinct and clearly separated from the start. In some towns, when speculator proprietors sold land to settlers, they sold proprietary rights with the land; in other towns they sold only parcels of land that carried with them no rights to future divisions. In cases where the proprietary meeting remained completely out of the control of the town residents, some serious conflicts arose between absentee proprietors and townspeople. After two such severe conflicts, the General Assembly passed a statute in 1714 requiring absentee proprietors to settle on their lands and improve them in three years or forfeit their claims. This law broke the efforts of absentee proprietors to dominate communities in which they invested only their money and not their physical presence, and assured each community self-government in land matters after the initial settling-in period.[10]

Because proprietorship was frankly an economic matter — after 1675, one bought a proprietary share — the problems of deciding the size of individual land allotments and of ascertaining membership were generally avoided. All people owning proprietary rights received an equal share in all divisions, and only people who had purchased shares were proprietors. Of course one could subdivide proprietary shares and one could own one-half or one-quarter of one and hence receive a fractional amount of a share in a division. All of the towns founded in this period were much more generous in the size of allotments in their initial divisions. Home lots were so much larger than in previous years that they severely diluted the conception of a nucleated village; Litchfield assigned fifteen-acre ones and Windham thirty-one-acre ones, and Lebanon's were farms in themselves at forty-two acres. The only town in this period that exercised the kind of restraint that characterized the earlier towns, Newtown, assigned only a total of twenty-two acres per family, including home lot and outlying land; however, Newtown could not maintain its sober testimony to the frugality of a bygone era and followed the first division with five more general divisions in five years. Voluntown, with its large number of proprietors, carried this extravagance to its logical conclusions and divided up all of the land at the town's inception; no empty land remained as commons except that which was forfeited for failure to build on or improve.[11]

As the proprietors became an increasingly important governing body, they were ironically doomed to oblivion in most towns by the very forces that gave them power. The proprietors' meeting was important only as long as there were common lands to regulate and divide. When the proprietors parceled out land, they were also parceling out their muscle. The proprietors lasted a surprisingly long time in the towns settled prior to the Narragansett War; the reason for their durability generally was that these towns were physically large and hence had large funds in their banks of land. In two of the smaller first towns, Lyme and Stamford, the common land was virtually all given out by 1700 and only a tiny amount remained, not nearly enough to sustain a general division. But these towns were exceptional. In Farmington, Norwich, Middletown, Guilford, and New Haven, sizable amounts of common land existed until the 1730s, when it was divided up because of the pressures placed upon it by the rising population. New Haven and Milford retained enough common land to make divisions as late as 1760 and 1769, respectively. By contrast, in almost no town founded between 1685 and the 1730s did the supply of common land last beyond the first three decades of the town's history. Three separate forces caused these towns to divide up their lands so quickly: (1) the social climate promoted land fever and self-indulgence and worked against restraint; (2) the land was lower in quality and more of it was needed to sustain a family farm; and (3) the towns were much smaller than the ones of the previous era, and there was simply not as much land to save. Whatever the reason — and the latter two economic reasons are just as plausible as the social one usually advanced by historians — in both the first-settled towns and the second-settled ones, the proprietors began to decline sharply in importance in the 1730s, only a few years after their formal organization. Vestiges of the proprietary meeting, however, sometimes survived as institutional anachronisms until the nineteenth century.[12]

In the towns settled after 1738 in Litchfield County, the proprietors were of crucial importance in the first years of a town's existence, but usually by the end of the first decade they ceased to be a vital force. As we have seen, the northwestern towns were organized by their proprietors, who authorized surveys, laid out highways, and supervised the divisions of land. The propensity of the proprietors, however, to divide up all of the common land almost immediately meant that their function was generally limited to initial organization, and they soon either withered or disbanded. One town, Hartland, laid out every acre of land into lots in the first year of its existence, and three years later every lot was assigned to a proprietor. In only one Litchfield County town, Cornwall, did an active proprietor's meeting last two generations, and even its role was minimal after the town's initial organization: nine-tenths of its land was allotted after twelve years; the final small amount that was husbanded until 1796 yielded only seven acres per proprietor. If the proprietor's organization lasted beyond two or three years, it would be under the control of residents and not absentee landlords, because of the colony's regulation requiring nonresidents to improve or forfeit their land. The domination of town business by greedy absentee landowners was a myth fostered by residents trying to weasel out of financial obligations to original proprietors. Proprietors did not dominate the towns' political lives after the initial organization, and what little power they did have was wielded by residents.[13]

The proprietors created after the organizing legislation of the 1720s and 1730s, those of the western towns, assigned the lands among themselves, usually in four or five divisions of fifty to one-hundred acres a division, but in some towns there were as many as fifteen divisions, each of which averaged only fifteen acres. Since each division invariably was in a different part of the town, a typical proprietor's holdings after a decade would be in several parcels widely scattered about the town. The wide geographical distribution of lands was made in an effort to ensure fairness in the quality of land assigned. The first two generations of each of these towns witnessed a mania of trading and selling of plots as everyone tried to put together the best possible farm out of contiguous lots. In the towns sold at auction, each proprietor received an equal amount of land, while in the towns owned by Hartford and Windsor land allotments were grossly unequal because each proprietor was assigned land based on the amount of his assessed wealth on the tax list. As in the case with land allotments in all of the towns settled before the 1730s, specific plot assignments were made by chance drawing; one "pitched" for land.[14]

FREEMEN

As proprietors became distinguished from townspeople during the seventeenth century, so too did the "freemen" of each town become increasingly differentiated from the "inhabitants." The Fundamental Orders of 1639 established two classes of voters: freemen and inhabitants. Anyone who possessed thirty pounds' worth of total estate was eligible to become a freeman, but only the General Court was empowered to admit him to freeman status. Under the Fundamental Orders, inhabitants could vote for all town officers and deputies to the General Court, but could not vote for the governor or assistants and could not be deputies. Under the Charter of 1662 the distinction between freemen and inhabitants was sharpened. Inhabitants could no longer vote for deputies and were reduced to voting only for town officers. The charter reduced the property qualification for freemen from thirty pounds to twenty and further required that they must be of "honest conversation," though it did not stipulate that they had to be church members. That confusion existed during elections over who was and who was not a freeman is evident from the fact that in 1669 the colony told the towns to try to alleviate this uncertainty by compiling lists of freemen.[15]

New Haven Colony employed a formula precisely the opposite of Connecticut Colony's for ensuring the sobriety and good character of its freemen. Only church members could be freemen in New Haven; but for them there was no property requirement. The church membership stipulation was important to the leaders of New Haven Colony; when they accepted Milford as a constituent town in the colony, a serious problem arose because Milford had admitted some freemen who were not church members. A few years later, when non-church members petitioned the colony gov-

ernment, asserting that they were being denied their full rights, the
General Court rebuked them as "troublers of our Israel." New
Haven was forced, however, by the amalgamation with Connecticut
to abandon her more restrictive views of freemanship.[16]

Twentieth-century estimates for percentages of adult white
males who were admitted as freemen show that the number in
seventeenth-century Connecticut differed from town to town. Before 1662, when it was not as important to be a freeman, few men
were recorded in the colony records as being admitted to freemanship. But many men never known to have been admitted nevertheless exercised the rights of freemanship. The distinction between freeman's meeting and town meeting was thus considerably
blurred. However, after 1662, when the distinction was heightened, the General Court carefully recorded all those admitted
to that status, and there were no more casual freemen. Because
traveling to Hartford, the capital, was a time-consuming process,
the percentage of adults admitted from each town varied proportionately with the town's distance from Hartford. Thus, in
Hartford, Wethersfield, Windsor, and Farmington, in 1669, about
63 percent of adult white males were freemen and about 75 percent of heads of households were. However, at Middletown, halfway down the river from Hartford, only 50 percent of the adult
white males were freemen; and in Saybrook, at the mouth of the
river, only 33 percent were. In even more remote towns, such as
Norwich, only 25 percent of the adult white males were admitted.
For many men the disadvantages of a long trip to Hartford out-
weighed the advantages of freeman status.[17]

This early system, whereby prospective freemen had to travel to
Hartford and be personally admitted by the General Court, was
burdensome for the individual seeking freemanship, and it became
onerous for the General Court as the population of Connecticut
grew. In 1678 the Court met this problem by instructing the town
selectmen to certify that each person applying to the Court for
freemanship met the property requirement and was of "honest,
peaceable, and civil conversation." Since the deputies would admit
the applicant if they were satisfied with the selectmen's recommen-
dation, control of the admission of freemen was thus shifted in
practice to the town, although in theory it remained with the central government. The laws regarding freemanship did not change
until 1729, when the formal power of admission was transferred to

the freemen of each town, owing to the administrative difficulty of central control. In actuality, after this date the freemen usually delegated the admitting power to the selectmen, even though the selectmen were officers not of the freemen but of the town, which included the inhabitants as well. The selectmen met a few hours in advance of the freemen's meeting, examined oral applications for freemanship, and admitted those whom they found satisfactory. The assembly specified that the town clerk had to record in writing the names of all new freemen.[18]

Until recently, historians commonly estimated that as few as 10 percent of the eligible adult white males were actually freemen in eighteenth-century Connecticut. These "guesstimates," however, are grossly inaccurate. It is possible to calculate with reasonable accuracy the percentage of adult white males who were freemen in nineteen towns in the period from 1750 to 1790. The estimates range from highs of 79 percent and 69 percent in two towns to lows of 25 percent in two others. This wide variety of experience averages out to a mean of 50.3, which would indicate that half of Connecticut's adult white males were registered to participate fully in the electoral processes.[19]

No significant positive correlation between the percentage of freemen and the population of towns can be established; this is because towns with small populations varied widely in their percentage of freemen. Towns with medium populations, however, were consistently above the median, and towns with large populations were consistently below it. No significant correlation can be established between the percentage of freemen and land size; both small and medium-sized towns varied widely, but large towns were consistently below the median. All of this suggests that, although no direct linkage can consistently be made among population, land size, and freemanship, the physically largest and most populous towns did have the smallest percentage of men achieving the status of freemanship — hardly surprising, inasmuch as each man's vote was potentially less meaningful in these towns and many men would have to walk long distances to attend freemen's meetings. This latter factor discouraged many men from becoming freemen, as case studies of freemanship and geography show; the farther away a man lived from the meetinghouse, the less likely he was to be a freeman. Connecticut towns were so large geographically that it was not unusual for an "outliving man" to have to walk ten or so miles to attend a meeting — a formidable undertaking even in good weather.[20]

In all of these towns at least 70 percent of the population could have qualified for freemanship, and admission after 1729 seemed almost effortless. The variability of the data on freemanship suggest that the freemen's meeting, like the town and society meetings, was normally quiescent but could become charged with excitement upon occasion. Many towns recorded the new freemen annually and in all cases the numbers varied greatly from year to year. The age profile of a town would account for some but not all of the variability; undoubtedly men were motivated to seek freemanship in years when political controversy made it seem more worthwhile. Many of the qualified men who were not freemen were young men in their twenties who almost certainly would seek admission when political events touched them closely.[21]

The freemen met twice a year — in the first weeks of April and of September. At each session they elected two deputies to the Assembly. It emphasizes the point that the freemen's meeting was legally distinct from the town meeting to note that the town meeting of Middletown addressed a petition to the Middletown freemen asking their deputies to act also as agents for the town. Similarly, Sharon's town meeting authorized the freemen's deputies to argue a case for Sharon at the next Assembly. In both instances, the deputies were not representatives of the town government specifically but of the freemen alone, and a special deputation of powers was required for them to act for the town. Usually, if a town was involved in a case before the General Assembly, it did not designate its deputies to act for it but instead appointed special agents. Presumably, if the deputies of a town were appointed town agents, they would disqualify themselves from voting in the Assembly because of a conflict of interest. Neither freemen's meetings nor town meetings issued instructions to the deputies, and they performed their duties as "virtual representatives" of the common good and not "direct representatives" bound by their constituents' wishes. That this concept was undergoing change in the Revolutionary years can be seen by the fact that Hartford started issuing instructions to its deputies in 1783. Although this practice was not widespread, demands in the Revolutionary years for a published list of votes cast by the deputies in each session shows the growing desire of freemen to make their deputies directly accountable to them.[22]

At the September meeting each freeman could vote for up to twenty men as nominees collectively for governor, deputy governor, and assistants. The constable of each town tallied the votes and forwarded them to the colony secretary, who announced at the October session of the Assembly the names of the top twenty vote-getters for the entire colony. At the April freemen's meeting each freeman could vote for one of these nominees as governor, one as deputy governor, and twelve as assistants. The results were announced at the May session of the Assembly.[23] Many towns took advantage of the gathering of the freemen in April to hold a town meeting on "freemen's day," but to emphasize the separate character of the two meetings, the freemen's meeting was held in the morning and the town meeting in the afternoon.

Lack of attendance at freemen's meetings was often a problem as it was at town meetings. In nine elections for colony-wide officers, vote totals are extant; in all of them less than half of the admitted freemen bothered to cast ballots. The historian of New London called a turnout of about 50 percent at a local freemen's meeting "a great assembly," and in Durham, so few were present at a freemen's meeting that men traveling by the meeting were importuned to come inside and vote in order to legitimize the election of deputies.[24]

As further evidence for a lackluster interest in colony-wide politics, towns commonly were willing to forego the privilege of electing deputies to the Assembly. Frequently in the pre-Revolutionary eighteenth century, a town asked to be relieved of paying the colony tax because of its "pressing circumstances" or because its inhabitants were "remarkably cut short in their crops." The Assembly usually abated the tax but required the town to withdraw its deputies until it paid its share of the colony's finances. The towns who fought a revolution for no taxation without representation were more than willing to accept the principle of no representation without taxation.[25]

Connecticut's legendary "steady habits" have been greatly exaggerated by folk culture, but undoubtedly the stability implied by this nickname was partially a function of freeman apathy about registration and attendance at meetings. Elections for deputy could be spirited at times, but the overall evidence suggests an exceptionally oligarchical pattern of officeholding. Much has been written about the length of the assistants' and governors' tenures in office, and although recent scholarship suggests that the stability of colony officeholding has been overemphasized, it still had a remarkably low turnover by today's standards. The method of balloting for assistants employed by the freemen also contributed to the oligarchical pattern sustained by deferential social attitudes. The nominees' names were called out orally in order of seniority and incumbents were called before challengers. Each freeman was given twelve ballots and would turn one in after a name was called if he wanted to vote for that person. To vote for a challenger a freeman was forced to save one of his blank ballots and in the words of one historian proclaim himself a "rebel against the Standing Order." This "political gimmickry" gave incumbents a marked advantage, although occasionally one of them who had grown senile or associated with an unpopular stand was thrown out of office. Local and regional loyalties also could overcome this gimmickry; the few vote totals of freemen meetings that have survived show that freemen voting in colony-wide elections often cast their ballots in disproportionate numbers for geographically proximate candidates.[26]

MILITIA

THE emergency created by the Pequot War of 1637, which threatened the survival of the colony, forced the General Court to think seriously about the nature of its defenses; the result was a series of acts in 1638 that organized the local militia. All men above the age of sixteen and younger than sixty, except church officers and magistrates, were required to bear arms and take part in regular training exercises unless specifically exempted by the Court. Ten training days a year were ordered held, but after the wartime emergency was over this figure was cut back to six. Since the winter was too cold for training and the summer was taken up by agricultural duties, the months of April, May, September, and October were set as the training months.[27]

The local militia between 1638 and 1650 was under the authority of the town constable, but the Code of 1650 removed him as the local commander and empowered the "soldiers [to] . . . make choice of their military officers, and present them to the court" for confirmation. The militia thus became a quasi-independent and electoral organization — within general guidelines they determined their own conduct and elected their own officers. The colony government could, of course, intervene in any local militia matter and could refuse to confirm an officer put forward by the man; in practice, however, the General Court in the seventeenth century interfered only when guidelines were broken and rarely refused to confirm an officer nominated by the men. Training was to be held six times a year at eight in the morning in the spring and fall; every soldier was required "to have in continual readiness a good musket or other gun fit for service"; and each town was ordered to maintain a "magazine of powder." Town government was not involved in the militia, except that the constable was told to provide the poor men with arms and ammunition and a way "to earn it out."[28]

One thing the militia clearly was not in colonial and Revolutionary Connecticut was an instrument of local government used to maintain peace or respond to civil strife. The *posse comitatus* of the towns under the authority of the constable performed this service, and if a riot broke out, the *posse*, not the militia, quelled it. Indeed, the militia was more likely to cause a local disturbance than to police one; training days were often riotous with drinking, brawling, horse racing, and shooting contests after the actual military exercises were over, and, according to the ministers of the colony, they occasioned much sinning. "We had a fine toot today," one militiaman wrote in his diary.[29]

The quality of the militia deteriorated steadily throughout the second half of the seventeenth century and the first three-fourths of the eighteenth. As local fears of Indian raids subsided, people felt less need to take preparedness seriously. The colony government at times tried to reverse this decline but proved powerless to do so; at times, however, the Assembly contributed to the deterioration. A large block of statutes passed between 1698 and 1708, the first major militia legislation passed since the Code of 1650, gave local officers more power over discipline, provided penalties for nonperformance of duty, prohibited plural militia officeholding by regimental commanders, and forbade privates' transferring from one company to another without the permission of local officers; yet training day continued to lack the seriousness of purpose and martial air one would associate with military excellence. Despite its attempt to instill discipline in the local troops, the Assembly added to the military weakness by reducing the number of training days from six to four after King William's War at the end of the seven-teenth century, and further reducing them from four to two after the French defeat in the Great War for Empire. Moreover, colony statutes continually widened the exemption clauses and added physicians and surgeons, schoolmasters, permanent herdsmen, ferry operators, lawyers, students and faculty at Yale, and all hold-ers of masters of arts degrees to those relieved of training obliga-tions. In addition, the upper limit of the age of responsibility was reduced from sixty to fifty-five.[30]

The structure of the local militia was remarkably simple; a full trainband was composed of sixty-four soldiers and officered by a captain, a lieutenant, an ensign, and four sergeants. To emphasize that the militia was indeed an expression of the local community and not a select group of military men: everyone who was in any way ever expected to have a part in the community's defense was eligible to vote for militia officers. All those exempted from train-ing because of occupation or old age were still required to own firearms and were specifically authorized to vote on training days. In a very real sense, then, the men of the community and not just the militiamen elected the officers. This distinction was important to the community because often its most respected leaders were exempt from training exercises. Elections were not annual but were held only when a vacancy occurred through resignation, re-tirement, or death. Despite a great deal of excitement and election fever, a strict seniority system characterized most elections, whereby each officer advanced a rung on the ladder; if a captain died, the lieutenant would be elected captain, the ensign would be elected lieutenant, and so on. Still, at least one vacancy had to be filled from the ranks and electing the new officer involved practices that would never be tolerated by the town, society, proprietors, or freemen. "Treating" with drink was expected, factions were formed, and electioneering was countenanced. Amidst this be-havior, so uncharacteristic of Connecticut political practices, one principle was uniformly adhered to: a candidate could not win by a mere plurality but had to have a clear-cut majority. In some cases where a man had a weak majority, the captain might call for an immediate "seconding" election to give people a chance to recon-sider. The most common system of voting was the "march round" method, whereby the men lined up and gave their votes orally to the captain as they filed past him. Militia companies aimed at concord, and usually, no matter how heated the contest, they would unite behind the victorious candidates; but as time went on, a larger number of controverted elections were appealed to the General Assembly. Also, the Assembly's occasional refusal in the eighteenth century to confirm a nominated officer shows that it began to take its confirmation power seriously and would not tolerate unacceptable candidates resulting from riotous practices.[31]

Besides elections, two other issues figured prominently in militia deliberations: the site of the training field and the division of a local trainband. After the population dispersed over a large area in each town, the location of the site for training frequently became a subject of controversy. The militia company always tried to settle the matter itself, usually selecting by majority vote an equitable site, but occasionally the decision would be appealed to the General Assembly. The colony government never required the training site to be fixed in advance by the colony government, however, as it did the site of meetinghouses; the location of a training field was not as important as the location of a meetinghouse, inasmuch as militia training occurred far less often than divine services; also, it was easier to change a training field than to build a new meetinghouse if an inappropriate site had been selected. The division of companies was a thornier problem. The society was the basic unit the militia trainband was based upon, and whenever a new society was created, so was a new trainband. However, when the population of a society grew sufficiently to swell the number of men in a trainband far in excess of the normal complement of sixty-four, whether to divide could become a controversial question. Many captains measured their status by the number of men they commanded and hence were anxious to prevent divisions. The colony government also wished to prevent small, undermanned, and perhaps undependable trainbands from coming into existence. However, many soldiers, anxious for officer status, were eager to divide a trainband and create new positions of leadership. Occasionally, some wanted to divide because they disliked the officers of a trainband and wanted to form their own unit for reasons of personality differences, a development the colony government also wanted to prevent. In the seventeenth century, the officers of a trainband made the decision on divisions; but in 1709 the power was transferred to the regimental officers appointed by the assembly to integrate and command the local militia in wartime. The local officers and men were consulted by the regimental officers, however, and protested vigorously if reorganization occurred without their consent. Many militia division cases reached the Assembly on appeal.[32]

Only two comprehensive lists exist that include all the militia trainbands in the colony, one for 1730 and one for 1739. However, from other evidence, the number of regiments, it is possible to make an estimate of the number of trainbands for later dates. In 1730 there were 134 trainbands in the colony and the average number of men per trainband was 63, or just one less than the 64 that was considered to be a company at full fighting strength. Between 1730 and the outbreak of the Revolution, although there was a significant increase in the number of trainbands, it did not keep pace with the population growth. By 1774, before the militia was reorganized for the war, the number of trainbands had increased to 234 but the number of men per band averaged 112. However, this trend towards larger trainbands was reversed during the Revolutionary years, and trainbands proliferated in extraordinary numbers. Once created, trainbands were not dismantled, and the Revolutionary experience had a lasting effect on their numbers. In 1790, eight years after the fighting ended, there were 390 trainbands, which represented a 66 percent increase over 1774; the average number of men per trainband declined to 80. This growth opened up 1,092 new officers' positions in local trainbands in a sixteen-year period; it also, of course, opened up nearly 100 new regimental officers' positions.[33]

The number of trainbands in a town in 1739 correlated most strongly with population and less strongly but significantly with square mileage (see table 15). Pressures of numbers on a company and long trips to the training field could both cause it to divide. In 1739 the largest number of trainbands in a town was six; slightly over one-third of the towns had but one. By the 1780s a couple of Connecticut's most populous towns had fourteen trainbands, enough to constitute more than an entire regiment. It seems reasonable to assume that the number of trainbands in a town still correlated with population and square mileage (see table 16). Although trainbands often were organized to include the same geographic area as a church society, a large number of societies had two of them. In 1739 there were 40 percent more trainbands than societies; in 1774 there were 23 percent more. In 1790, with the

TABLE 15
Militia Trainbands in 1739

No. of trainbands in town	No. of towns	Average population in 1756	Average square mileage
6	5	4,736	124
5	8	3,503	137
4	4	2,878	77
3	13	2,148	80
2	9	1,634	68
1	21	964[a]	56

Source: See note 33 to this chapter, below.
[a] Includes only ten towns because the other eleven in the category were in the process of being founded, and population figures for 1756 would bear little relationship to their populations in 1739.

TABLE 16
Militia Trainbands, 1730–90

Date	No. of trainbands	Total of men in militia	No. of men per trainband
1730	134	8,500	63
1739	164	11,184	68
1774	234	26,260	112
1790	390	31,332	80

Source: See note 33 to this chapter, below.

great increase in militia trainbands occasioned by the Revolution, there were about twice as many as Congregational church societies. Of course, because of the Toleration Act of 1784, there were by 1790 over one-hundred new societies of dissenters, and if they were included in calculations, trainbands would exceed societies by only 27 percent.

The Revolutionary War affected the militia in the short run but did not permanently change its nature or structure, as it did its numbers. In response to the Coercive Acts, the General Assembly passed a series of reforms in 1774 and 1775 designed to upgrade the militia's fighting capabilities. Punishment for missing training was increased; six shillings pay per day was authorized for training days, which previously had been unpaid; and the number of training days was increased from two full days to twelve half-days. During the war itself, the exempted householders were required to meet and train as a "home guard," militia activity greatly increased, and training took on a much more serious demeanor. After the war, however, the number of training days was cut to four half-days and the old rowdy ways resumed. While the growing number of exemptions before the Revolution had, in the words of one historian, "chipped" away from the model of universal military duty, the militia membership in the 1780s still was nearly synonymous with the male membership of a community, and the trainband still was a local citizens' defense organization; the Revolution neither separated the militia from the community nor imbued it with a sense of professionalization. Not until the 1790s did training cease to be a community activity and the militia start to become a select group of expert military men.[34]

IN addition to the growth in size and independence of the proprietors, freemen, and militia, there was a change in the legal system. The judiciary, although staffed with judges appointed solely by the colony government, grew more rapidly than either the population or the number of new towns and became increasingly decentralized. Justices of the peace and probate judges were not responsible to a local electorate, but by 1790 the 4.4 justices that towns averaged and the 27 probate districts spread across the state brought the courts to within a short distance of most people and guaranteed easy access.[35]

The proliferation of instruments of justice and of the other units of local government, when coupled with the growth of town and society government, illustrates a process of institutional expansion and differentiation in eighteenth-century Connecticut that created thousands of new positions of leadership and brought governmental services significantly closer to the homes and neighborhoods of the colony's and state's inhabitants. The creation in 1784 of the state's first five cities was in keeping with this process; the acts of municipal incorporation brought a large measure of autonomy and self-government to the central business districts of the largest towns.[36] Only the development of the proprietors as an organized entity failed to enlarge the role of local inhabitants in decision making; and in their case they were usually forced by local pressure to take an expansive view of their membership, with the colony acting to curtail control of them by absentees. This proliferation and decentralization of institutions was a two-edged sword that could affect government in conflicting ways. First, by creating more potential for participatory involvement of individuals and neighbors, it could soothe social tensions and prevent the alienation of the governed from the governors. On the other hand, the proliferation led to an institutional framework of more bodies who were less closely supervised by a stable central elite and whose jurisdictions overlapped and were frequently unclear; this situation could easily lead to local squabbling. Moreover, the local elite making the decisions, by virtue of being better known to the nearby community, may have lacked some of the ability to inspire awe that more distant governing figures had possessed. In a sense the lessened physical distance between the governors and the governed may have led to a lessened social distance. Certainly, communities wanted more institutions, more leadership positions, closer government, and more initiative in local government. As the court records and General Assembly appeals cases show, however, achieving these goals did not stem the rise of disorder that characterized eighteenth-century Connecticut. Whether the disorder would have been greater or lesser without the massive growth of local decision making is a question that can probably never be answered; it depends on which edge of the sword one thinks was sharper.

[VI]

THE EMERGENCE OF CENTRAL PLACES

ADMINISTRATIVE, intellectual, and economic criteria can each be used to define central places. In modern America, for example, it could quite plausibly be argued that Washington, D.C., is the administrative center; Cambridge, Massachusetts, the intellectual center; and New York City the economic center. For colonial Connecticut, however, administrative and intellectual criteria are not very helpful in classifying towns. Too few distinctions among towns can be made if one tests centrality by administrative importance; Hartford and New Haven, the co-capitals of the colony, were the most important seats of government, followed by the four other county seats; however, all other towns were administratively equal and would have to be lumped together as "the rest." Yale College gave New Haven preeminence as an intellectual center, but intellectual pursuits generally developed in proportion to a town's economic importance; hence, intellectual centrality followed economic centrality, and to designate certain Connecticut towns as intellectual centers simply is to note a concomitant growth that accompanied economic development. Classifying towns by economic function allows for many distinctions, and the distinctions made are the meaningful ones for colonial society.

A chronological overview of the development of Connecticut's economy is essential to any discussion of economic function. The colony progressed from a primarily internal economy before 1710, through a transition stage from 1710 to 1740, into an external economy in about 1740. Before 1710 Connecticut consumed most of its own agricultural produce and imported only the minimum of manufactured goods needed to sustain a farming economy. Although merchants and trade existed in this period, their importance was not paramount, and in many ways the economy of the period resembles the idyllic subsistence life of relative prosperity and economic democracy so extolled by the mythologizers of history. Wasteful farming practices; the rough, hilly land of the new towns, which was unsuited to cultivation; and the growth of population destroyed this early economy by creating the first major crisis in the colony's economy — a shortage of good land. In response to the crisis, Connecticut evolved from 1710 to 1740 from an internal to an external economy; it changed from a society of subsistence farmers who produced primarily for themselves and the local market to a society of producers of commercial crops for export. Intertown transportation systems were developed, artisanal and manufacturing activities were accentuated, agricultural specialization by region and town developed, trade greatly increased, and large-scale merchants appeared, developing contacts with much of the Atlantic world. In short, Connecticut was transformed from a relatively homogeneous economy of largely subsistence farmers to one of a complex and differentiated nature dependent on commerce — from a backwater of the British Empire to an active participant in the Atlantic trading community. Although the metamorphosis did not solve the basic land-shortage problem completely, and although the events of the Revolutionary years badly distended trading patterns, the commercial economy that developed at the mid-eighteenth century propelled the colony into an apparent boom and still characterized the new state in 1790. This commercialization of the economy had potent effects upon the towns and resulted in a clear economic differentiation of town types.[1]

In classifying towns by degrees of economic centrality or importance, or in delineating urban as opposed to nonurban areas, one of the more common errors made by historians is to use aggregate population as the criterion. Urban scholars are unanimous in denouncing population numbers as a test for urbanization; yet some demographers continue to use them and administrators almost always do so. Population is used as a classification tool because it is overwhelmingly the most convenient one. But the absurdity of using population as the test can be seen by looking at the censuses of colonial Connecticut. Towns such as Farmington and Woodbury, with little mercantile development and no economic influence beyond their own borders, and with decentralized residential patterns, are among the highest in absolute population; to consider them more urban than towns with lesser numbers but with sizable clusters of population engaged in external trade is to negate the meaning of the word. Density of population is a far better criterion; many sociologists would argue, however, that even density can be misleading and that it must be used in conjunction with an analysis of the economic function and role of the town in relation to the surrounding countryside and towns.[2]

To a certain extent no Connecticut town was an economic central place, yet to a certain extent all of them were, once they passed beyond the frontier stage. No one metropolis dominated the Connecticut economy as Boston and New York City did the economies of Massachusetts and New York. Each Connecticut town, however, included some merchants, and with the commercialization of agriculture each acted as a collection depot for produce on the way to export and reciprocally as a retail center in which farmers could buy goods brought in from afar. To a similar extent all Connecticut towns were rural in nature; each of them, including the most commercially developed, such as Hartford and New Haven, included large numbers of farmers. The distinctions made, then, must be on the mix of merchants and farmers and on the relative importance of the mercantile community of a town to the town as a whole, the surrounding region, and the colony. Thus, the degree of urbanization is defined by the quantity of economic services a center performed and by the center's position relative to other centers.

Importance changes with time, and economic power is always in a state of flux; towns grow and decline. Differentiation of economic town types first became manifest to Connecticut inhabitants at the mid-eighteenth century, when mercantile activity became crucial to the colony's economic life. It was then that Connecticut's largest towns made the transformation from villages into provincial cities.[3] Thus the quarter of a century preceding the Revolution is the period when economic central places were clearly established, and it is the period for which classification of towns is most meaningful. The Revolution did not alter the hierarchy of towns, although some shifts in importance did occur and some centers added manufacturing functions to their market functions, making them both trading and manufacturing centers. The incorporation of five cities in the 1780s was a political act designed to recognize the preeminent central places that had emerged prior to the Revolution.

Scholars drawing upon many disciplines, among them archaeology, anthropology, sociology, and geography, agree that urban clusters of living can usually be classified as either of two types: (1) those organized for social reasons, where economic considerations are subordinated to religious, moral, or military precepts; or (2) those created by the self-regulating market mechanism whose functions are economic. Type one is planned by the leaders of society and is dedicated to preserving a link with the past and with tradition. Type two is unplanned, occurs from the many individual decisions of buyers and sellers, and is inclined to be innovative and a foe of traditional values.[4] Connecticut's Puritan villages of the seventeenth century, insofar as they can be construed as pockets of urban existence, are examples primarily of the first type; their main functions were to ensure social control, promote the New England version of Christianity, and provide defense against Indians. Even the most mercantile of villages, New Haven, could not sustain itself as a commercial town and within two years of its inception had become more of a social and religious center for farmers than an economic central place. The desire for land proved too strong for the Puritan ethos to withstand; as religious purpose weakened and the need for defense waned, the villages that had been organized for social purposes disappeared and were replaced by the second type of urban unit — those organized for economic reasons. Of course the dichotomy between the two ideal types is never perfect — Connecticut's social villages of the seventeenth century served as the trade centers of the community, and the economic villages of the eighteenth century promoted religious and social norms — but the main thrusts behind the Puritan village and behind those of the late colonial and early national periods are starkly different. One could draw a continuum from 1636 to 1790 and put social villages on one end and economic villages on the other.

Planned centers can be imposed upon a landscape and planted virtually anywhere; they frequently overcome "natural forces" through sheer will and purpose. For example, the economic conditions of seventeenth-century Connecticut militated against any urban type of existence; the most natural and efficient use of resources in a pure economic setting would have been through each farmer living on his land: farmsteads would have been in accordance with the "least work" principle that geographers argue is the economic ideal in distributing population. But to satisfy noneconomic needs, farmers lived in villages and walked to their lands regardless of some loss of efficiency. As several historians have shown, when the efficiency loss became too great, the population tended to disperse.[5]

One of the questions that has remained unanswered by historians, however, is why Connecticut's Puritans were so willing to jettison the agricultural village. Despite inefficiencies, it has shown more tenacity in other societies. Breaking down a pattern of nuclear villages requires strong forces; farmers often maintain them for social reasons long after they are economically burdensome. In England, when the enclosure movement consolidated farmers' landholdings in the second half of the eighteenth century and the first half of the nineteenth, it was much more economically advantageous to build homes on farmsteads; yet most English farmers stayed in the villages. In the 1960s the Italian government, in an attempt to improve the standard of living of the peasants, implemented a program to force them out of the villages to which they clung with an uneconomic ferocity.[6]

The ease with which Connecticut farmers embraced "outliving" can be explained by economic circumstances that were impelling, but it must also be seen as a measure of the rise of individualism and independence. Modern empirical studies show that the costs of production rise by 20 percent for every kilometer farmers have to walk to their lands. A distance of 1 kilometer between farm land and residence occasionally evokes a response by the farmer, but a distance of 3 or 4 kilometers invariably produces changes in living patterns, because it is so grossly uneconomic. The large size of early Connecticut towns and the extensive farming methods meant that in each Connecticut town, unlike most peasant societies, the 3- to 4-kilometer threshold was quickly realized. In England, for instance, in the midlands, where dispersal did not take place, villages were located 1.6 kilometers apart for a maximum walking distance of .8 kilometers; this figure compares to maximum walking distances in Connecticut that were frequently in excess of 8 kilometers. Connecticut's farmers would have had to pay an extraordinary price to maintain their communal ideal; their refusal to pay the price, however, indicates the growth of an individualistic spirit, and, of course, the dispersal process itself accelerated the growth.[7]

Unplanned centers not created by purpose or will are sited according to transportation routes, as the original developer of central-place theory, Walter Christaller, showed, or are located by the "connectivity" principle, as a recent geographer shows in a refined version of central-place theory. Economic central places develop when an area produces a surplus for market — that is why differentiation among towns became so pronounced at mid-eighteenth century. When this differentiation among roughly equivalent villages began, those areas best connected to the outside world were best suited to dispose of the surplus. Thus, while transportation accessibility is the prime criterion for the location of economic central places, they can develop on nonnatural transportation routes simply because they are in a position to connect a region with outside markets; perhaps they may be at the center of an area with no access to a transportation route, or perhaps they may be at the edge of a region and at the mouth of a natural funnel for its produce. Modern Chicago, for example, is a city at the heart of a productive region, whereas Omaha and Kansas City are "gateway" centers located between contrasting areas to secure exchange benefits. Although spatial relationships are important in developing central places, seldom are centers evenly spaced; transportation routes almost always abridge perfect spacing patterns.[8]

Seldom in a society is there a single type of economic central place; usually there is a range of higher- and lower-order centrality. The essential difference between higher- and lower-order centers in preindustrial society is that the higher provides all the services the lower provides, but the lower does not have some of the services of the higher. Of course, while the scholar seeks to type towns into neat categories of centrality, most urban centers in a society could best be evaluated for centrality by being placed on a continuum; pre-Revolutionary towns in Connecticut, for instance, would range from New Haven, the most developed, at one end of the continuum, to Union, the least developed, at the other end. However, classification, while blurring some distinctions and necessitating some arbitrary cut-off lines, does allow one to generalize about an otherwise endless variety of experiences. When differentiation of communities became pronounced in Connecticut, three distinct types emerged: (1) urban centers that were major entrepôts of importance to many towns in a surrounding region and that engaged heavily in a direct export trade; (2) secondary centers of two kinds — those that engaged in the direct export business but were not vital to the commerce of other towns, and those that were not engaged in the direct export of goods but did serve as inland market centers for several surrounding towns; and (3) country towns that neither engaged in the direct export business nor served as centers for other towns. In 1776 there were five urban centers, twenty-five secondary centers, and forty-three country towns. These numbers may at first seem to depart substantially from the normal ratio of one:two:four that geographers have established for central places of the three ranks, but if one adds to the urban centers Albany, New York City, Newport, Providence, and Boston, all of which were "gateway" central places for Connecticut, the ratio corresponds closely to the norm.[9]

While anthropologists correctly argue that any cluster of people living in close proximity constitutes an urban pocket and that village development is part of the urbanization process, the analysis presented here will use "urban center" to mean only the major entrepôts of the first order of centrality and will use the terms "secondary center" and "country town" for the two lower-order types of urbanization.

The five urban centers, Hartford, Middletown, New Haven, New London, and Norwich, owed their preeminence primarily to geography and secondarily to historical circumstances. All five were river ports or seaports. Hartford's location at the juncture of the Farmington River with the Connecticut made it the ideal site for the trade of the Connecticut River Valley immediately south of Springfield. The importance of the small rivers to the development of trading sites has not been fully appreciated. Flatboats and canoes carried extensive cargoes on these smaller streams to points like Hartford, where they could be transferred to oceangoing vessels. Middletown, sited, as the name suggests, on the Connecticut River midway between Hartford and the coast, drained the hinterland in the river valley too far south to be serviced by Hartford and too far north to be serviced by a coastal port. Middletown had the additional advantage of being just south of a dangerous sandbar in the river that led some shippers to unload their cargoes there rather than continue upstream to Hartford. New Haven and New London, both located on the coast, possessed the two best harbors on the shoreline; New Haven's in the west was ideal for the New York trade, and New London's in the east was equally so for that of Boston and Rhode Island. Separated by fifty miles, the two towns each had enough trade area not to undercut each other's commerce seriously. Both were connected to the interior by rivers: New London lay at the mouth of the Thames, the colony's second most important river; and the Quinnipiac emptied into New Haven harbor. Norwich, situated at the headwaters of the Thames, was the most inland point to which seagoing vessels could penetrate in eastern Connecticut. Two rivers, the Shetucket, which connected to the Quinebaug, and the Yantic, met in Norwich to form the Thames; the Shetucket-Quinebaug system extended over thirty-five miles into the interior. Norwich, sited only twelve miles up-stream from New London, in many ways was located too near the latter town and deprived it of much of its hinterland. The two perceived each other as rivals and as threats to one another's pros-perity. Norwich, because of its better contact with the hinterland of eastern Connecticut, emerged as the stronger of the two in the 1760s. It was a tribute to New London's harbor, the finest in the colony — John Winthrop, Jr., said of it that "ships of 500 tons may go so close they may toss a biscuit ashore" — that the town could compete at all with its upstream rival.[10]

These five urban towns all nurtured impressive mercantile communities. Of the 54 leading merchants identified in a study of Revolutionary Connecticut, the five towns were home to 41. In Hartford, 153 individual merchants advertised imported goods during the Revolution. In 1782 at least 68 Norwich men called themselves merchants when a trade association was formed to pro-hibit illegal imports. In Middletown, the least developed of the five towns before the Revolution, nine merchants and nine ship cap-tains operated stores and warehouses on Main Street in 1770; in Middletown, as in the other four towns, supplementing the domi-nant main street, seven or eight additional streets in the business district were devoted to retailing. Extant maps of Hartford, New London, and New Haven in the 1770s show complex street plans consisting of two or three major streets and several lesser ones devoted to business. Almost every known commodity in the West-ern world could be obtained. Stores in New London and Norwich sold chandlery wares, rum, sugar, molasses, beeswax, furs, clothes, drygoods, books, drugs, linen, jewelry, silver, pewter, tin, and wide assortments of merchandise loosely advertised as "French goods," "goods from Holland," or "all European goods." Artisans offered services unlikely to be found in other towns, such as wigmaking, bookbinding, and barbering, and tended to specialize much more in single products than did the smaller-town part-time gen-eralists.[11]

Mainly, the merchants in the five urban centers were generalists, importing a wide range of goods and receiving their country prod-uce from a variety of sources; not until the 1790s did mercantile specialization begin and merchants separate into wholesale and retail sales. Merchants in each of the five towns were wholesalers for shopkeepers and merchants in at least six surrounding towns

and also operated their own retail outlets. Many formed partner-
ships, of varied duration, with merchants in the surrounding towns
or employed relatives to operate "branch stores" in some other
locale. The successful urban merchants seemed to have a penchant
for setting up nephews, brothers-in-law, sons-in-law, and so on in
nearby towns to run their secondary operations. The urban merchants relied on three sources for goods: their own retail custom-
ers, merchants and shopkeepers from other towns who brought
goods to the urban center, and agents who traveled in the hinterland buying produce for export. Most large merchants employed
all three sources, and a few owned commercial farms that gener-
ated produce for export. They usually wholesaled their imported
goods to the merchants of surrounding towns, who came to the
urban towns to purchase them or distributed them through family
connections. Occasionally, they would sell "goods afloat" at auctions held directly at shipside.[12]

A detailed map drawn of the center of New Haven in 1748,
which lists all buildings and their residents' occupations, provides
the material for an occupational analysis of the business district of
that town (see table 17). This district, the "compact part," as it was
called by Ezra Stiles, contained only about one-fourth of the entire
town's population; between 1748 and 1776 the compact part more
than doubled in size as New Haven shared in the great mid-century
growth of all urban towns; hence, the figures for 1748 seriously
understate the degree of commercial development achieved in the
pre-Revolutionary years. In 1748, twenty-nine farmers comprised
the largest occupational group, but merchants, numbering twelve,
were the second largest group. A total of eighty-five men made

TABLE 17
Occupations in New Haven's Business District, 1748

Farmers	29	Lawyers	3	Tanners	2
Merchants	12	Hatters	3	Clockmakers	2
Shoemakers	11	Innkeepers	3	Millers	1
Joiners	7	Physicians	3	Silversmiths	1
Mariners	7	Ship carpenters	2	Wheelwrights	1
Gentlemen	5	Tailors	2	Laborers	1
Coopers	4	Ministers	2	Yale president	1
Barbers	4	Clothiers	2	Saddlers	1
Smiths	3	Schoolmasters	2	Unspecified	11

their livings from nonfarming occupations. Of the artisans, most did not serve farming needs per se but produced goods and services for a retail market; there were, for instance, only three blacksmiths and one miller, compared to ten shoemakers, seven joiners (carpenters), and four barbers. Three lawyers practiced in the town and, according to Ezra Stiles, were the only ones in the entire county.[13]

Detailed plans of Middletown's and Hartford's main streets three decades later, in the 1770s, suggest an even higher emphasis on retailing in the central part of town and a correspondingly lower percentage of farmers. Of the forty-two buildings listed on Middletown's main street, thirty-seven were occupied by people involved in some aspect of business while only five were inhabited by farmers; on Hartford's main street only five of the forty-seven buildings housed farmers.[14]

These urban towns, containing as they did well over one-hundred businesses each in the late colonial period, must have presented an impressive picture to the rural visitors from the Connecticut countryside or to those from smaller towns. The mere clustering together of that many buildings — New Haven's center had 328 houses in 1772, Hartford had 250 in 1786, and Middletown had 190 in 1783 — told observers that they were viewing a major center of activity. English visitors frequently expressed amazement at finding such well-developed centers of civilization in a land they thought of as containing mainly trees and savages.[15] Thomas Pownall, an English official traveling through Connecticut in 1754, voiced his admiration for New Haven and his obvious surprise at its resemblance to an English trading center: "The traveler has from the hills an enchanting view of the vale and the town; a town of trading, and the harbor full of vessels. The town is built on a regularly designed plan. Is a square, has a place or square in the middle, from the angles of which go off in right lines eight streets. The houses are all built in the English fashion. In the center of the square is a fine meeting house with its spire like our English churches."[16]

A cosmopolitan air pervaded the urban centers on the eve of the Revolution. Wives of the leading men, clad in silk dresses with long trains, with calashes on their heads and high-heeled shoes, adorned themselves with much jewelry and carried long fans. Alert to changing styles, they seized eagerly on news of fashion from recent travelers to Boston or New York. One can imagine the excitement in 1775 when Marie Gabriel, "a mantuamaker and milliner from Paris," opened up a shop in Hartford. Men also carefully cultivated their appearances. When Samuel Edwards of Hartford died, he left, besides his large and elegant wardrobe, a "noted wig," "best bob wig," and "natural white wig." The social life of the fashion-conscious urbanites also reflected a growing sophistication and love of pleasures. Dancing became extraordinarily popular and balls were held to celebrate most occasions. One European visitor to New Haven expressed amazement that the normal course of events at one of the frequent balls was to dance both the minuet and the "country dances" until one o'clock in the morning. Many of the balls were large affairs with "a hundred charming girls . . . dressed with elegant simplicity." Wedding celebrations sometimes lasted three days; at one in Norwich, ninety guests danced ninety-two jigs, fifty-two contra dances, forty-five minuets, and seventeen hornpipes. Taverns in the five towns became numerous enough to attract specialized clienteles. The use of carriages became common among men of distinction by the outbreak of the Revolution, and a group of men appeared whose occupation was listed as "Gentlemen."[17]

The urban towns developed other attributes of provincial cities. Of the five, only Middletown lacked a newspaper by the Revolution; the *Connecticut Gazette* in New Haven and the *New London Summary*, founded respectively in 1755 and 1758, were the first two in the colony, followed by the *Connecticut Courant* in Hartford in 1764 and the *Norwich Packet* in 1773. Each of the towns had established Latin grammar schools that attracted students from the surrounding countryside who were preparing for college entrance. Starting with the appointment of a postmaster in Hartford in 1764, the urban towns became the centers of a regularized postal system for the colony; previously, letters were irregularly delivered to local taverns, which were used as mail depositories. With the accumulation of wealth by a few prosperous merchants, individuals began building up large personal libraries. A Middletown merchant opened Connecticut's first slave market in the 1760s, and it proved profitable.[18]

An indication of the growth of urbanization in Norwich can be seen in the declining number of rattlesnakes killed and presented to the selectmen for the ten-shilling bounty. From a high of seventy-eight rattlesnakes brought in for the bounty in 1738, the number declined throughout the 1740s, 1750s, and 1760s until it was rumored that just one rattlesnake was left in town. For a dozen years none was killed; then in 1786 the so-called last rattlesnake was killed and presented for the bounty.[19]

In New Haven, Yale College added a cosmopolitan air that other urban towns lacked; with over two-hundred students, it had the largest enrollment of any colonial college in 1776.[20]

A growing heterogeneity characterized the five centers as they emerged as economic central places. Although only one-half of Connecticut's towns spawned Separatist parishes during the Great Awakening, all five of the urban towns did so. The urban communities lost a higher percentage of converts to the Anglican church than did many of the smaller towns surrounding them. Anglicans also had greater success in officeholding in the urban areas than in secondary centers and country towns, indicating that Anglicanism was no longer a crushing burden for aspirant officeholders. The few Catholics in the colony lived mostly in the five urban areas, and Jewish worship appeared in New Haven. The plurality of worship in the five towns reflected an increase in the settlement of new nationalities, among them Spanish, Portuguese, French, Dutch, and West Indians. Before mid-century, and in the other towns even later, only an occasional French Huguenot or Dutch Protestant diluted the almost totally English population. Most of the non-English came to the urban towns to engage in trade and readily merged with the mercantile classes. While non-English merchants were not elected as leaders in the communities, some became influential and moved in the select social circles.[21]

The two groups of secondary centers, those ports that imported goods directly from outside the colony and those four that served as inland market centers, varied greatly in their development of business districts and merchant communities. All towns on the Connecticut River south of and including Windsor and all towns on the coastline participated in the direct import-export trade; this inclusiveness accounts for their variety. Fairfield, the most developed of the secondary centers, could have been included in the group of urban towns; the least developed of these centers, river ports like Glastonbury and Haddam and coastal ports like Killingworth and Saybrook, had a minimal amount of commercial activity. Yet, as an entrepôt, Fairfield was clearly less developed than any of the five urban towns — as an indication of contemporary opinion, it was not incorporated as a city in the 1780s — and the small river and coastal ports all did possess merchants who imported goods directly from outside. The river and coastal ports of this group owed their secondary status to inferior harbors, lack of tributary rivers giving access to a large hinterland, or locations too near one of the five urban centers to enable them to compete successfully for large-scale trade. The inland centers never achieved centrality of the first order precisely because they were inland and could not take part directly in oceangoing commerce.

The secondary centers contained far fewer stores than the five urban towns and their central street grids were much simpler. The center of Fairfield, the largest of the secondary towns, contained thirty stores and shops and eighty-five houses during the Revolutionary years. They were arranged on two intersecting streets and two small lanes. Fairfield's harbor, less built-up than those of the urban towns, contained seven warehouses and wharves. Guilford and Greenwich were more typical of medium-sized secondary centers; a map of Guilford center in the 1770s shows approximately fifty buildings; one of Greenwich in 1773 shows thirty-eight. Lebanon, the least developed and least nucleated of all the inland market towns, scattered its thirty-seven buildings up to a mile from the two central buildings in the town: the store of the leading merchant, Jonathan Trumbull, and the First Society meeting-house.[22]

The number of men dignified by the title of merchant ranged from two to fifteen in the secondary centers that were ports; in several, however, one or two merchants or merchant firms dominated local commerce. In Lyme, while fifteen merchants engaged in the coasting trade, importing and exporting goods from New York and Boston, only two merchants traded regularly with the West Indies and one, John McCurdy, dominated the town's trade by the Revolutionary period. The Selleck family of Stamford controlled most of that town's direct trade with the West Indies, and in Glastonbury only Thomas Wells did a "brisk trade" with the other colonies and the West Indies. The number of major traders could go much higher, however; the largest secondary center on the Connecticut River, Wethersfield, had six merchants with a direct Caribbean import-export trade, and Guilford similarly housed six large-scale merchants.[23]

The inland secondary centers varied greatly in numbers of merchants. It is impossible to determine precisely the number of merchants in Windham, the leading inland market town, but in view of the extensive debts owed them by the farmers and shopkeepers of the surrounding countryside, at least eight men in 1776 were major importers and exporters. Danbury's center contained twenty-two stores and shops in 1777, and when the town's first newspaper appeared in 1790, several merchants advertised to the surrounding area that they would ship "country produce" to New York City. Ten different Litchfield merchants advertised during the Revolutionary years that they would collect goods from and distribute them to nearby towns. Lebanon was unique in that it had only one major merchant, Jonathan Trumbull, who alone accounted for Lebanon's position as a market town.[24]

The records of the customshouses for the late colonial period have not survived intact; hence, one cannot say with certitude how many ships used the secondary centers as home ports. However, local evidence and indirect evidence would suggest that in the last years before independence the secondary ports averaged about 2 or 3 vessels, ranging from 5 in some to just 1 in others. In 1774, 200 ships were registered at Connecticut ports, of which 72 showed New London as home port. By qualitative assessments, New Haven, the second largest home port, harbored about half the number of New London, and the other three urban towns had still fewer. A traveler counting the ships docked at New Haven and Hartford recorded that Hartford usually had about half as many as New Haven. If Hartford, Middletown, and Norwich each had 15 ships, it would yield a rough estimate of 153 vessels using the five urban towns as home ports. This would leave 47 that were using the secondary ports, or roughly 2 or 3 each. Local sources show that 4 or 5 ships sailed from Wethersfield; at least 1 each from Glastonbury, East Haddam, and Windsor; and at least 4 or 5 from Stamford.[25]

Not always were the ships at either urban or secondary centers owned by merchants from the vessels' home ports. Inland merchants frequently invested in ships to carry their goods and maintained branch stores and warehouses at the ports through which they imported and exported. Many of the ships in New London, undoubtedly most, were owned by merchants of Hartford, Middletown, and Norwich who utilized its superior harbor as an initial port of entry for large ships. Not infrequently, shopkeepers in country towns or in the secondary centers would own shares in a ship operating out of one of the ports: Jonathan Trumbull of Lebanon owned ships in New London and East Haddam, Suffield's leading merchant owned a small ship that probably sailed out of Hartford, and several merchants and sea captains in Preston owned shares in ships based in Norwich.[26]

The reason for the commercial development of the river and coastal ports is obvious — when ships could dock at their centers it was almost inevitable that some enterprising man would serve his community and himself by promoting commerce — but similar development of each of the four inland centers requires further explanation. Windham and Litchfield, the two shire towns of their counties, were the first-settled areas of their respective regions, giving each an initial, crucial lead over future towns. Neither town had a particularly advantageous location; both Kent which was closer to the Hudson Valley, and Plainfield, which was on the Quinebaug River, had equal or better areas. Litchfield, however, had a twenty-year lead on Kent, and Plainfield's first twenty years were ones of turmoil. For the areas served by Litchfield and Windham some central town was needed: both northwest and northeast Connecticut were at great distances from the urban and secondary ports. The northwest lay near New York Colony and the Hudson Valley, the northeast near Boston and Rhode Island; it would have been extraordinary, given the Connecticut farmers' desire to produce crops for export, if some inland center had not developed to organize the overland trade. Trade thrives on capital, credit, and stability, which Windham and Litchfield offered. Moreover, because they were the first two towns in their areas, the highway transportation system was oriented to them; Litchfield had the two major highways of the west running through it. As transportation specialists show, an area that is initially favored, for whatever reason, obtains the best communications first; transportation reinforces its early advantage and leads to even greater development. In addition, being the shire towns of their counties was basic to Windham's and Litchfield's regional preeminence, as other towns in the areas realized. Towns frequently vied for county-seat status; Woodbury, for example, fought in vain to become the seat of Litchfield county. As well as seating the county court government, the county shire town was the location of the sheriff's office, with its importance to the regulation of business, and was the scene of thriving retail trade and professional activity. Prominent men, aware of the impact the new status would have on the town's future, were quick to establish residence in each of the newly designated shire towns. When Brooklyn, a crossroads village, temporarily replaced Windham as the county seat in the early nineteenth century, it became a major market town within a few years.[27]

Lebanon owed its emergence as a market town to the singleminded determination of the Trumbull family, which, it appears from indirect evidence, in 1739 assumed the business of the town's other most important merchant, Nathaniel Porter. Lebanon had no natural advantages and, adjacent to Windham, was forced to compete with the shire town for the commerce of the region. The two, Windham and Lebanon, are the only cases of an inland market center being forced to compete with any nearby center of primary or secondary importance. The Trumbulls spanned a half century as major merchants and made Lebanon a collection point for surrounding towns, not only by operating a wholesale business in the town center but by actively scouring the countryside and soliciting business. In addition, Lebanon was nearer than any other center to large parts of Hebron, Coventry, and Colchester. However, Lebanon's limited hinterland and its total dependence on the Trumbulls, a few lesser merchants notwithstanding, was most fully demonstrated when Jonathan Trumbull went bankrupt in the late 1760s and Lebanon declined to the status of a country town. Trumbull's energy and political connections could not overcome the economic fact that Windham County did not need two market centers. It should be added that Trumbull's business judgments were often less than astute; a more solidly based community, however, could have weathered the lack of ability of one businessman.[28]

Danbury, on the other hand, had a substantial hinterland including six surrounding towns. Located in the western part of the colony midway between the coastal ports and Litchfield, Danbury served as a collection point for produce on its way to the Hudson Valley and New York City. Why Danbury emerged as the center for this area, instead of New Fairfield, Newtown, or Ridgefield, which had equally advantageous locations, can best be explained by its founding date; it was settled twenty years before the surrounding towns and had the early advantages of better transportation, more capital, and stability. Despite being burned by the British in 1777, Danbury experienced a phenomenal growth in economic complexity during the Revolution, which survived the end of hostilities. Indeed, the British march inland to burn Danbury was a tribute to its economic importance. Shortly after the war Danbury was made a half-shire town for Fairfield County, an act that attests to its centrality.[29]

Most Connecticut towns, of course, were not accessible to ships and did not serve surrounding towns as central places; these were the country towns. It should not be assumed, however, that they lacked a commercial life or some economic sophistication. All possessed an artisanal community, several grist- and sawmills, many taverns, a majority of farmers who raised crops for export, and at least one and usually several retail shops. Normatively, in a pre-modern rural society, the lowest-order central place serves a hexagonal hinterland within a maximum distance of 4.5 miles, which is slightly over one hour's walk. The number of country-town villages and parish villages in Connecticut would indicate that they were slightly closer than 9 miles (2 × 4.5) apart; this spacing was probably occasioned by the difficult terrain in the eastern and western uplands, which made it nearly impossible to cover 4.5 miles in an hour.[30]

The villages of these country towns were invariably small, seldom larger than eighteen buildings, and organized on one street or at most two intersecting streets. Yet these villages served as central economic places for societies or towns. Sharon, for example, had a village in 1776 consisting of a lawyer, local merchant and shop, blacksmith, school, tavern, brickyard, tannery, Congregational meetinghouse, and Anglican church. Other buildings of a service nature — three gristmills, a sawmill, two forges, a tavern, a meetinghouse, and six schools — were decentralized around the town. Simsbury contained six separate little villages ranging from eight buildings to eighteen. Tolland's center comprised only eight buildings. In a few towns, like Voluntown and Hebron, there was no village and economic services were scattered across the countryside. It is impossible to establish how many retail shops of a crossroads store nature existed in these country towns, since most of the account books for these shopkeepers are not extant. However, every town history has shown at least one store in each town once it was past the frontier stage, and the few in-depth studies with good sources have uncovered more. The range would probably be from one or two shops to four or five.[31]

Even when located outside a village, the retail stores served the country towns as central places. They acted as brokers between farmers and the merchants involved in external trade. Occasionally, inland merchants or port merchants traveled to country stores, but more normally, the country shopkeeper transported his merchandise for export to an inland market town or port and brought back goods for retail sale. The goods of the country stores were surprisingly varied and complete: 62 percent cloth and wearing apparel; 10 percent hardware; 10 percent provisions; 10 percent leather, lime, and salt; 6 percent stationery and books; 1 percent tea; and 1 percent coal.[32]

TABLE 18
Numbers of Taverns in Towns

Town	No. of taverns	Year
Bolton	4	1776
Coventry	7	1774
Farmington	16	1750
Hartford	24	1776
Litchfield	17	1783
Winchester	5	1783
Windham	12	1760

Sources: Connecticut Archives, Finance and Currency, Connecticut State Library, Hartford, Series I, vol. V, 214a; Bruce P. Stark, *Lyme, Connecticut: From Founding to Independence* (Old Lyme, Conn., 1976), 52; Ezra Stiles, *Extracts from the Itineraries and Other Miscellanies of Ezra Stiles*, ed. Franklin Bowditch Dexter (New Haven, 1916), 367; *A History of Litchfield County* (Philadelphia, 1881), 183; Samuel Alvord, *A Historical Sketch of Bolton* (Bolton, Conn., 1920), 25; William D. Love, *The Colonial History of Hartford* (Chester, Conn., 1974), 232–50; Ellen Larned, *History of Windham County, Connecticut*, 2 vols. (Worcester, Mass., 1874; reprint ed., Chester, Conn., 1976), II, 48.

Taverns, including ordinaries and public houses, far more numerous than stores in all types of towns, also served as central places for the farming community. Because taverns are so regularly mentioned in travelers' accounts, so often indicated on maps, and so "quaint" to the sensibilities of modern man, historians are familiar with them as part of the colonial landscape; scholars have not fully realized, however, the ubiquity of the tavern in the village and countryside alike. At least one was integral to every neighborhood, and a tavern usually occurred on intertown highways at three- or four-mile intervals. Probably no Connecticut man was more than three miles from one, and most were far closer. Country towns usually maintained at least five, secondary centers ten, and the urban towns still more. Taverns served as social centers, and one would assume that farmers and merchants meeting there found the setting conducive to discussions of agriculture, prices of crops, patterns of trade, and matters of politics. Abetting such social functions, rural taverns sometimes stocked a few shelves of goods for retail sale and took merchandise for payment. In itself, the prevalence of taverns indicates the importance attached to them by contemporaries and their role in ameliorating the isolation of rural life (see tables 18 and 19).[33]

TABLE 19

Taverns on the Main Road from the Massachusetts Border
to New Haven during the Revolution

Tavern	Distance in miles from last one	Tavern	Distance in miles from last one
Kibbe, Enfield	5	Kilburn, Wethersfield	3
Ellsworth, Windsor	7	Shayler, Middletown	11
Bissel, Windsor	1	Camp, Durham	6
Porter, Windsor	3	Doolittle, Wallingford	8
Benjamin, Hartford	4	Mansfield, New Haven	5
Bull, Hartford	2	Killyer, New Haven	8

Source: Albert E. Van Dusen, "The Trade of Revolutionary Connecticut" (Ph.D. diss., University of Pennsylvania, 1948), 48.

The role of the society meetinghouse as a central place in rural life is so well known that one fears belaboring the obvious by mentioning it. There, most people met at least twice a week, and few matters could so arouse a community as the location of a new one. Controversies over meetinghouse sites were endemic to colonial society and are an ironic testimony to their importance in the community life. Physical centrality was the guiding principle in locating a new meetinghouse, but establishing centrality was not always easy; distances of less than a mile could cause bitter differences engendering conflict for years.[34]

Mills, artisans' shops, physicians' houses, and occasionally a lawyer's office also served as central places in rural towns. All four types of activity, however, correlated more positively with other factors than with economic centrality.

A rare extant list of taxes paid by the artisans and millers in each of the towns shows that the amount of artisanal and milling activity varied almost directly with population size; country towns with decentralized populations had as many craftsmen and millers per capita as did the urban centers. Understandably, since the urban towns and secondary centers had significantly larger populations than the country towns, their workshops and mills were more numerous in absolute terms. Also, the distribution of artisans throughout types of communities was different; it was more centralized in urban and secondary centers than in country towns, and the types of craftsmen differed by town types — more produced luxury items in the urban and secondary centers and more serviced farmers in the country towns. Moreover, while artisans in country towns also farmed, in the urban towns and to a lesser extent in the secondary ones, some craftsmen practiced their trades full-time.[35]

By 1763 at least 64 percent of Connecticut's towns had acquired physicians — most of them more than one. The majority of towns without them were those in newly settled Litchfield County. The presence of physicians correlates not with economic centrality but with population and land size. Farmington, for example, physically the largest town in the colony, had the most, (eight), compared to three in Hartford and two in New London. The three other urban towns, Middletown, New Haven, and Norwich, each had five physicians, but Killingly also maintained this number, suggesting that specific localized circumstances could also account for the number of practitioners in each town. Neighboring towns with similar economic circumstances, populations, and land size varied widely in numbers of physicians — Windham had six and Lebanon two, Coventry four, and Preston and Groton one each. Towns occasionally advertised for physicians if they had none, offering them land if they would move to the community; physicians also were sometimes a subject of discussion at town meetings. Most physicians practiced medicine part-time and were also involved in farming or commerce.[36]

The number of lawyers in a town can more readily be explained by general principles than by particular circumstances. The majority of lawyers gravitated to the two capitals or to the four county seats as the prime sources of legal business. New Haven, for example, had five lawyers in 1761, while not another practiced in the county. Litchfield, a county seat, had four lawyers at the end of the Revolution; Stamford, a port with 40 percent more population but not a county seat, had only two. Though a lawyer would occasionally set up practice in a country town, rural young men interested in the law usually moved to a governmental center.[37]

Although stores, taverns, meetinghouses, and a variety of businesses and services could serve as central places, they could not, by themselves be considered villages. As a step towards urban living, the village imparts a social experience different from rural life. The story of the destruction of the nucleated village as the home for all townspeople is often told, but it is unclear how complete the movement to farmsteads had become in the eighteenth century. It is equally unclear how much the trend towards increased commercial activity acted as a countervailing force against the farmstead movement. What percentage of people in Connecticut towns were country dwellers, and what percentage were villagers?

From two sources, contemporary maps and travelers' accounts, it is possible to determine the number of houses in the centers of eighteen of Connecticut's seventy-three towns. The number of houses in town centers ranged from the 328 in New Haven and the 250 in Hartford to none in two nonnucleated towns, Hebron and Harwinton. When these dwellings are multiplied by six, a conversion figure that a variety of evidence suggests as accurate,[38] they yield a population figure for each of the town centers. Of the sixteen towns with a village at the center, the percentage of the population living in the center ranged from 31 percent in Hartford to 3 percent in the tiny village of Washington.

From this broad spectrum some conclusions can be drawn by analyzing the percentage of village residents according to town type. Four of the eighteen towns in the sample were urban, six were secondary centers, and eight were country towns. The town centers, prior to the hiving off of suburbs in the Revolutionary years, contained 21.2 percent of the urban towns' population; the centers contained 9 percent of the population in the secondary towns; and the centers of the country towns contained 4.6 percent of their populations. It seems hardly surprising that, with higher mercantile activity, a town would have a higher percentage of village inhabitants. When the three types of towns have their percentages multiplied in proportion to the total population of towns

TABLE 20
Inhabitants of Town Centers in 1774

Town type	No. of towns in sample	No. of towns in category	% of population living in center
Urban	4	5	21.9
Secondary	6	25	9.0
Country	8	43	4.6
Total			9.1

Source: See appendix ten below.

of that type, they reveal that probably 9 percent of the colony's total population lived in town centers (see table 20).

Unfortunately for the purposes of historians, the percentage of people living in town centers is not the same as the percentage of people living in villages. Many towns had several other villages that lay distant from the town center, often at the center of a society. Simsbury, for example, had four other small villages besides the town center, ranging from eight to thirteen houses; the Third Society of Hartford was organized in a large village on the east bank of the Connecticut River; the New Cambridge Society of Farmington contained a small parish village; Sharon had a small village surrounding a sawmill five miles away from the town center. The maps of towns indicate that about half of the Congregational societies had parish villages usually containing about nine houses. Thus, approximately sixty-five more small villages existed in colonial Connecticut, containing approximately 3,510 inhabitants. This raises the total number of the population living in villages to approximately 11 percent (see table 21).

TABLE 21
Villagers in the Colony in 1774

Type of village	No. of people
Urban	7,275
Secondary	6,832
Country	4,091
Parish	3,510
Total	21,708[a]

Source: See appendix ten below.
[a] 10.9 percent of colony total.

While this figure may appear large, it indicates that nearly 90 percent of the population were country dwellers. Moreover, where a man lived did not necessarily determine his occupation; many artisans and shopkeepers lived in the countryside, and even the largest urban town contained some farmers living in the village center. The correlation of village size with economic type does show that commerce was the wellspring of villages and that, although some farmers resided in them, villages were primarily centers of business. The villages of early seventeenth-century Connecticut were farming villages containing a few merchants and shopkeepers; the villages of late eighteenth-century Connecticut were basically commercial, containing the homes of but a few farmers. The near ubiquity of villages in country towns and their presence in half of the societies suggests that they played a role disproportionately important to their populations.

The distribution of wealth in a town directly related to its age and to the development of its economic system. The urban towns showed a greater maldistribution of wealth and larger groups of wealthy and poor at opposite ends of the scale. As a town grew in mercantile activity, more amounts of wealth were concentrated in the hands of a few; poverty existed in direct relation to the numbers of landless people in menial occupations. The most egalitarian wealth structure existed in the country towns. Not surprisingly, as towns grew older, the inequality of wealth distribution increased; as population growth placed pressures upon land, some men responded more ably to the crisis than others and the generally middle-class structure became more variegated. Even in prosperous secondary centers and country towns, the care of the poor became a problem of public debate and concern in about mid-eighteenth century. Almshouses, a symptom of the growth of poverty, appeared in at least one of the urban towns on the eve of the Revolution. Ironically, this first appearance of serious poverty occurred as Connecticut entered a period of seemingly great prosperity. In the second half of the eighteenth century there was a trend towards greater inequalities of wealth; personal property was distributed in much the same ratio as earlier, but land became more concentrated in the hands of the wealthier people in society. Labeling the distribution of wealth "middle class" or "stratified" at any given time is problematic, since historians do not agree on definitions for these concepts. However, it is not problematic to say that

Connecticut towns grew less middle class and more stratified after 1750 as their mercantile community and population increased and as the economy became increasingly devoted to commercial agriculture.[39]

Within individual towns, wealth distribution correlated strongly with both occupation and age. Merchants, shopkeepers, professionals, manufacturers, and farmers who owned land were substantially above the mean level of wealth; artisans, however, were 47 percent lower than the mean, and the landless laborers who comprised 30 percent of the pre-Revolutionary population were 89.5 percent lower. Age was also strongly associated with poverty; young men tended to be substantially below the mean. For both the landless and the young, the means of escaping their lowly position lay in acquiring land; this became increasingly difficult after the settlement of Litchfield County at mid-century, when no more uninhabited land was available for new towns. A hint at the dimensions of this problem and at its consequences for upward social mobility can be found in a recent case study of the status of fathers and sons in Hartford County in the early eighteenth century; 14 percent of sons advanced beyond their fathers' level of wealth, 56 percent stayed the same, but 30 percent declined in wealth and died poorer than their fathers had been. In a society of high expectations that enshrined self-improvement and upward social mobility, the prospect of a declining status and a life near the poverty level could only have produced alienation in some form.[40]

Political patterns in towns, like wealth distribution patterns, varied according to town types (see table 22). At the supra town level, the urban towns and, to a lesser but significant degree, the secondary centers dominated the leadership of the colony. Within the towns, the three types of towns had different patterns of officeholding; other variables, such as region, date of settlement, and population, also affected local officeholding in measurable ways.

The major figures in politics on the colony level were the governor and deputy governor and the twelve assistants who collectively advised the governor and constituted the upper house of the legislature; these fourteen figures were elected at-large in the colony and were the only leaders selected in colony-wide elections. Between 1701 and 1784 40 percent of the assistants came from the five urban towns, 50 percent came from the secondary centers, and

TABLE 22
Homes of Assistants, Deputy Governors, and Governors,
1701–84

Town	No. of men serving	Town	No. of men serving
Urban towns			
Hartford	7	Norwich	4
New London	7	Middletown	3
New Haven	6		
Secondary centers			
Fairfield	6	East Haddam	1
Stratford	4	Glastonbury	1
Guilford	3	Haddam	1
Milford	3	Lyme	1
Wethersfield	3	Norwalk	1
Windsor	3	Saybrook	1
Lebanon	2	Stamford	1
Litchfield	2	Stonington	1
Windham	2		
Country towns			
Colchester	1	Suffield	1
Durham	1	Tolland	1
Farmington	1	Wallingford	1
Mansfield	1	Woodbury	1
Plainfield	1		

only 10 percent came from the country towns. Of the governors in this period, 56 percent came from the five urban towns, with the rest originating in secondary centers. During the Revolutionary years five of Connecticut's seven leading military figures came from the five urban towns; one was from a secondary center, Wethersfield, but lived in New Haven while attending Yale; only one, the legendary Israel Putnam of Pomfret, lived in a country town. The Loyalists, too, drew their leaders primarily from the urban towns.[41]

For at least two reasons the political domination of the urban and secondary towns in colony politics is logical. First, to win colony elections one had to be widely known and respected; in the leading towns were merchants with regular intertown contacts, and these towns were usually the first-settled areas in the colony, with a continuity of old respected families of traditional leadership. Second, talented and ambitious men from the country towns frequently moved to the urban centres to exploit their abilities; one might say there was a "brain drain," to use a modern phrase for the same phenomenon.[42]

On the local level, the urban towns were the most oligarchical in their election of deputies to the General Assembly; fewer persons served in office than in the secondary centers and country towns, and they served larger numbers of terms. However, while family connections were important in all types of towns, they were less so in the urban towns than in the secondary centers and country towns. This is no paradox; while the urban towns possessed many extraordinarily wealthy and influential men who were frequently returned to office, these towns also offered so much economic opportunity for upward mobility and attracted so many talented men from other communities that the resulting larger pool of leadership material diluted the influence of a few select families. Family connections were more important for local officeholding success in secondary centers and most important in country towns. The secondary centers provided some mobility and attracted some new able inhabitants who, joining the mercantile community, enlarged the leadership pool; the country towns, with generally smaller and more stable populations, had fewer such infusions of new wealthy people, minimizing any challenge to the leadership of the established families. The differences in officeholding between urban towns and other large towns were not based on populations — the urban ones were not more populous than the other large towns — but were based instead on the differences in the social structures caused by the economic centrality of the urban towns.[43]

These conclusions about the polity of Connecticut towns mesh almost perfectly with the typology developed recently by Edward Cook in the most comprehensive study yet written on officeholding in colonial New England. Cook found that, throughout New England, urban towns tended to allow for more mobility, to rely less on family connections, and to produce a higher percentage of provincial leaders than did other towns. Secondary towns, according to Cook, had more stable elites, and family connections played a more important role. In both urban and secondary towns Connecticut's patterns were identical to those identified by Cook. At first glance it seems that the present typology of Connecticut towns would differ from Cook's in the assessment of small towns; but the difference is caused by differing population patterns between Connecticut and the rest of New England. Connecticut's smallest towns were much larger in population than the smallest towns in other colonies, and hence the towns the present study labels "small" would not be small in Cook's typology. Connecticut's small towns correspond most to

the towns called "rural secondary centers" or "suburbs" by Cook.
When Connecticut's small towns are compared with these, they
reveal similar patterns of high family domination and oligarchical
officeholding; they also were poor bases for an entry into provincial politics.[44]

Noneconomic factors, however, also played a role in the distribution of power within a community. Family connections were most
important in the western part of the colony and in the Connecticut
River Valley, least important in the east; turnover in office was
most pronounced in the east, less so in the west, and least in the
river valley; family connections were more important in towns
founded before 1675 than in towns founded later; the smaller the
town the greater the predominance of a few families in its
officeholding.[45] In general the eastern towns had more democratic
officeholding patterns than those of western and river areas; this
conclusion meshes well with the qualitative literature, which always
stresses the radical nature of the east and the conservative mould of
the west. Thus, the kind of people who for religious and cultural
reasons were attracted to the independence of the Baptists in eastern Connecticut were inclined to an open polity, whereas the
people in the West, attuned for similar reasons to the sober ways of
the Anglicans, were inclined towards a closed one. The river valley,
comprised totally of urban and secondary towns, had a political
structure like that of the west. It merely confirms expectations to
note that the older and smaller towns were more likely to be dominated by a few select families; families had more chance to establish
themselves in kinship units in the older towns and had less competition in small towns. Table 23 summarizes these findings.

A TRAVELER on any Connecticut highway after 1740 would be
struck by the presence of large centers of urban life, by the
ubiquitous villages, by the all-pervading commercial activity, and
by the mills, meetinghouses, taverns, and shops that dotted the
landscape. One Englishman traveling the highway from Hartford
to New Haven wrote in his diary: "I don't think any part of England is thicker settled than this state. There are houses about the
whole way from New Haven (to Hartford)." Another going down
the Connecticut River recorded his impression that the Connecticut River Valley was "one continuous town."[46]

TABLE 23

Officeholding Patterns of General Assembly Deputies
by Town Type, in Comparison to the Average of All Towns

Variable	Domination by few individuals	Family dominance	Oligarchy measured by turnover rate
Economic Factor			
Urban	Higher	Lower	Higher
Secondary	Same	Same	Same
Country	Same	Higher	Same
Geography factor			
East	Lower	Lower	Lower
West	Higher	Higher	Same
River	Higher	Higher	Higher
Population factor			
Large[a]	Lower	Lower	Same
Medium[a]	Same	Same	Same
Small[a]	Higher	Higher	Same
Age factor			
Founded before 1675	Same	Higher	Same
Founded 1675–1700	Same	Lower	Same
Founded 1700–1735	Same	Lower	Same

Source: See appendix twelve below.

[a] Large is here defined as over 4,000 inhabitants in 1774; medium as between 2,500 and 4,000; and small as less than 2,500.

In its history Connecticut could never be considered a society of equal, homogeneous communities. From the beginning the three River Towns and New Haven and New London were more important and cosmopolitan than their sister towns. Nor was the colony ever comprised completely of subsistence farmers. Ideal types never existed in Connecticut; when we consider change from one stage to another or trends, we are talking of changes in emphasis and of degrees. The degree of heterogeneity among towns and within towns, however, showed a sharp increase in the eighteenth century. Among towns the economic centers became more distinct from the country towns as trade became more important; towns with favorable locations for mercantile activity developed differently from others; old towns and new ones, urban, secondary, and country towns, developed different social structures. Within towns commercial activities increased; the landscape was transformed by the growth of population and the central buildings that provided the people with services; social distinctions based on wealth, occupation, age, religion, and family connections could increasingly be made.

Connecticut's experience approximates that of the normative-type society described by social scientists and parallels that of the other mainland colonies. The six stages of living patterns listed below, through which most areas pass successively, characterize man's experience to the present:

1. Decentralized stage — farmers live on the land they farm;
2. Village stage — small villages arise to facilitate the local exchange of produce;
3. Town stage — higher- and lower-order wholesale and retail centers arise to promote interregional trade;
4. Manufacturing stage — manufacturing centers arise coextensively with some of the trade centers;
5. Conurbation stage — enormous centers arise with satellite centers and create a gross imbalance in the distribution of population;
6. Dispersion stage — people flee the largest urban centers because of their many problems and bring urban values to rural society.[47]

Modern Connecticut is presently in stage six of development; industry and commerce are fleeing to the less-developed areas of the Sun Belt and other desirable locations, and people, weary of high crime and dehabilitating pollution, are moving to the suburbs and countryside. It is clear that by 1790 Connecticut had progressed through stages one, two, and three and was beginning stage four. Stage one had not been implemented at the colony's inception and the first towns had not been decentralized from the start, because the Puritans, as have many peasant civilizations, imposed villages for social reasons on an economic situation that would otherwise not have created them. Their English background as well as their religious precepts inclined them towards nucleated living arrangements. However, economic forces overcame this pattern of village life and Connecticut moved to a primarily decentralized existence similar to stage one. The necessity for some imported goods, for milling of grains and sawing of wood, and for local trade maintained some of the social villages as economic units, and as they grew in function Connecticut paralleled the ideal society of stage two. With the development of surplus produce and surplus population, Connecticut moved into a trading economy that created wholesale and retail towns of higher orders than the villages, and the colony entered stage three. The declining ratio of land to people combined with the Revolutionary emergency to thrust the state into the beginnings of stage four.

Other colonies had also proceeded along these stages of development, and Connecticut was not alone on the road towards an urbanized society. Interspersed among the five major colonial cities of Boston, Newport, New York, Philadelphia, and Charlestown, whose rise has been chronicled by Carl Bridenbaugh, waves of secondary and tertiary urbanization occurred throughout the colonies in the eighteenth century. Secondary urban centers — like Portsmouth, New Hampshire; Providence, Rhode Island; Albany, New York; Wilmington, Delaware; Annapolis and Baltimore, Maryland; Norfolk, Williamsburg, and Richmond, Virginia; and Savannah, Georgia — joined Connecticut's five urban centers as well-established provincial cities. A group of only slightly less important centers, such as Medford, Marblehead, and Salem, emerged in Massachusetts, and almost overnight a ring of centers, Lancaster, Easton, Harrisburg, Chambersburg, and Gettysburg, sprang up in western Pennsylvania safely distant from the fatal gravitational pull of Philadelphia. In the eighteenth-century South a number of crossroads locations attracted enough commerce and artisanal activity to establish themselves as villages serving as economic central places, bringing a certain embryonic degree of urbanization to a formerly all-rural backcountry.[48]

All of this urbanization, like Connecticut's, stemmed from the market mechanism; none was planned or resulted from the will of a governmental body, and none was for a purpose other than economic — these were economic central places. Presumably, the urbanization brought with it everywhere the concomitant rearrangement of the social structure that was occurring in Connecticut: a growing heterogeneity in class, status, and wealth; economic mobility; the growth of dissenting religions and emancipation from controlling social forces; changed patterns of officeholding and leadership that differed by types of community; political splits between urban and rural dwellers; increasing individualism and a growing innovative spirit; and greater disparities in population densities. According to sociologists and anthropologists, these attributes all characterize a society passing from a folk to an urban culture. To be sure, the precise patterns differed from colony to colony and none was the same as Connecticut's; but they were merely variants caused by unique circumstances within the same model, and the overall process shared a fundamental sameness of which Connecticut was exemplary.[49]

[VII]

URBANIZATION AND
EARLY NEW ENGLAND SOCIETY

BECAUSE it is a widely held belief in today's world that change is presently occurring at an unprecedented pace, the extraordinary growth and development of the American colonies is apt not to be fully appreciated. However, by 1790 — just four generations after its founding — Connecticut had grown from a land inhabited by 6,000 Indians to a state of 238,127 people that included 101 towns and 307 ecclesiastical societies. It had a varied economy tied intimately into the Western world and a series of constitutional arrangements sanctioned by time and custom, and it elected or appointed over 18,000 civil and military officers. When one thinks that the elderly people of 1790 could look about themselves at this complex world and realize that it was their great grandparents who had been the first generation of whites born in the "howling wilderness," the pace and dimensions of the growth and development make more of an impact on the senses. It is a supreme conceit of today's generation, who have witnessed the changes wrought in society by the automobile, atomic energy, and television, to think that only twentieth-century man lives in an era when the world is being transformed. If modern industrialization has changed the world of 1979 beyond the recognition of its great grandfathers, no less did the growth and development of Connecticut's towns change the world of 1790 beyond the recognition of its great grandfathers.

Radical change occurs in every era, but the forces effecting the change and conditioning the directions it takes are different. Many forces come into play: in today's society secularism and education are important agents of change, but most historians would probably agree that technology is the pervasive factor shaping everything else; secularism and education, for example, are closely related to it. In colonial Connecticut, the decline of Puritanism, the rise of an Atlantic trading community, and ideological influences from England and abroad all influenced the ways in which Connecticut towns grew and developed, but the pervasive factor was land; the initial abundance of land, its quality, its location, and finally its lack of availability were the dominant forces that make the story of colonial Connecticut towns the story that it is.

Land first brought Puritans from Massachusetts to Connecticut; they came primarily as farmers and settled towns in the areas that were most fertile and most accessible. They made the towns they settled physically large because the land for doing so was available and they wanted to have enough acreage to launch their children and grandchildren successfully into the world. If they quarreled among themselves, if they felt a need to follow a particularly inspiring minister, if they felt they were limited in their economic aspirations, there was land elsewhere in Connecticut that enabled them to move and found more towns. The abundance of land allowed them to be a people of farmers who satisfied the centuries-old English desire to own land and make a living from it. Merchants, ministers, government officials, and artisans were all farmers and landowners. Even the nature of the farming process was conditioned by the availability of more land if the present wore out.

But the world of the founding generation did not last; the land euphoria contained within it the seeds of its own destruction and created problems unforeseen by the settlers of the first towns. No matter how plentiful the land may have seemed, the supply was finite, not infinite; the productiveness of the land itself created a high rate of population growth, which put pressures upon the supply. As land became more scarce, with the unclaimed land having uneven quality, towns were settled that were away from major waterways; the square mileage of each town was substantially reduced; population densities differed sharply among towns; the economy was transformed; and ultimately people left the colony in search of a future elsewhere. The change in the land supply made the towns of the eighteenth century vastly different from the towns of the seventeenth.

Of lesser importance only when compared to the supply and quality of land was its location. Distance was a crucial factor in the development of Connecticut towns. Their distance from navigable water, from the cities of nearby colonies, or from each other shaped their economic lives. The distances of neighborhoods from the town centers, the meetinghouses, and the militia training fields shaped the towns' internal polities. One need only see the ubiquity with which distance is cited in petitions from disaffected inhabitants to the General Assembly during local controviersies to appreciate how important was the location of a town or a neighborhood.

If land was the factor that conditioned the process of growth and development in Connecticut towns, the magnitude of the growth and development itself transformed the colony. Towns became differentiated by population density, region, economic function, and age; a multitude of government officers emerged in place of a relatively unified leadership; religious dissent grew and the Congregational church fragmented; great disparities in wealth among the populace developed; and the increasing difficulty of making a living caused geographical and occupational mobility. In short, the political, social, and economic structures of the colony grew progressively heterogeneous and complex through the differentiation within and among the towns.

This rapid growth in local heterogeneity and complexity — this process of urbanization — serves as a base of evidence to make some comments on early New England society in general and town life in particular, as well as on the recent treatment these subjects have received from historians. For the last two decades scholarly debate on New England town life has centered on three major questions: were towns democratic or oligarchic? communal or individualistic? harmonious or contentious? Almost every historian who has dealt with the New England community has come to grips with one of these questions, and many have dealt with two or all three of them. In two seminal works, Richard Bushman and Kenneth Lockridge have both argued that the early Puritan world was one of relative concord based on a collectivist impulse that accepted the authority of an elite, and that the late seventeenth century and the eighteenth century witnessed a gradual retreat from these values and a growth in a "yankee" world of democracy, individualism, and discord. Other major studies of town life, such as those of Charles Grant and Philip Greven, Jr., support this interpretation. The interpretation received one of its most explicit and persuasive statements in a widely cited essay by T. H. Breen and Stephen Foster, which emphasized the importance of Puritanism as a force for social cohesion in the seventeenth century. The hypothesis of a distinct evolution, however, is questioned by the scholarship of Sumner Powell, Darrett Rutman, and John Demos, and most recently Richard Gildrie and Paul Lucas, who all argue that the seventeenth century was neither tranquil nor deferential and that individualism and acquisitiveness were well advanced in the founding years of New England and produced a contentious society from the start. On the other hand, Michael Zuckerman has written eloquently that New England towns were still "peaceable kingdoms" in the late eighteenth century.[1] My present account indicates that all of these scholars and most of the others who have written on these themes have properly identified some phenomena; they have identified them in isolation, however, and only when they are placed in a wider perspective can the totality of the experience be evaluated and appreciated.

It is doubtful if one should label the change in town polity a transition from a lesser to a greater form of democracy. Although it would be misleading to claim that the first towns were democracies, there were democratic elements in the seventeenth-century local communities — the town meetings met frequently; the relatively small populations lent themselves to participatory involvement; every town officer, no matter how minor, was elected; and among the founders, family traditions and patterns of leadership were not as firmly established as they would be later, when distinctions could be drawn between early arrivals and newcomers. Growth and development in the towns resulted in changes that in some cases diminished and in some cases enhanced these early democratic elements. In the eighteenth century the town meeting met less frequently, population growth diluted each man's potential importance, and more distinctions based on tradition and economic criteria were drawn among "better," "middlin'," and "meaner" families, all of which served to reduce the relative weight of democracy. Moreover, in the eighteenth century, there is no indication that officeholding was less oligarchical, and in some cases there are indications that it was more so. Yet, one can just as easily identify democratizing elements in the eighteenth century: town and society meetings, although less frequent, did assert themselves stridently when an issue aroused tempers; local officers increased dramatically in numbers, giving many more men an entry into decision making; the franchise was freely available at little inconvenience to most adult white men; and townspeople did not hesitate to appeal decisions that aggrieved them. To call the sum of these changes, which worked in both directions, a progression from lesser to greater democracy or from greater to lesser is to make a value judgment that will always be subject to dispute — change occurred, but change is not always amenable to being placed on a linear evolutionary scale.

The transition from communalism to individualism is on firmer scholarly ground, but even here one must enter disclaimers. That the first towns were more communal in the seventeenth century than they were in the eighteenth cannot be denied, nor can it be denied that they were more communal than newly founded towns in the eighteenth century. The striking difference can be seen in many ways. The group settlement of towns, the "Christian" method of distributing land, the congruence of church and town, the "village elder" attitude by which leaders enforced morality, the ubiquity of subsistence farming as an occupation, and the nucleated living patterns that included all townspeople characterized the towns created prior to 1675. These attributes can all be contrasted profitably to the individual settling of towns, the distribution of land by the auctioneer's block, the growth of competing churches, the decline in morality enforcement, the development of a variegated economy with differing and competing interest groups, and the dispersal of much of the population, which characterized the towns created in the late colonial period. Merchants and farmers, Anglicans and Congregationalists, villagers and outlivers, wealthy and poor, and first settlers and newcomers often felt that they had antagonistic interests and were impelled to act out individualistic impulses and look after themselves in a world where one less readily sacrificed to the public good.

Lest this contrast be stated too baldly, however, one caveat and two problems of definition must be raised.

First, the founders of towns in the most communal years of the seventeenth century, while not indulging in the heady individualism of absentee speculators out for a windfall profit, did practice on-the-site speculation. The attempt made by each group of founders to maximize its town's lands reveals an acquisitive impulse that, although couched in group solidarity, was in itself an embryonic form of economic assertiveness; and this form of speculation had potent consequences for the development of the towns.

Second, while the communalism of the towns was severely weakened over the course of the colonial and Revolutionary period, other forms of communal interests arose that, although they were inadequate replacements, did alter the definition of community. Economically and socially, the community of many townspeople in one sense was expanded and partially changed from a geographic base to one of group interest. Whereas in the seventeenth century the colony and the town would have constituted the primary social and economic community to which one gave loyalty, in the eighteenth century merchants and artisans might feel a wider kinship with their counterparts elsewhere; commercial farmers had to concern themselves with getting a good price for their crops in the Atlantic trading world, whereas previously the cost of milling grain at the local mill was more important. Yet these wider communities, except for that of the large-scale merchants, were too amorphous and too remote to have much effect on the everyday social orientation of the average inhabitant. He may have been tied into an economic community with West Indian planters, middle-colony artisans, or sailors in port cities, and he may have even felt a certain empathy for them, but they were not part of his social experience. He related to them through the impersonal marketplace. The expanded economic and social communities did not fill the void created by the decline of homogeneity and loss of unity.

Third, in a certain sense, the weakening of the communal spirit that knit all the early towns of Connecticut into one large Puritan community resulted in an enhancement of the nearby community as a primary unit of loyalty and thus enhanced the local community at the expense of the commonwealth spirit. Towns were physically removed from the watchful eye of the General Assembly; outlying areas within towns brought society and militia government to their own neighborhoods and had an allotted share of local leadership; distant societies became towns; and urban centers became cities. This atomization of community moved the locus of authority away from the center of the colony and towards the town and the society or neighborhood. There was a new American nation and there was a new state of Connecticut, each of which constituted a political community to which Connecticut residents gave a measure of loyalty; but loyalty to a political community diminished proportionately to the distance of the community from the individual. Both the founding world and the Revolutionary world of Connecticut could be represented as a series of concentric circles of different political communities. At the center of the circles of the founding world would be the community of Englishmen, followed by the community of Puritans, the colony of Connecticut, and so on, until the last circle would inscribe the individual. At the center of the circles of the Revolutionary world would be the individual, followed by the society or neighborhood, the town, and so on until the final circle would inscribe the nation.[2]

Asserting that a transition from communalism to individualism did indeed occur in Connecticut's towns through the colonial and Revolutionary period seems to lead inevitably to the corollary that a transition was also made from a harmonious to a contentious society — and it was, but sharp limits must also be placed on this interpretation, and it must be qualified.

First, one should not overestimate the harmony of the founding towns. Doctrinal differences were endemic and were acted upon; the faction-ridden Wethersfield church, for example, chipped off three religious fragments that dissented strongly enough to leave Wethersfield and found other towns. Political differences surfaced frequently: several towns resisted amalgamation with New Haven, and New Haven Colony in turn resisted joining Connecticut, submitting to its jurisdiction only after years of political fighting; within two decades of its founding, each town squabbled over which residents had and which did not have proprietary status; and towns continually fought one another over boundaries.

Yet, amidst these controversies, a large amount of concord existed and overcame circumstances that could easily have lent themselves to much more discord. The Fundamental Orders adopted in 1639 and the Code of 1650 both represent successful attempts to bring order and structure to the towns and prevent what easily could have become a disparate collection of local entities feuding with one another. The unity of local government in the town meeting and the high level of participation in the meeting and its high frequency militated against local contention. Resident proprietorship prevented conflicts between residents and outside speculators, and the essential fairness of the land-distribution system created few disgruntled townspeople anxious to challenge local authority. Threats of Indian raids worked in the direction of maintaining harmony, and, despite doctrinal differences, the all-pervasive force of a piety that regarded a lack of uniform faith as sinful promoted peace. The similarity of interests in a largely homogeneous population mitigated disorder; and, above all, when the local peace was threatened the General Court quickly interceded.

Almost all of the evidence indicates that the level of contention increased after the third quarter of the seventeenth century. While the degree of discord caused by the land scramble in eastern Connecticut has been exaggerated, so that it obscures the peaceful settling of most of the towns there, the battles in some of the towns with rival claimants to their lands were intense. Religious dissent could not be contained; Anglicans, Baptists, and finally Separatists fought for toleration and, upon achieving it, vied with the established church for members. Doctrinal differences did not go away in the established church, and secular struggles over meetinghouse locations, ministers' salaries, and pew assignments exacerbated the spiritual strife. The vast acreage the founders of the first towns had carved out of the wilderness in the hope of sustaining their progeny instead haunted their descendants, as distances between homes and meetinghouses, town centers, and militia training fields became prohibitive. Demography itself worked against maintaining harmony, as rapid population growth strained the social fabric and increased competition for a decreasing amount of available land. The Assembly was deluged with appeals from disgruntled local inhabitants who refused to acquiesce in local decisions that they felt injured them. The Revolutionary experience quickened the impulse towards disorder, as people learned to question authority more readily and to accept external decision making less willingly. The revolts of outlying areas of large towns against distant town centers during the Revolutionary years and the rhetoric used to justify the revolts were the ultimate expression of willingness to sacrifice stability and concord for the sake of self-realization.

This rebelliousness, however, had its limits, and the contention must be placed in its proper perspective. The "peaceable kingdom" always remained the goal of each community, and the legitimacy of conflict as a proper way for a people to live was never accepted. While societies fought bitter battles over the choice of a new minister, it was never agreed that a majority had the right to impose a candidate upon an unwilling minority—unanimity remained an elusive but pervasive goal. Outlying societies may have *demanded* town status from the Assembly in Revolutionary rhetoric, but none resisted negative responses by the Assembly except by drafting new petitions, and the Assembly carefully scrutinized all petitions and acted upon them with caution and forbearance. Connecticut's level of contention may have seemed high to contemporaries and to recent historians, but both judged it against the earlier low level that engendered the nickname "land of steady habits." Fights between resident and absentee proprietors may have appeared vicious to contemporaries, but they were fought with petitions, rhetoric, and meetings and not with mobs, guns, and arson, as were the Hudson River Valley land riots. Nor did Connecticut's pre-Revolutionary agitation, such as the Stamp Act demonstrations, ever approach the degree of terror and violence spawned in centers like Boston.

Besides the maintainance of the goals of concord and harmony, other factors combined to limit rebelliousness. Connecticut's elite was frequently challenged, but the local officeholding patterns show that it maintained much of its sway over the population. The widespread involvement of inhabitants in all levels of local government and the decentralization of the institutions of government created a participatory system that seemed responsive to people's needs. And finally, apathy, a word seldom used to explain eighteenth-century society, was rampant at the local level. Most people simply did not attend town, society, or freemen's meetings and preferred to trust the few who did with most of the decision making. Many historians explain this phenomenon by calling it a "deferential" system in which average men deferred to society's natural leaders. There is much truth in this explanation, but the occasional willingness of Connecticut townspeople to be defiant, to pack meetings, to contest elections, to revolt against outside authority, to enroll en masse as freemen, and to turn long-serving leaders out of office does indicate that at times they were outrightly undeferential. Although they did tender respect to natural leaders, most of the time they deferred because they did not care or because they were pleased with the decisions being made. When they did care, however, or were displeased, they raised their voices; and they wanted someone to listen.

In many ways eighteenth-century Connecticut produced a world of men usually quiet and apathetic but occasionally loud and defiant. When what they perceived as their rights and privileges were threatened, eighteenth-century townsmen were loud and defiant to degrees their seventeenth-century ancestors would have found appalling. They did not want to be dominated by a church in which they did not believe, by groups of ministers in churches in which they did believe, by distant parts of the towns or societies in which they lived, or by a central General Assembly. Seen in this light, the decision to revolt against England was just another variant of the spirit of independence, contention, and defiance that always lay just beneath the surface.

Historians often employ the parent-child metaphor to explain the American Revolution and write that the colonies had grown to a point of maturity that made them want to cast off their dependent status and be autonomous adults in the world. While there is much truth in this explanation, it was not only the growth that occasioned the rebellious spirit; it was also the nature of the growth. The child had developed a personality of independence during a maturation process that had been punctuated by fights over land rights in towns, over locations of meetinghouses and training fields, over choices of ministers and religions, and over the many other aspects of life at the local level. Whether leaving his hometown for land in a new town located on the frontier, joining a new church, or moving to a trading center to begin a career as a merchant, the young man of the eighteenth century was imbued with a spirit of independence. And he did not hesitate to exercise that independence for fear of being disruptive. His social experience forced him to locate himself as an individual in a world of neighbors who worshipped differently, moved frequently, and made their living variously. His normal means of expressing his individualism was to be not overly involved in the community and to pursue his own interests. But his political experience taught him to assert his individualism stridently when he felt the occasion demanded.

TOWNS INCORPORATED, 1635–1675

Town	No. of families at date of incorporation[a]	Years elapsed between first settlement and incorporation[b]	Square mileage[c]
Windsor[d]	U[e]	0	173.8
Wethersfield[d]	U	1	105.2
Hartford[d]	U	0	80.7
Saybrook	37	13	78.8[f]
New Haven	60	0	110.8
Stratford	U	1	130.0
Fairfield	U	1	138.5
Guilford	25	0	83.9
Milford	54	0	77.5
Stamford	12	1	57.5
Farmington	44	2	224.1
New London	32	1	90.5
Stonington	U	9	99.0
Middletown	30	4	145.5
Norwalk	38	1	67.8
Branford	35	0	53.7
Greenwich	12	6	50.6
Norwich	35	3	97.0
Killingworth	23	4	53.2
Lyme	H[g]	H	134.6
Haddam	28	6	104.3
Wallingford	47	6	105.5
Simsbury	30	6	144.6
Woodbury	15	0	183.6
Derby	12	33	69.0
Average	31.0	2.9[h]	106.3

[a] Figures compiled from town histories, Connecticut Archives, Connecticut State Library, Hartford; *Connecticut State Register and Manual* (Hartford, 1976), and maps in the Connecticut State Library.

[b] Many of these towns were acting like incorporated entities several years before they joined Connecticut Colony and had any official recognition extended to them. In these cases, the figures given here represent the point at which the settlement first started functioning as a governmental body and a clearly defined entity.

ᶜ The square mileage of few of the towns was determined at the town's inception. For example, the three River Towns purchased land from the Indians that extended westerly for six miles and easterly "into the wilderness." The boundaries were hammered out by negotiations with the Indians and with neighboring towns. Most towns were involved in boundary disputes throughout the colonial period, although many of the disputes were over relatively insignificant amounts of land. The area of each town was here calculated from modern surveys and from the most accurate extant colonial map of Connecticut, the Earl of Shelburne Map. I am indebted to Professor Anthony Philpotts of the Department of Geophysics at the University of Connecticut for showing me how to measure areas on maps with the aid of an analytical balancer.

ᵈ I have chosen 1635 as the date at which Hartford and Windsor started functioning as towns. A small party of Englishmen from Plymouth Colony had settled in the area of Windsor in 1634, and one could conceivably date its formation to their arrival. Or the creation of the River Towns could just as plausibly be argued to have occurred later than 1635; no Connecticut community actually organized any *town* government until towns were formally organized by the Fundamental Orders in 1639. However, Hartford and Windsor were heavily settled, maintaining order, and holding church meetings in 1635, and this date is as accurate as any for the two towns' inceptions. Wethersfield's church was organized in 1636, and I have selected this date as the start of the organized community of Wethersfield.

While no precise figures can be given for the population of the three River Towns at their inception, it was undoubtedly higher in each of the three than it was in most of the other towns in this period. By 1639 Hartford had over ninety proprietors, most of whom were heads of families. Their large initial population accounts partially for the strength of the River Towns and their ability to people other towns.

ᵉ U = unknown.

ᶠ This is the area of Saybrook after Lyme separated from it.

ᵍ H = hived off from a previously settled town.

ʰ Without Derby.

TOWNS INCORPORATED, 1686–1734

Town	No. of families at date of incorporation	Years elapsed between first settlement and incorporation	Square mileage
Waterbury	28	8	156.1
Danbury	20	2	79.7
Preston	Hᵃ	H	68.9
Windham	11	1	65.2
Glastonbury	H	H	57.1
Colchester	21	5	64.1
Plainfield	30	7	42.7
Lebanon	15	5	77.9
Mansfield	23	Hᵇ	50.2
Canterbury	10	Hᵇ	46.7
Durham	34	9	23.3
Groton	H	H	78.8
Hebron	9	5	70.7
Ridgefield	20	3	57.7
Killingly	15	16	118.8
Newtown	22	3	66.3
Coventry	16	6	38.6
New Milford	Uᶜ	U	119.7
Pomfret	23	19	53.1
Ashford	34	6	68.9
Tolland	25	4	40.4
Litchfield	47	0	85.4
Stafford	12	1	60.8
Bolton	15	2	36.8
Voluntown	U	14	71.2
Willington	U	7	34.8
Union	19	7	29.9
East Haddam	H	H	57.6
Average	20.4	10.5	64.9

ᵃ H = hived-off.

ᵇ Mansfield and Canterbury, although hived-off towns, were incorporated so soon after the parent town was incorporated that in many ways they were new towns.

ᶜ U = unknown.

TOWNS INCORPORATED, 1737–1766

Town	No. of families at date of incorporation	Years elapsed between first settlement and incorporation	Square mileage
Harwinton	30	4	31.4
New Hartford	31	4	38.3
Canaan	Uª	1	53.0
Sharon	28	0	72.9
Goshen	28	1	45.6
Kent	32	0	64.9
Cornwall	36	1	46.8
Torrington	25	5	34.9
New Fairfield	30	10	49.3
Salisbury	U	2	60.5
Somers	Mᵇ	M	M
Suffield	M	M	M
Woodstock	M	M	M
Enfield	M	M	M
Norfolk	27	14	46.7
Hartland	37	11	34.5
Winchester	28	17	37.3
Barkhamsted	40	26	39.0
Colebrook	U	14	33.0
Average	30.8	7.2	45.9

ª U = unknown.
ᵇ M = settled as part of Massachusetts.

TOWNS INCORPORATED, 1767–1790

Town	Years petitions were presented to Assembly for incorporation	Year incorporated	Square mileage
Redding	1754, 1767	1767	32.7
Chatham	1767	1767	60.5
East Windsor	1756, 1760, 1768	1768	55.3
Washington	1778	1779	38.7
Southington	1771, 1772, 1779	1779	45.1
Watertown	1780	1780	64.2
Cheshire	1770, 1780	1780	41.6
East Hartford	1769, 1774, 1780, 1782	1783	45.3
Woodbridge	1780, 1783	1784	40.3
Berlin	1783, 1785	1785	40.3
Bristol	1785	1785	67.2
Thompson	1770, 1782, 1783	1785	59.2
East Haven	1706, 1755, 1785	1785	12.6
Brooklyn	1786	1786	28.7
Franklin	1786	1786	26.7
Bozrah	1782, 1786	1786	20.0
Hamden	1785	1786	33.0
Hampton	1768, 1784, 1786	1786	32.8
North Haven	1781, 1785	1786	21.0
Ellington	1767, 1786	1786	34.8
Montville	1786	1786	51.3
Granby	1768, 1786	1786	55.3
Lisbon	1786	1786	23.2
Warren	1786	1786	28.0
Bethlehem	1787	1787	19.7
Southbury	1786	1787	45.3
Weston	1787	1787	49.6
Brookfield	1772, 1780, 1785, 1787, 1788	1788	19.8
Huntington	1780, 1786, 1789	1789	57.8

Source: Compiled from Connecticut Archives, Town and Lands, Connecticut State Library, Hartford, Series I and II.

LAND TYPES BY TOWN

THE classifications on the map presented in this appendix are based on the overall attributes of the land in each town. Of course, some land is productive for some types of farming and not for others; hence, by specialization farmers can extract the highest possible yield from their land's potential. Also, Connecticut land, formed during a very recent geological era, has not been rendered uniform in regions by the homogenizing effects of climate, and each town in the colony contained several types of land, varying considerably in quality; the most productive town contained some barren and the least productive contained some that was fertile. The table shows the percentage of the types of soil in each town, and the three keys at the end of the table indicate what each soil was like and what it would produce.

The sources for this appendix are the forty-five quadrangle maps found at the end of Mont Morgan, *The Soil Characteristics of Connecticut Land Types* (New Haven, 1939).

Land Types by Town

Town (in order of founding)	% of soil types	Overall productivity
Windsor	A 25, B25, G 25, H25	6
Wethersfield	F 75, G 15, J 10	8
Hartford	X 25, A 25, E 25, H 25	6
Saybrook	X 60, XX 39, D .5, C .5	1
New Haven	D 35, X 25, B 20, C 20	5
Stratford	D 40, E 30, F 20, A 10	7
Fairfield	F 50, X 30, D 15, E 5	6
Guilford	XX 50, X 20, D 15, E 15	3
Milford	A 31, E 27, E 27, G 15	6
Stamford	D 70, E 25, C 5	7
Farmington	X 45, J 30, B 15, F 10	4
New London	D 30, X 30, XX 30, C 10	3
Stonington	XX 35, F 30, X 20, A 15	3
Middletown	X 40, F 30, E 15, A 15	5
Norwalk	F 60, D 30, E 5, X 5	8
Branford	XX 40, G 20, D 20, E 20	4
Greenwich	D 40, A 40, F 10, A 10	5

Town (in order of founding)	% of soil types	Overall productivity
Norwich	X 40, D 40, F 10, E 10	5
Killingworth	X 60, XX 30, D 5, C 5	1
Lyme	XX 75, D 15, C 5, L 5	2
Haddam	XX 85, X 10, D 2.5, E 2.5	1
Wallingford	E 70, A 20, F 5, G 5	7
Simsbury	X 70, D 10, J 10, K 10	2
Woodbury	X 25, XX 25, F 25, A 25	4
Derby	X 55, E 25, A 10, D 10	4
Woodstock	X 30, XX 30, F 30, D 10	3
Waterbury	D 40, A 30, E 20, C 5	6
Danbury	D 40, XX 30, F 15, A 15	5
Preston	D 50, X 40, C 5, F 5	5
Windham	X 55, D 20, E 15, XX 10	4
Glastonbury	X 40, XX 20, G 20, E 20	4
Colchester	D 40, E 25, X 20, XX 15	5
Plainfield	X 60, D 20, E 10, J 10	3
Lebanon	D 45, E 25, C 15, F 15	6
Mansfield	X 75, D 15, E 10	3
Canterbury	X 45, D 35, J 15, F 5	5
Durham	XX 80, E 10, A 5, C 5	2
Groton	XX 40, X 30, D 15, C 15	3
Hebron	X 50, XX 40, D 5, E 5	1
Ridgefield	F 40, XX 30, E 15, A 15	5
Killingly	X 60, D 20, XX 20	3
Newtown	F 40, A 30, XX 20, D 10	5
Coventry	X 60, D 15, F 15, J 10	3
New Milford	XX 35, X 35, A 15, F 15	3
Pomfret	X 40, F 40, D 20	5
Ashford	X 65, D 20, A 8, F 7	3
Litchfield	F 40, A 30, X 25, E 5	6
Stafford	X 65, XX 30, D 5	1
Bolton	XX 60, X 25, F 10, E 5	2
Voluntown	X 45, D 35, C 19, J 1	3
Tolland	X 65, D 25, J 5, C 5	3
Willington	XX 50, X 45, D 5	1
Union	X 90, D 5, C 3, E 2	1
East Haddam	X 55, XX 25, D 10, E 10	2
Harwinton	X 60, E 20, A 10, D 10	3
New Hartford	X 50, XX 30, A 10, E 10	2
Canaan	XX 75, E 10, D 10, C 5	2

Town (in order of founding)	% of soil types	Overall productivity
Sharon	XX 40, X 40, F 10, D 10	2
Goshen	A 50, F 40, C 5, E 5	6
Kent	XX 65, E 15, A 10, L 10	3
Cornwall	X 60, XX 30, D 5, E 5	1
Torrington	A 25, F 25, X 25, XX 25	4
New Fairfield	XX 65, A 25, E 5, A 5	3
Salisbury	XX 70, A 10, C 10, E 10	2
Norfolk	XX 70, A 20, J 5, D 5	1
Hartland	XX 50, X 40, D 5, E 5	1
Winchester	X 55, E 15, F 15, A 15	4
Barkhamsted	X 40, XX 40, D 10, E 10	2
Colebrook	XX 45, X 45, D 10	1

KEY TO SOIL TYPES

XX = very stony or mountainous land
X = stony, hilly land of light-textured glacial till soils
A = stony, hilly land of medium- to heavy-textured glacial till soils
B = excessively sandy land of level topography
C = permanently wet muck and peat land
D = hilly land of light-textured, rapidly drained glacial till soils
E = hilly land of light- to medium-textured, moderately drained glacial
     till soils
F = hilly land of medium- to heavy-textured, slowly drained glacial till
     soils
G = rolling land of medium-textured, perfectly drained till or outwash
     soil
H = valley land of light-textured, moderately drained soils over stratified
     clay
J = valley land, irregular surface, of gravelly and sandy soils over sand
     or gravel
K = valley land, level surface, of moderately sandy soils over sand or
     gravel
L = valley land, level surface, of medium-textured soils over sand or
     gravel

Note: Other land types exist in Connecticut in addition to these but only in small percentages in any town.

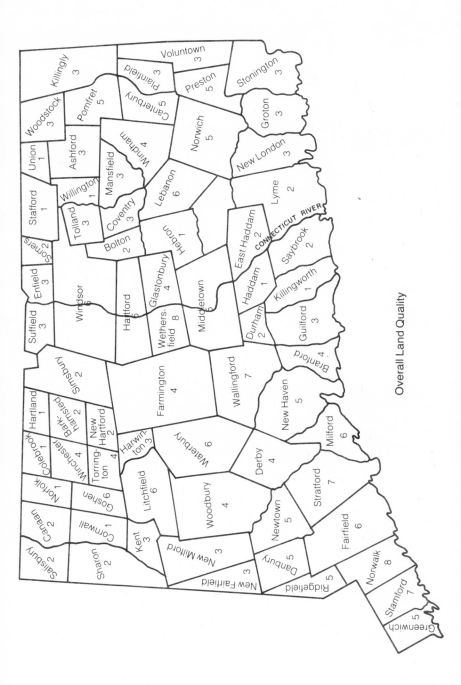

Overall Land Quality

KEY TO OVERALL PRODUCTIVITY

12 = superior
 9 = favorable
 6 = fair
 3 = poor
 0 = not productive

KEY TO ADAPTABILITY OF
LAND TYPES TO CROPS

Land type	Early vegetables	Other vegetables	Orchard fruits	Grain	Grass, hay	Pasture
XX	0	0	0	0	0	0
X	0	0	3	3	3	6
A	0	0	6	3	6	6
B	0	0	0	3	0	0
C	0	0	0	0	3	3
D	9	6	6	6	6	6
E	6	6	9	9	9	9
F	3	6	6	12	12	12
G	6	6	6	12	12	12
H	6	9	3	9	9	6
J	6	6	3	6	3	3
K	12	6	3	6	3	3
L	9	12	3	9	6	6

12 = superior
 9 = favorable
 6 = fair
 3 = poor
 0 = not productive

NUMBER OF TOWN OFFICERS IN RELATION TO LAND SIZE AND POPULATION IN 1775

Town	Officers		Land size		Population	
	Rank[a]	No.	Rank[a]	Square miles	Rank[a]	No.
Farmington	1	206	1	224	3	6,069
Middletown	2	135	7	85	6	4,878
New Haven	3	133	4	111	1	8,295
Fairfield	4	130	5	106	6	4,863
Norwich	5	116	6	97	2	7,327
Waterbury	6	115	2	156	11	3,536
Stratford	7	112	3	130	4	5,555
Lebanon	8	103	10	78	9	3,960
Norwalk	9	86	13	68	8	4,388
Windham	10	85	15	65	12	3,528
Sharon	11	83	11	73	15	2,012
Newtown	12	81	14	66	13	2,229
Hartford	13	76	8	81	5	5,031
Branford	14	75	18	54	14	2,051
Canaan	15	71	19	53	19	1,635
Groton	16	69	9	79	10	3,848
Derby	17	69	12	69	17	1,889
Salisbury	18	60	16	61	16	1,980
Ridgefield	19	59	17	58	18	1,708
New Hartford	20	41	20	38	20	1,001

[a] Spearman's Rank Correlation Coefficient: 0 = no correlation; 1 = perfect correlation (significant at the .39 level). Number of officers to land size: .80; number of officers to population size: .84.

FREEMANSHIP AND TOWNS

Town	% of adult white males admitted as freemen[a]	Population[b]	Square mileage[c]	Economic function[d]
East Guilford[e]	79	M	S	S
Waterbury	69	M	L	C
Newtown	66	S	M	C
East Haddam	64	M	S	S
Salisbury	63	S	S	C
Brooklyn[e]	60	S	S	C
Lebanon	54	M	M	S
Kent	51	S	S	C
Litchfield	50	M	M	S
Norwich	47	L	L	U
Mansfield	44	S	S	C
New Haven	42	L	L	U
Middletown	42	L	L	U
Ridgefield	41	S	S	C
Derby	40	S	M	S
Durham	31	S	S	C
Farmington	30	L	L	C
Coventry	25	S	S	C
Ashford	25	S	M	C

[a] The percentage of freemen in each town was derived from both secondary sources and primary sources. Secondary sources used were Chilton Williamson, *American Suffrage from Property to Democracy, 1760–1860* (Princeton, N.J., 1960), 27 (for East Guilford and East Haddam); Bruce P. Stark, "Lebanon, Connecticut: A Study of Society and Politics in the Eighteenth Century" (Ph.D. diss., University of Connecticut, 1970), 208 (for Lebanon) Charles Grant, *Democracy in the Connecticut Frontier Town of Kent* (New York, 1961; reprint ed., New York, 1972), iii (for Kent); and Marvin Thompson, "A Social and Economic Analysis of Political Leadership in Colonial Litchfield, Connecticut, 1719 to 1784" (Ph.D. diss., University of Connecticut, 1977), 118–22 (for Litchfield). Two methods were used for calculating the percentage of freemen from primary sources. First, for some of the towns a list of the total number of freemen for a given date is available. This number was compared to the number of adult

white males in the town for the same date. The figure for the adult white males can be calculated by dividing the total population by 4.7, which was the ratio in the census of 1774 of total population to adult white males over twenty-one. Second, in several towns, although no totals are available for freemen, the number admitted each year is recorded in the town-meeting records. A ten-year total of new admissions was compared to the probable number of men who would reach age twenty-one in a ten-year period. This latter figure can be determined from the census of 1774; for one year the ratio of general population to white men reaching twenty-one was 86.6 to 1.

[b] L = large, defined as over 4,000; M = medium, defined as 2,500 to 4,000; and S = small, defined as less than 2,500. All definitions are based on the census of 1774.

[c] L = large, defined as over ninety square miles; M = medium, defined as sixty-five to ninety square miles; and S = small, defined as less than sixty-five square miles. All definitions are based on the town's area in the year the estimate for freemanship was made.

[d] U = urban town; S = secondary center; C = country town. See chapter six above.

[e] A society, not a town.

Note: Spearman's Rank Correlation Coefficient: freemanship to population size .30 (not significant); freemanship to square mileage .11 (not significant) (significant at the .39 level).

Contingency Table for Freemanship

	Population variable			Square mileage variable			Economic function variable		
	S	M	L	S	M	L	C	S	U
> Median	5	4	0	5	3	1	5	4	0
≤ Median	6	0	4	4	2	4	6	1	3

ARTISANAL ACTIVITY AND POPULATION

Town	Population rank[a]	Artisan rank[b]	Town	Population rank[a]	Artisan rank[b]
New Haven	1	2	Ashford	37	43
Norwich	2	1	Newtown	38	44
Farmington	3	3	Milford	39	37
New London	4	7	Windsor	40	31
Stratford	5	6	Glastonbury	41	42
Stonington	6	11	Coventry	42	47
Woodbury	7	4	Woodstock	43	35
Hartford	8	5	Branford	44	36
Wallingford	9	10	Suffield	45	39
Middletown	10	9	Sharon	46	51
Fairfield	11	8	Kent	47	40
Norwalk	12	12	Killingworth	48	38
Lyme	13	15	Salisbury	49	52
Lebanon	14	19	Derby	50	49
Groton	15	17	Haddam	51	48
Simsbury	16	14	Ridgefield	52	53
Stamford	17	14	Canaan	53	50
Waterbury	18	16	Plainfield	54	58
Windham	19	22	Voluntown	55	54
Wethersfield	20	18	Enfield	56	56
Killingly	21	20	Stafford	57	55
Colchester	22	30	New Fairfield	58	57
East Windsor	23	24	Tolland	59	—
Guilford	24	21	Redding	60	60
East Haddam	25	32	Goshen	61	59
Greenwich	26	46	Durham	62	62
New Milford	27	26	Somers	63	67
Saybrook	28	23	Harwinton	64	63
Litchfield	29	28	Bolton	65	61
Danbury	30	25	New Hartford	66	65
Mansfield	31	33	Willington	67	68
Canterbury	32	41	Cornwall	68	66
Chatham	33	29	Norfolk	69	64
Preston	34	34	Torrington	70	69
Hebron	35	45	Hartland	71	70
Pomfret	36	30			

Note: Spearman's Rank Correlation Coefficient: population to artisanal activity .97 (significant at the .20 level).
[a] From census of 1774.
[b] From Connecticut Archives, Finance and Currency, Connecticut State Library, Hartford, Series II, V, doc. 164.

For only one town, Greenwich, is there a substantial difference between population and artisanal activity rank. The artisanal activity rank is based on 1778 figures, and Greenwich's location as the nearest town to British-occupied New York City and Greenwich's burning may have affected its craft assets. At any rate, it is the exception that proves the rule. It may appear that Hebron and Killingworth have disproportionate ratios between population and artisans but that is because they are in the middle of the series, where towns are bunched closely together. An addition or subtraction of 6 percent of their populations would put their ranks in a perfect ratio.

PHYSICIANS IN CONNECTICUT IN 1763

Farmington	8	Saybrook	3	Willington	2
Windham	6	Stafford	3	Windsor	2
Killingly	5	Woodstock	3	Andover	1
Middletown	5	Guilford	2	Cornwall	1
New Haven	5	Killingworth	2	Fairfield	1
Norwich	5	Haddam	2	Glastonbury	1
Coventry	4	Lyme	2	Enfield	1
Hebron	4	New London	2	Groton	1
Ashford	3	Milford	2	Lebanon	1
Branford	3	Plainfield	2	Preston	1
Canterbury	3	Stamford	2	Sharon	1
Hartford	3	Stonington	2	Stratford	1
Litchfield	3	Tolland	2	Somers	1
Mansfield	3	Wallingford	2	Voluntown	1
Pomfret	3	Wethersfield	2		

Source: Ezra Stiles, *Extracts from the Itineraries and Other Miscellanies of Ezra Stiles,* ed. Franklin Bowditch Dexter (New Haven, 1916), 193–94.

RESIDENTIAL DENSITY

Town	Inhabitants in main village	Date	% of population
Fairfield	510	1777	8
Farmington	300	1781	5
Greenwich	228	1773	8
Guilford	300	1776	10
Hartford	1,500	1786	31
Harwinton	0	1786	0
Hebron	0	1786	0
Lebanon	222	1772	6
Litchfield	300	1781	10
Middletown	1,140	1783	14
New Haven	1,968	1772	25
New London	780	1776	14
Plainfield	180	1781	12
Sharon	60	1776	3
Simsbury	108	1736	8
Tolland	54	1756	6
Washington	48	1781	3
Windham	300	1781	9

Note: Density is computed as if the town divisions of the Revolutionary years had not occurred.

Sources: Marquis De Chastellux, *Travels in North America in the Years 1780, 1781, 1782,* 2 vols. (Williamsburg, Va., 1963), II, 71, 77, 81, 83; Ezra Stiles, *Extracts from the Itineraries and Other Miscellanies of Ezra Stiles,* ed. Franklin Bowditch Dexter (New Haven, 1916), 265, 395; Elizabeth Schenck, *The History of Fairfield,* 2 vols. (New York, 1889), II, 393; Connecticut Archives, Ecclesiastical Connecticut State Library, Hartford, Series I, vol. 20, 351; vol. IX, 351; Map of Greenwich in Spencer Mead, *Ye Historie of ye Town of Greenwich* (New York, 1911), 86; Map of Guilford by Lois North, copy in Connecticut State Library; Map of Lebanon, copy in Connecticut State Library; Map of Middletown, copy in Connecticut State Library; Map of New London, original in Trumbull Papers, XXIV, doc. 18, Connecticut State Library; Map of Sharon, copy in Connecticut State Library.

INDIVIDUAL AND FAMILY

DOMINANCE AMONG

GENERAL ASSEMBLY DEPUTIES, 1700–1780

Town	Number of terms served by longest officeholder	% of total terms			
		5 men	1 family	3 families	5 families
Branford	50	48	27	60	74
Colchester	28	43	22	46	65
Danbury	59	57	22	44	61
Durham	59	70	27	64	80
Fairfield	30	44	40	65	78
Farmington	35	42	20	50	67
Glastonbury	44	54	30	74	87
Greenwich	42	43	36	55	67
Groton	40	39	34	51	65
Guilford	42	47	20	48	65
Haddam	52	64	55	76	86
Hartford	28	43	25	44	58
Killingworth	24	42	25	51	66
Lebanon	44	48	24	48	63
Lyme	28	34	13	38	53
Middletown	64	54	20	44	59
Milford	69	54	22	48	59
New Haven	59	47	18	40	53
New London	36	45	11	30	48
Norwalk	55	51	23	53	67
Norwich	35	42	23	63	82
Plainfield	28	37	17	33	50
Preston	31	39	11	32	52
Saybrook	34	38	20	47	63
Simsbury	38	40	25	53	72
Stamford	73	56	33	52	68
Stonington	27	36	21	38	53
Stratford	42	36	13	37	54
Wallingford	36	46	40	57	69

Town	Number of terms served by longest officeholder	% of total terms			
		5 men	1 family	3 families	5 families
Wethersfield	42	53	18	47	67
Windham	42	44	19	40	57
Windsor	31	30	27	47	59
Woodbury	47	56	21	60	83
Averages	44.9	46.8	24.1	49.9	66.0

OFFICEHOLDING PATTERNS OF DEPUTIES
TO THE GENERAL ASSEMBLY, 1700–1780

Town	Average no. terms served per deputy	Turnover rate (%)	Average no. terms served per deputy	Turnover rate (%)	Average no. terms served per deputy	Turnover rate (%)	Average no. terms served per deputy	Turnover rate (%)	Average no. terms served per deputy	
	1701–20		1721–40		1741–60		1761–80		1701–8c	
Ashford			4.22	39	4.75	39	6.67	54	6.08	4
Bolton					4.00	55	6.00	3		
Branford	6.00	32	6.08	39	5.13	44	4.56	32	6.98	4
Canaan[b]										
Canterbury	2.75	43	4.76	48	7.27	44	3.96	47	6.16	4
Colchester	7.84	30	7.80	36	6.07	35	8.00	35	9.16	3
Coventry			12.83	35	5.69	44	7.18	39	6.95	4
Danbury	5.2	41	6.82	49	5.07	49	4.68	42	7.24	4
Derby	7.00	32	6.27	28	6.17	46	4.27	47	7.28	3
Durham	4.13	40	6.16	39	7.27	34	7.18	19	8.56	3
East Haddam			5.14	48	3.08	60	8.00	30	6.74	4
Enfield					6.00	22	6.67	34		
Fairfield	5.27	62	5.27	46	7.70	35	5.64	33	8.51	4
Farmington	5.33	50	6.00	46	4.59	51	7.90	42	7.71	4
Glastonbury	7.5	32	9.5	24	8.22	19	6.15	39	8.71	2
Goshen							4.44	64		
Greenwich	3.92	63	5.54	46	4.80	46	5.07	41	6.49	4
Groton	3.11	68	4.15	61	4.81	60	3.43	66	6.19	6
Guilford	5.64	46	6.50	29	7.90	30	5.71	40	9.29	3
Haddam	7.38	34	5.71	48	6.14	42	5.42	54	7.39	4
Hartford	6.50	28	11.00	13	6.50	4.	6.67	27	10.3	2
Harwinton							5.47	48		
Hebron			7.75	35	9.38	35	6.81	35	8.50	3
Kent[b]										
Killingly			3.86	64	4.21	61	3.71	83	4.68	6
Killingworth	7.70	56	7.27	51	6.25	58	5.00	56	9.95	5
Lebanon	4.21	68	7.90	27	6.67	34	4.19	32	7.43	3

Town	1701–20 Average no. terms served per deputy	1701–20 Turnover rate(%)	1721–40 Average no. terms served per deputy	1721–40 Turnover rate (%)	1741–60 Average no. terms served per deputy	1741–60 Turnover rate (%)	1761–80 Average no. terms served per deputy	1761–80 Turnover rate (%)	1701–80[a] Average no. terms served per deputy	1701–80[a] Turnover rate (%)
tchfield					4.88	41	6.66	29	6.33	35
me	5.07	58	6.91	59	4.28	67	5.71	59	7.8	61
ansfield			8.44	53	6.15	30	4.06	53	6.72	44
iddletown	5.64	25	6.08	34	8.77	18	10.00	31	9.32	26
ilford	5.58	40	8.33	22	7.09	37	6.15	28	8.91	33
ewtown					3.29	55	4.87	51		
ew Hartford							6.66	55		
ew Haven	4.44	45	8.89	14	7.27	33	6.15	21	7.80	28
ew London	4.59	54	4.21	57	5.00	50	8.00	18	6.36	44
ew Milford			4.88	34	3.64	54	4.21	41	4.85	48
orwalk	3.50	70	4.63	69	4.73	45	4.24	42	4.28	56
orwich	6.82	40	4.88	58	4.27	48	4.15	43	7.21	46
ainfield	3.91	53	4.44	56	5.58	53	3.81	57	5.82	53
omfret			5.36	36	4.53	43	5.50	51	6.36	44
eston	4.93	64	4.59	58	4.16	86	2.93	85	5.08	73
dgefield					6.46	41	5.14	46	6.11	43
lisbury[b]										
ybrook	7.18	38	5.00	41	7.60	30	4.53	57	8.24	42
aaron							5.20	42		
msbury	7.09	38	3.70	59	6.59	49	3.39	60	5.25	52
omers							5.85	40		
afford[b]										
amford	4.86	50	7.5	28	7.4	27	6.17	31	8.82	33
onington	3.18	85	3.55	71	4.16	68	3.81	71	5.29	73
ratford	3.60	75	4.21	70	4.21	58	4.44	38	5.22	61
ffield					4.88	46	4.11	42		
olland					6.58	30	6.15	36		
oluntown					6.07	35	5.57	40	7.13	38
allingford	5.71	55	7.50	33	5.27	32	3.80	38	7.69	37
aterbury	6.08	47	3.95	59	3.89	50	6.08	30	6.94	47
ethersfield	5.92	47	9.62	27	5.83	49	7.60	29	8.67	38
indham	10.28	40	4.44	58	5.00	63	4.71	45	7.61	52
indsor	7.09	32	10.00	29	5.38	43	5.57	48	9.27	37
oodbury	3.93	51	5.27	58	5.43	41	11.43	19	7.74	41
oodstock					5.11	33	5.42	42		

Compiled only when fifty years or more were available.

No data available.

NOTES

INTRODUCTION

1. The twelve major books I refer to are, in order of publication: Charles Grant, *Democracy in the Connecticut Frontier Town of Kent* (New York, 1961); Sumner Chilton Powell, *Puritan Village: The Formation of a New England Town* (Middletown, Conn., 1963); Darrett B. Rutman, *Winthrop's Boston: A portrait of a Puritan Town* (Chapel Hill, N.C., 1965); John Demos, *A Little Commonwealth: Family Life in Plymouth Colony* (New York, 1970); Philip Greven, Jr., *Four Generations: Population, Land, and Family in Colonial Andover, Massachusetts* (Ithaca, N.Y., 1970); Kenneth Lockridge, *A New England Town: The First Hundred Years* (New York, 1970); G. B. Warden, *Boston, 1689–1776* (Boston, 1970); Michael Zuckerman, *Peaceable Kingdoms: New England Towns in the Eighteenth Century* (New York, 1970); Dirk Hoerder, *Society and Government, 1760–1780: The Power Structures of Massachusetts Townships* (Berlin, 1972); Richard P. Gildrie, *Salem, Massachusetts, 1626–1683: A Covenant Community* (Charlottesville, Va., 1975); Edward Cook, Jr., *The Fathers of the Towns: Leadership and Community Structure in Eighteenth-Century New England* (Baltimore, 1976); and Robert A. Gross, *The Minutemen and Their World* (New York, 1976). An example of one of the fine professional monographs published by a local press is Estelle Feinstein, *Stamford: From Puritan to Patriot* (Stamford, Conn., 1976). Although New England dominates the local history field, community case studies are now being written on other areas of the colonies. For example, two major ones on Pennsylvania were published recently: see Stephanie Grauman Wolf, *Urban Village: Population, Community, and Family Structure in Germantown, Pennsylvania, 1683–1800* (Princeton, N.J., 1976); and Jerome H. Wood, *Conestoga Crossroads: The Rise of Lancaster, Pennsylvania, 1730–1790* (Harrisburg, Pa., 1975). Before the last few years, besides New England, only such urban areas as Williamsburg, Philadelphia, and New York City had been the subject of book-length work. As it is for New England, the dissertation, journal, and conference literature is rapidly proliferating for the communities of the middle and southern colonies.

2. The first historian to utilize the records of many towns in his work was Michael Zuckerman, in *Peaceable Kingdoms*, but as he admitted at a session of the American Historical Association Conference in Boston in 1970, he sampled only towns of one type and in one area of Massachusetts. Hoerder, *Society and Government, 1760–1780*, included five towns in his sample but studied only officeholding in communities and for only a twenty-year period. Charles E. Clark, in *The Eastern Frontier: The Settlement of Northern New England, 1610–1763* (New York, 1970), while not focusing

explicitly on community structure, does provide a charming overview of the northern New England town. However, his impressionistic work lacks sufficient data and a conceptual framework to give it authority. James A. Henretta, "The Morphology of New England Society in the Colonial Period," *Journal of Interdisciplinary History*, 2 (1971), made the first attempt to integrate the various community studies into an overview. The best published works that rely on large samples of towns are Cook, *The Fathers of the Towns;* and Darrett B. Rutman, "People in Progress: The New Hampshire Towns of the Eighteenth Century," *Journal of Urban History*, 1 (May, 1975). A collection of nine essays, Bruce C. Daniels (ed.), *Town and County: Essays on the Structure of Local Government in the American Colonies* (Middletown, Conn., 1978), provides surveys of local institutions of government in the three regions of colonies. Most of these essays are based on a wide sample of communities. David J. Russo in an ambitious and provocative study places town studies in a long-range perspective: see Russo, *Families and Communities: A New View of American History* (Memphis, 1974). Ruth E. Sutter provides an even longer and wider perspective and discusses the North American community in the context of Indian, Spanish, French, and English culture: see Sutter, *The Next Place You Come To: A Historical Introduction to Communities in North America* (Englewood Cliffs, N.J., 1973). Page Smith's study of the town in American history is insightful and creative but, even more than Clark's work on the eastern frontier, it is impressionistic and lacks the grounding in data and social science techniques that is essential for secure generalizations: see Smith, *As a City upon a Hill: The Town in American History* (New York, 1966).

3. John Friedman, "Two Concepts of Urbanization," *Urban Affairs Quarterly*, 1 (1966), 79–81.

4. See Philip Hauser, "Urbanization: An Overview," *The Study of Urbanization*, eds. Philip Hauser and Leo Schnore (New York, 1965), 9; and David Popenoe, "On the Meaning of 'Urban' in Urban Studies," *Urban Affairs Quarterly*, 1 (1965), 29, for the two definitions of urbanization. The literature on definitions is conveniently summarized in John H. Baker, *Urban Politics in America* (New York, 1971), 3–27.

CHAPTER I. THE PROCESS OF TOWN SETTLEMENT
AND FORMATION

1. The story of how Connecticut's boundaries were drawn is an interesting one, but it has been told elsewhere and need not be repeated here. See Richard Dunn, *Puritans and Yankees: The Winthrop Dynasty of New England, 1630–1717* (Princeton, N.J., 1962; reprint ed., New York, 1971, *passim.*

2. A narrative of the River Town's settlement can be found in most general histories of Connecticut and in many specialized accounts. See especially Charles Andrews, *The River Towns of Connecticut* (Baltimore,

1889), *passim;* William Deloss Love, *The Colonial History of Hartford* (Hartford, 1914; reprint ed., Chester, Conn., 1974), 3, 17–21, 65–67; and Albert E. Van Dusen, *Connecticut* (New York, 1961), 19–24.

3. Dorothy Deming, *The Settlement of the Connecticut Towns,* VI, *Connecticut Tercentenary Series* (New Haven, 1930), 6–10; Love, *Hartford,* 36, 37.

4. Deming, *Connecticut Towns,* 11–14. See appendix five above, for detailed listings of land quality by towns.

5. Deming, *Connecticut Towns,* 19, 20; J. L. Rockey (ed.), *History of New Haven County, Connecticut,* 2 vols. (New York, 1892), II, 104, 105. New Haven's street pattern was laid out according to a plan based on scriptures and unintentionally may have retarded the development of commerce because it was not conducive to trade. See John Archer, "Puritan Town Planning in New Haven," *Journal of the Society of Architectural Historians,* 34 (May, 1975), 140.

6. Deming, *Connecticut Towns,* 20–22; Rockey, *New Haven County,* II, 112–15; Bernard Steiner, *A History of the Plantation of Menunkatuck and of the Original Town of Guilford, Connecticut* (Baltimore, 1897), 14–18, 22, 23; Works Projects Administration, *History of Milford, Connecticut, 1629–1939* (Milford, Conn., 1939), 2–16.

7. Frances Manwaring Caulkins, *A History of New London, Connecticut* (New London, 1895), 41–47.

8. Material for most of these data is found in the following: Deming, *Connecticut Towns,* 24–31; Frances M. Caulkins, *A History of Norwich, Connecticut* (Hartford, 1866), 1–61; William Haynes, *Stonington Chronology* (Stonington, Conn., 1949), 1–10; Samuel Orcutt and Ambroise Beardsley, *The History of the Old Town of Derby, Connecticut* (Springfield, Mass., 1880), 2–19, 46, 47; Susan Reik, "Genesis of a New England Town: The Growth of Farmington, Connecticut" (M.A. thesis, Columbia University, 1972), 2–11; Rockey, *New Haven County,* II, 3, 4, 341, 343, 366; and William Vibert, *Three Centuries of Simsbury, 1679–1970* (Simsbury, Conn., 1970), 33–35.

For an analysis of the founding of two towns that emphasizes the desire of the first settlers to amass large amounts of land, see Christopher Collier, "Saybrook and Lyme: Secular Settlements in a Puritan Commonwealth," *A Lyme Miscellany,* ed. George Willauer (Middletown, Conn., 1977), 9–28.

9. The relative priority on a 10-point scale of the various attributes of a village location are: 10 for water, 5 for arable land, 3 for grazing land, 3 for fuel, and 1 for building materials. See Michael Chisholm, *Rural Settlement and Land Use: An Essay in Location* (London, 1962), 114–15; and James Lemon, *The Best Poor Man's Country: A Geographical Study of Early Southeastern Pennsylvania* (New York, 1976), 62–63.

10. J. Hammond Trumbull and Charles Hoadley (eds.), *The Public Records of the Colony of Connecticut,* 15 vols. (Hartford, 1850–90), III, 296.

11. The change in the policy of the General Court and the impact of land speculation on the politics of Connecticut and on the character of its inhabitants are discussed fully in Richard Bushman, *From Puritan to Yankee: Character and the Social Order in Connecticut, 1690–1765* (Cambridge, Mass., 1967), part 2.

12. Rockey, *New Haven County*, II, 626–29; James Montgomery Bailey, *History of Danbury, Connecticut, 1684–1896* (New York, 1896), 25, 26, 41–54; Lynn Wilson *History of Fairfield County, Connecticut, 1639–1928*, 3 vols. (Hartford, 1929), I, 91.

13. William Chauncey Fowler, *History of Durham, Connecticut, from the First Grant of Land in 1662 to 1866* (Hartford, 1866, 3–21; Deming, *Connecticut Towns*, 46, 47; Jane Eliza Johnson, *Newtown's History and Historian* (Newtown, Conn., 1917), 3–25; Wilson, *Fairfield County*, I, 97, 98.

14. Payne Kilbourne, *Sketches and Chronicles of the Town of Litchfield, Connecticut* (Hartford, 1859), 33; Alain C. White (comp.), *The History of the Town of Litchfield, Connecticut, 1720–1920* (Litchfield, Conn., 1920), 14.

15. Bushman, *Puritan to Yankee*, chap. 1; Ellen Larned, *History of Windham County, Connecticut*, 2 vols. (Worcester, Mass., 1874; reprint ed., Chester, Conn., 1976), I, 6–18.

16. Larned, *Windham County*, I, 105–37.

17. *Ibid.*, I, 221–29.

18. D. Hamilton Hurd, *History of New London County* (Philadelphia, 1882), 386–87; John Betal Porter, "Notes on the Early History of Coventry, Connecticut," ms., Connecticut State Library, Hartford, 3–5; John Sibun, *Our Town's Heritage, 1708–1758* (Hebron, Conn., 1975), 13; Bruce P. Stark, "Lebanon, Connecticut: A Study of Society and Politics in the Eighteenth Century" (Ph.D. diss., University of Connecticut, 1970), 8–12; Larned, *Windham County*, I, 160–66, 181–83, 238–43, 519–20; Loren Waldo, *The Early History of Tolland* (Hartford, 1861), 1–40; Samuel Alvord, *A Historical Sketch of Bolton* (Bolton, Conn., 1920), *passim;* Stafford Library Association, *The History of the Town of Stafford* (Stafford Springs, Conn., 1935), 7, 8, 9; Charles Hammond, *The History of Union, Connecticut* (New Haven, 1893), 38–45; Elmer S. Johnson, "Willington: Two Hundred Years Ago," ms., Connecticut State Library, Hartford, 5, 6, 21, 22. The two most exceptional towns to this pattern were Tolland and Voluntown. Tolland was settled by a group migration reminiscent of the earlier period, and Voluntown was deeded to 150 war veterans who were "middlin" men and did not possess the high social standing of most absentee proprietors. Deming, *Connecticut Towns*, 71–74, overstates the degree of disputation surrounding the planting of these towns. The individual town studies reveal that controversy was minimal and, even more importantly, that it occurred among rival speculators prior to the settling of the towns and did not involve actual settlers.

19. Deming, *Connecticut Towns,* 35.

20. Connecticut Archives, Towns and Lands, Connecticut State Library, Series I, vol. II, 105. Hereafter cited as C.A., T.L.

21. Deming, *Connecticut Towns,* 36–38.

22. Jackson Turner Main, "The Economic and Social Structure of Early Lyme," *Lyme Miscellany,* 29.

23. Dorothy Deming, *The Settlement of Litchfield County,* VII, *Connecticut Tercentenary Series* (New Haven, 1933), 1–3; Ray Bentley, *History of Harwinton* (Harwinton, Conn., 1972), 11–13.

24. Bentley, *Harwinton,* 13, 14; Deming, *Litchfield,* 2, 3; *A History of Litchfield County* (Philadelphia, 1881), 237; Stanley A. Ranson, *History of Hartland, the 69th Town in the Colony of Connecticut* (Hartland, Conn., 1961), 9.

25. Bentley, *Harwinton,* 11–17; Deming, *Litchfield,* 3–5; *Litchfield County,* 374–75.

26. Ransom, *Hartland,* 5–9.

27. *Sketches of the People and Places of New Hartford* (New Hartford, Conn., 1883), 2.

28. Edward C. Starr, *A History of Cornwall, Connecticut: A Typical New England Town* (New Haven, 1926), 34–36.

29. Deming, *Litchfield,* 1–5; *Litchfield County,* 264, 385, 527, 566, 577; Starr, *Cornwall,* 36.

30. Larned, *Windham County,* I, 487–95; Van Dusen, *Connecticut,* 94.

31. David Grayson Allen, "In English Ways: The Movement of Societies and the Transferal of English Local Law and Custom to Massachusetts Bay, 1600–1690" (Ph.D. diss., University of Wisconsin, 1974), 399. In Massachusetts, also, the Revolutionary spirit fueled the desire of neighborhoods and parishes to attain town status, and sixty hived-off towns were created in the 1770s and 1780s. See Allen, "In English Ways," 310. For in-depth analyses of the creation of new towns from old ones in Massachusetts prior to the Revolution, see Richard Gildrie, *Salem, Massachusetts, 1626–1683: A Covenant Community* (Charlottesville, Va., 1975), 68–69; and Kenneth Lockridge, *A New England Town: The First Hundred Years* (New York, 1970), 94–100.

32. Bruce P. Stark, *Lyme, Connecticut: From Colony to Independence* (Old Lyme, Conn., 1976), 1.

33. C.A., T.L., Series I, vol. IX, 336, 345; vol. X, 82, 83, 84, 172, 182, 183.

34. Chisholm, *Rural Settlement,* 146–47, discusses hiving off in past peasant societies and in present Sudan and Rhodesia and shows its universality.

35. C.A., T.L., Series I, vol. X, 41a.

36. C.A., T.L., Series I, vol. X, 124.

37. C.A., T.L., Series I, vol. IX, 285a.

38. I am indebted to Professor Christopher Collier for pointing out to me this difference between the pre-Revolutionary and the Revolutionary petitions. The same rhetoric characterized the movement for new towns in Massachusetts. See Robert Gross, *The Minutemen and Their World* (New York, 1976), 160–68.

39. C.A., T.L., Series I, vol. IX, 285a.

40. C.A., T.L., Series I, Vol. IX, 220–22.

41. C.A., T.L., Series I, vol. X, 61.

42. C.A., T.L., Series I, vol. IX, 212; vol. X, 40, 162.

43. See Bruce C. Daniels, "Emerging Urbanism and Increasing Social Stratification in the Era of the American Revolution," *The American Revolution: The Home Front,* ed. John Ferling (Carrollton, Ga., 1976), 15–30. See also Christopher Collier, *Roger Sherman's Connecticut: Yankee Politics in the Age of the American Revolution* (Middletown, Conn., 1971), 197, 198; Carl Bridenbaugh, *Cities in Revolt: Urban Life in America, 1743–1776* (London and New York, 1970), 10, 11; Ernest Griffith, *The History of American City Government: The Colonial Period* (New York, 1938), 262, 263; and John Murrin, "Anglicizing an American Colony: The Transformation of Provincial Massachusetts" (Ph.D. diss., Yale University, 1966), 267. For specific examples of fights in Massachusetts between town centers and outlying residents, see Gildrie, *Salem,* 127; Gross, *The Minutemen,* 143–45; and Lockridge, *A New England Town,* 106–15.

44. Edward Atwater (ed.), *The History of the City of New Haven by an Association of Writers* (New York, 1887), 80, 81; Collier, *Roger Sherman's Connecticut,* 198; Love, *Hartford,* 348, 349; Rollin Osterweis, *Three Centuries of New Haven, 1635–1938* (New Haven, 1953), 165; David Roth, *Connecticut's War Governor: Jonathan Trumbull,* IX, *Connecticut Bicentennial Series* (Chester, Conn., 1974), 74. Gross, *The Minutemen,* 153–60, shows that while the Revolution temporarily ended local divisions, they reappeared with more virulence after the original unified response. Towns could agree to oppose British coercion but they could not agree how; nor could they agree who should make the sacrifices.

45. C.A., T.L., Series I, vol. X, 40.

46. C.A., T.L., Series I, vol. IX, 45.

47. C.A., T.L., Series I, vol. X, 149–70.

48. C.A., T.L., Series I, vol. X, 113a–21.

49. C.A., T.L., Series I, vol. X, 113a–21, 182, 183.

50. C.A., T.L., Series I, vol. X, 82a, 82b, 82c.

CHAPTER II. THE GROWTH AND DISTRIBUTION
OF POPULATION

1. Charles Grant, *Democracy in the Connecticut Frontier Town of Kent* (New York, 1961), 83–85; Richard Bushman, *From Puritan to Yankee: Character*

and the Social Order in Connecticut, 1690–1765 (Cambridge, Mass., 1967), *passim;* Philip Greven, Jr., *Four Generations: Population, Land, and Family in Colonial Andover, Massachusetts* (Ithaca, N.Y., 1970), *passim;* Kenneth Lockridge, "Land, Population, and the Evolution of New England Society, 1630–1790," *Colonial America: Essays in Politics and Social Development,* ed. Stanley Katz (Boston, 1971), 467–91; Kenneth Lockridge, "Social Change and the Meaning of the American Revolution," *Journal of Social History,* 6 (Spring, 1973), 403–39. Earlier scholars have dealt with population growth and land: men ratios in New England, but their work has been largely ignored. See Albert Olson, *Agricultural Economy and the Population in Eighteenth-Century Connecticut,* XL, *Connecticut Tercentenary Series* (New Haven, 1935).

2. The censuses can be found in the published colony and state records for those years and in Evarts B. Greene and Virginia D. Harrington, *American Population before the Federal Census of 1790* (Gloucester, Mass., 1966), and in Robert Wells, *The Population of the British Colonies in America before 1776: A Survey of Census Data* (Princeton, N.J., 1976).

3. Stella Sutherland, *Population Distribution in Colonial America* (New York, 1966), 37–40; Daniel Scott Smith, "The Demographic History of Colonial New England," *Journal of Economic History,* 32 (March, 1972), 171, 175. Smith lists the Rossiter and Sutherland growth rates per decade.

4. David Humphreys, *An Historical Account of the Incorporated Society for the Propagation of the Gospel* (London, 1730), 42, cited in Greene and Harrington, *American Population,* 48; George Chalmers, *Political Annals of the Present United Colonies, 1607–1763,* Book II (London, 1780), 27, cited in Greene and Harrington, *American Population,* 49; J. Hammond Trumbull and Charles Hoadley (eds.), *The Public Records of the Colony of Connecticut,* 15 vols. (Hartford, 1850–90) I, "Report of Connecticut to the Board of Trade," 584.

5. Glenn Weaver, "Industry in an Agrarian Economy: Early Eighteenth-Century Connecticut," *Bulletin of the Connecticut Historical Society,* 19 (June, 1954), 82–92, suggests this explanation for Connecticut's practice of consistently understating her numbers and wealth in reports to the Board of Trade.

6. Greene and Harrington, *American Population,* 50.

7. "Account of New England," *New England Historical and Genealogical Register,* 38 (1884) 380, cited in Greene and Harrington, *American Population,* 47; Albert E. Van Dusen, "The Trade of Revolutionary Connecticut" (Ph.D. diss., University of Pennsylvania, 1948), 11. See James Henretta, *The Evolution of American Society, 1700–1815: An Interdisciplinary Analysis* (Lexington, Mass., 1973), *passim,* for a convenient summary and analysis of recent literature on demographic trends; and *Documents Relative to the Colonial History of New York,* 15 vols. (Albany, 1856–87), IV, 183, cited in Greene and Harrington, *American Population,* 49.

8. Ezra Stiles, *Extracts from the Itineraries and Other Miscellanies of Ezra Stiles,* ed. Franklin Bowditch Dexter (New Haven, 1916), 93. The polls are listed yearly in the colony records until 1709. Greene and Harrington, *American Population,* 51–58, reprint them. One can see the acts forgiving new towns their taxes by thumbing through any volume of the colony records. For the list of polls reported in 1779, 1788, and 1791, see Connecticut Archives, Finance and Currency, Connecticut State Library, Hartford, Series II, vol. V, 163a.

The ratio 1 to 4 was first used by Ezra Stiles, an eighteenth-century commentator on Connecticut society who is usually distinguished for his reliability; it may be that in this case Stiles was wrong, but his normal precision has made historians less inclined to question his judgment. At any rate, the 1 to 4 ratio remains to be tested. However, even if it is accurate, the aggregate polls listed in the colony records would not yield the proper population of pre-census Connecticut. Stiles used the 1 to 4 ratio for individual towns, but, in the colony totals that are listed in the archives and that have been used by historians, many settlements containing large numbers of people are not included: well-established towns paying their taxes late, as many did, are frequently not listed; newly incorporated towns and parishes were customarily forgiven their taxes for a period of three to five years and hence are not listed; and unincorporated settlements were never listed. Estimates made from lists of polls such as this would seriously understate the population even if the 1 to 4 conversion ratio were correct. A quick look at the list of total polls reported by the colony also shows why it is not a reliable guide to the population as a whole in the colony—reporting was not consistent. In 1701–10, the last decade the polls were listed, they totaled 3,695 at the beginning, rose to a height of 4,668 in 1708, and dropped the next year to 3,688, a figure below that of the beginning of the decade. Had the population of Connecticut suffered a 25 percent loss in the year 1708 we would be aware of it through qualitative sources. A document entered in the Connecticut Archives in 1791 that gives the total number of polls reported by the towns in the new state for 1779, 1788, and 1791 shows that the conversion factor for polls to population for the entire colony or state should be much higher than the 1 to 4 ratio. When the polls listed are divided into the population derived from the censuses they yield conversion ratios of 4.58, 6.45, and 6.54. Were the 1 to 4 figures used for this data, they would grossly understate the population.

9. Benjamin Trumbull, *Complete History of Connecticut, 1630–1764,* 2 vols. (New Haven, 1818), I, 451; J. G. Palfrey, *History of New England,* 5 vols. (Boston, 1890–97), IV, 372–73; Franklin Bowditch Dexter, "Estimates of Population in the American Colonies," *Proceedings of the American Antiquarian Society,* 5 (October, 1887), 32; Bushman, *Puritan to Yankee,* 83;

Smith, "The Demographic History," 165–183. Bushman cites Anthony Garvan, *Architecture and Town Planning in Colonial Connecticut* (New Haven, 1951), as his source, and Garvan almost exclusively uses the unreliable tax lists; see Garvan, *Architecture*, 3.

10. See chapter seven above.

11. Henretta, *Evolution of Society*, 14; Smith, "The Demographic History," 182, 183.

12. See Ellen Larned, *History of Windham County*, 2 vols. (Worcester, Mass., 1874; reprint ed., Chester, Conn., 1976), II, *passim*.

13. I am indebted to a personal conversation with Marvin Thompson, associate editor of the Jonathan Trumbull papers and author of a doctoral dissertation on the town of Litchfield, for the information on Litchfield County's out-migration in the early nineteenth century.

14. I wish to thank James Richtik, Chairman, Department of Geography, University of Winnipeg, for providing valuable guidance to me on the subject of modern soil maps and their historical uses. For examples of their use by historical geographers in a manner similar to my own, see James Lemon, *The Best Poor Man's Country: A Geographical Study of Southeastern Pennsylvania* (New York, 1976), 37–40; and T. R. Weir, "Settlement in Southwest Manitoba, 1870–1891," *Papers of the Historical and Scientific Society of Manitoba* (1960–61), 54–64. See appendix five for a complete listing and analysis of the soil maps data.

15. See chapter six above for figures on the proportion of population living in villages.

16. Wilbert Moore, "Social Change," *Encyclopedia of the Social Sciences*, 14, 365–75, discusses population growth as one of the strongest causes of social change.

CHAPTER III. THE EVOLUTION OF TOWN-MEETING GOVERNMENT

1. The best statement of the uniqueness and the frontier origins of the New England town can be found in the work of Alexis de Tocqueville, published nearly seventy years before Frederick Jackson Turner wrote his famous essay on the frontier. See John Sly, *Town Government in Massachusetts, 1620–1930* (Cambridge, Mass., 1930), 53–54. The ultimate statement on the Germanic origins of town government is Herbert Baxter Adams, "The Germanic Origins of New England Towns," *Johns Hopkins University Studies in Historical and Political Science*, I (Baltimore, 1882). Sumner Chilton Powell, *Puritan Village* (Middletown, Conn., 1963), 142, treated the problem of the origins of town government with a great deal of sophistication, but he was probably the last major scholar to emphasize the unique American nature of town-government origins. Three years earlier, George Haskins, *Law and Authority in Early Massachusetts: A Study in Transition and*

Design (New York, 1960), 75–76, had shown through a comparative study of English and New England law how Massachusetts town government paralleled parish vestries and manorial courts. This was a reinvigoration of a thesis first sketched out by Edward Channing, "Town and County Government in the English Colonies of North America," *Johns Hopkins University Studies in Historical and Political Science,* X (1884), 5–57. John J. Waters, "Hingham, Massachusetts, 1631–1661: An East Anglian Oligarchy in the New World," *Journal of Social History,* 1 (1967–68, 351–70, shows how important Old World origins were to New England politics. Kenneth Lockridge, *A New England Town: The First Hundred Years* (Norton, 1970), xiii, explicitly states that Powell overemphasized the uniqueness of New England town government. Research into the English origins of the New World town has reached a new level of understanding in two recent studies: David Grayson Allen, "In English Ways: The Movement of Societies and the Transferal of English Local Law and Custom to Massachusetts Bay, 1600–1690" (Ph.D. diss., University of Wisconsin, 1974), iv, vi, and chap. 1; and David Thomas Konig, "English Legal Change and the Origins of Local Government in Northern Massachusetts," *Town and County: Essays on the Structure of Local Government in the American Colonies,* ed. Bruce C. Daniels (Middletown, Conn., 1978). Both Allen and Konig conclude that New England town government was an adaption of English institutions to the New World. The most detailed study of English local government remains Sidney Webb and Beatrice Webb, *English Local Government,* 10 vols. (London, 1906–29). A good analysis of English local government at the time of the planting of the colonies is Wallace Notestein, *The English People on the Eve of Colonization* (New York, 1954).

2. Charles Andrews, *The River Towns of Connecticut* (Baltimore, 1889), 27–28. Thomas Jodziewicz, "Dual Localism in Seventeenth-Century Connecticut: Relations between the General Court and the Towns, 1636–1691" (Ph.D. diss., William and Mary College, 1974), 85, notes the "distinct appearance of sameness."

3. Andrews, *River Towns,* 121–24; A. E. Van Dusen, *Connecticut* (New York, 1961), 40–43; J. Hammond Trumbull and Charles Hoadley (eds.), *The Public Records of the Colony of Connecticut,* 15 vols. (Hartford, 1850–90), I, 2, 3, 37, 91, 100, 106, 509–63 (hereafter cited as *Col. Recs.*).

4. For the early proprietors see Roy Akagi, *The Town Proprietors of the New England Colonies* (Gloucester, Mass., 1963). For suffrage laws and the admission of freemen see Albert McKinley, *The Suffrage Franchise in the Thirteen English Colonies in America* (Philadelphia, 1905), 382–406. For the militia see *Col. Recs.,* I, "Code of 1650," 542–44.

5. Andrews, *River Towns,* 104; Charles Grant, *Democracy in the Connecticut Frontier Town of Kent* (New York, 1972), 129.

6. "Hartford Town Votes, 1635–1716," Connecticut Historical Society,

Collections, VI (Hartford, 1897), *passim;* Erna Green, "The Public Land System of Norwalk, Connecticut, 1654–1704: A Structural Analysis of Economic and Political Relationships" (M.A. thesis, University of Bridgeport, 1972), 12, 137; Norwich Town Meeting Minutes, Norwich City Hall, I, 1674–75; William Deloss Love, *The Colonial History of Hartford* (Chester, Conn., 1974), 56, 59. Jodziewicz, "Dual Localism," table 4, 318, in a careful analysis of the frequency of town meetings in eight towns, found that in six of them it declined markedly between the 1650s and 1680s. This trend is similar to the one described by Powell for Sudbury, Massachusetts. See *Puritan Village,* 75.

7. "Hartford Town Votes," January, 1638; Green, "Norwalk," 136; Joan Ballen, "Fairfield, Connecticut, 1661–1691: A Demographic Study of the Economic, Political, and Social Life of a New England Community" (M.A. thesis, University of Bridgeport, 1970), 128–30.

8. All the powers and duties of the townsmen were outlined in the General Court meeting of October, 1639. See *Col. Recs.,* I, 37. The role of the selectmen as jacks-of-all-trades seems similar to the situation in Massachusetts towns. See Richard Gildrie, *Salem, Massachusetts, 1626–1683: A Covenant Community* (Charlottesville, Va., 1975), 44–45.

9. These enjoinders are found frequently throughout the Connecticut colony records of the seventeenth century. For the acts concerning children see *Col. Recs.,* I, "Code of 1650," 520–21. For the enforcement of morality see Edmund Morgan, *The Puritan Family* (New York, 1966), *passim.*

10. Frances Manwaring Caulkins, *A History of New London, Connecticut* (New London, 1895), 92–93.

11. The office of constable was created in 1636. See *Col. Recs.,* I, 2. Andrews, *River Towns,* 110–15, discusses the role of the constable at length. For all these powers of the constable see *Col. Recs.,* I, "Code of 1650," 522–23.

12. *Col. Recs.,* I, 23, 39, I, "Code of 1650," 523, II, 190; Andrews, *River Towns,* III. The constable was also the arm of the General Court in Massachusetts. See Allen, "In English Ways," 22.

13. *Col. Recs.,* I, "Code of 1650," 551–52.

14. See "Hartford Town Votes," 1650–70; Norwich Town Meeting Minutes, 1660–70; Green, "Norwalk," 141; Ballen, "Fairfield," 120–21, 180.

15. *Col. Recs.,* I, 91, 101.

16. *Col. Recs.,* I, 100.

17. *Col. Recs.,* I, "Code of 1650," 548–49.

18. *Charter of the Colony of Connecticut of 1662* (Hartford, 1900), 14.

19. *Col. Recs.,* I, 48; Bernard Steiner, *A History of the Plantation of Menunkatuck and of the Original Town of Guilford, Connecticut* (Baltimore, 1897),

216; Caulkins, *New London*, 135; Jodziewicz, "Dual Localism," *passim*. Haskins, *Law and Authority*, chaps. 1 and 2, makes the point about the inability of charter colonies to incorporate other bodies. Judith Diamondstone, "The Government of Eighteenth-Century Philadelphia," *Town and County*, ed. Daniels, discusses how narrowly seventeenth-century Englishmen construed delegated power.

20. For a comparison of colony-town relations in Connecticut and Rhode Island, see Bruce C. Daniels, "Contrasting Colony-Town Relations in the Founding of Connecticut and Rhode Island prior to the charters of 1662 and 1663," *Bulletin of the Connecticut Historical Society* (April, 1973), 60–64.

21. Konig, "English Legal Change"; Haskins, *Law and Authority*, 59, 106; and Michael Zuckerman, *Peaceable Kingdoms: New England Towns in the Eighteenth Century* (New York 1970), 17, 18, 19, argue that Massachusetts towns were closely supervised by the colony government in the seventeenth century. Yet supervision was lax enough that Powell, *Puritan Village*, and Lockridge, *A New England Town*, who examined the relationship from local sources, conclude that the towns enjoyed a near autonomy. While both Powell and Lockridge probably overstate the freedom enjoyed by the towns, Allen, "In English Ways," 388, 411, shows that despite some restrictions on town autonomy, Massachusetts was not rationalized into a structured bureaucracy until after 1660. T. H. Breen, "Persistent Localism: English Social Change and the Shaping of New England Institutions," *William and Mary Quarterly*, 32 (January, 1975), 24–27, and Jodziewicz, "Dual Localism," x, show that the nature of the power flow between the two levels was a matter of vital concern in both Massachusetts and Connecticut. Jodziewicz, "Dual Localism," 33, 54, shows how the growth in towns and population forced the colony of Connecticut to concede more independence to the towns and "necessitate[d] more compromise and more general legislation," as opposed to a stricter central control. Gildrie, *Salem*, 33–38, 88–95, also shows that the colony and towns frequently clashed over questions of authority. See Konig, "English Legal Change," for a description of the centralizing activities of the monarchy in Tudor-Stuart England and their impact on New England government.

22. Estelle Feinstein, *Stamford: From Puritan to Patriot, 1641–1774* (Stamford, 1976), 50–53; Charles Hoadley (ed.), *Records of the Colony and Plantation of New Haven*, 2 vols. (Hartford, 1857), I, 113, 191–93, II, 172 (hereafter cited as *N.H. Col. Recs.*).

23. *N.H. Col. Recs.*, II, 493–94; Feinstein, *Stamford*, 74.

24. Jodziewicz, "Dual Localism," 33, 53, 54. See chapter six above for the development of the other bodies. The change described in Richard Bushman, *From Puritan to Yankee: Character and the social Order in Connecticut, 1690–1765* (Cambridge, Mass., 1967), is nowhere else analyzed as bril-

liantly, but it is not a new theme. It is implicit in Van Dusen, *Connecticut,* for example, and has long been an accepted part of the historiography.

25. See table 6 above.

26. Kenneth Lockridge and Alan Kreider, "The Evolution of Massachusetts Town Government, 1640–1740," *William and Mary Quarterly,* 23 (October, 1966), 565. In the definition of a town meeting, meetings that met by adjournment are not counted as separate meetings unless the adjourned portion of the meeting was held more than three weeks after the original meeting—then the adjourned meeting is counted as a separate meeting. This is a compromise between counting no adjourned meetings and counting them all. Hence, an election meeting held on December 3 and adjourned once to December 7 and once again to December 14 would count as only one meeting. However, a meeting of December 3 that adjourned to January 20 or February 10 would count as two separate meetings. This satisfies a definition of meeting that measures it not in a legalistic sense but in the spirit in which the analysis is intended. Many towns met once in December and then adjourned to April, and to count this as only one meeting would unfairly distort the analysis: the town was clearly meeting twice to discuss town business. Also, different towns were often not similar in what was an adjourned or a new meeting; but the definition of a meeting has to be made the same for all towns in the sample to ensure valid comparisons.

27. Lockridge and Kreider, "Massachusetts Town Government," 565.

28. Norwalk had an extra meeting on oysters in 1722, and Salisbury had the extraordinary meeting about Elizabeth Crary in 1762.

29. Hartford Town Meeting Minutes, Hartford City Hall, December, 1769; Waterbury Town Meeting Minutes, Waterbury City Hall, December 1754; Sharon Town Meeting Minutes, Sharon Town Hall, December, 1763, January, 1767, and December, 1776; Norwich Town Meeting Minutes, September, 1716; Ellen Larned, *History of Windham County, Connecticut,* 2 vols. (Worcester, Mass., 1874; reprint ed., Chester, Conn., 1976), I, 59–62, 201; Connecticut Archives, Towns and Lands, Connecticut State Library, Hartford, Series I, vol. X, 90; Ezra Stiles, *Extracts from the Itineraries and Other Miscellanies of Ezra Stiles,* ed. Franklin Bowditch Dexter, (New Haven, 1916), 31; Caulkins, *New London,* 400; Ray Bentley, *History of Harwinton* (Harwinton, Conn., 1972), 20. Lack of attendance at town meeting was also a problem in Massachusetts: see Gildrie, *Salem,* 43.

30. *Col. Recs.,* VII, 245; Middletown Town Meeting Minutes, Middletown City Hall, 1700–1720, esp. December, 1702; Farmington Town Meeting Minutes, Farmington Town Hall, December, 1709; Ridgefield Town Meeting Minutes, Ridgefield Town Hall, December, 1722 and 1720s–50s, *passim;* Norwich Town Meeting Minutes, August, 1715. See Zuckerman, *Peaceable Kingdoms, passim.* Consensus was a traditional goal of

English local government. See George Homans, *English Villagers of the Thirteenth Century* (New York, 1975), 104.

31. Middletown Town Meeting Minutes, December, 1712, 1717, and 1720; Ridgefield Town Meeting Minutes, December, 1722, 1749, and 1751; Branford Town Meeting Minutes, Branford Town Hall, October, 1781 and 1782; Norwich Town Meeting Minutes, February, 1702; Sharon Town Meeting Minutes, December, 1748, and December, 1751; Steiner, *Guilford*, 144; Alain White (comp.), *The History of the Town of Litchfield, Connecticut, 1720–1790* (Litchfield, Conn., 1920), 40.

32. Farmington Town Meeting Minutes, December, 1765, and December, 1702; Newtown Town Meeting Minutes, Newtown Town Hall, December, 1766; Guilford Town Meeting Minutes, Guilford Town Hall, December 1781; Ridgefield Town Meeting Minutes, December, 1722; Norwalk Town Meeting Minutes, Norwalk City Hall, December, 1748, 1752, and 1756; Norwich Town Meeting Minutes, December, 1728, and adjourned meeting of December, 1728.

33. *Col. Recs.*, II, 61, III–V, *passim*, V, 324; Herbert Baxter Adams, *Saxon Tithingmen in America, Johns Hopkins University Studies in Historical and Political Science*, IV (Baltimore, 1883), 8.

34. *Col. Recs.*, VI, 277, XI, 499.

35. *Col. Recs.*, VI, 277, 463–64, XIII, 74, XI, 499.

36. *Some Early Records and Documents of and Relating to the Town of Windsor, Connecticut, 1639–1703* (Hartford, 1930), December, 1642; Fairfield Town Meeting Minutes, Fairfield Town Hall, 1734, 1756, *passim;* Middletown Town Meeting Minutes, 1708, 1712–19, 1720; Derby Town Meeting Minutes, Derby City Hall, December, 1707; Jackson Turner Main, "The Economic and Social Structure of Early Lyme," *A Lyme Miscellany*, ed. George Willauer (Middletown, Conn., 1977), 31.

37. See appendix six for data on numbers of officers in relation to land size and population.

38. *Col. Recs.*, IV, 32, 455, V, 73, VI, 112, XII, 255, XV, 193–94; Charles J. Hoadley (ed.), *The Public Records of the State of Connecticut* (Hartford, 1894), I, 228. Grant's study of Kent and Van Dusen's study of Revolutionary trade strongly support the conclusions of this paragraph. See Grant, *Kent*, 134, 135, and Albert E. Van Dusen, "The Trade of Revolutionary Connecticut" (Ph.D. diss., University of Pennsylvania, 1948), 267. See Jane Eliza Johnson, *Newtown's History and Historian* (Newtown, Conn., 1917), 133–36, and Payne K. Kilbourne, *Sketches and Chronicles of the Town of Litchfield, Connecticut* (Hartford, 1859), 119, for accounts of the extraordinary powers the meetings conferred on the selectmen during the Revolution. During the Revolutionary years the activities of the town meeting and of the selectmen greatly increased. The Revolution was obviously a "crisis" situation that politicized the town meeting.

39. Hartford Town Meeting Minutes, December, 1706; Farmington Town Meeting Minutes, December, 1708, April, 1710, December, 1756; Norwalk Town Meeting Minutes, February, 1702, December 1709.

40. The increased activity can easily be seen by casually glancing through the published records of the Assembly and the governor and Council. See table 6 above.

41. Actually, very little change occurred in local institutions in the Revolutionary era. See Daniels (ed.), *Town and County,* introduction and *passim.*

42. See Wilbert E. Moore, "Social Change," *International Encyclopedia of the Social Sciences,* 14, 365–75, for the relationship among population growth, economic complexity, and government. The relationship between government and authority is discussed in a brilliant essay by Leonard Krieger: "The Idea of Authority in the West," *American Historical Review,* 82 (April, 1977), 249–70. For a perceptive discussion on the growth of the propensity to question authority in Connecticut, see James M. Poteet, "Unrest in the 'Land of Steady Habits'": The Hartford Riot of 1722," *Proceedings of the American Philosophical Society,* 119 (June, 1975), 223–32. See also Bushman, *Puritan to Yankee, passim.*

43. Krieger, "The Idea of Authority," 261–63.

CHAPTER IV. THE GROWTH AND GOVERNMENT OF CHURCH SOCIETIES

1. The dates for the founding of all Congregational church societies can be found in an immensely valuable volume, Albert Bates, *List of Congregational Ecclesiastical Societies* (Middletown, Conn., n.d.). See George C. Homans, *English Villagers of the Thirteenth Century* (New York, 1975), 382–83, for a discussion of English parishes and villages.

2. Ola Winslow, *Meetinghouse Hill, 1630–1783* (New York, 1952), 39–42.

3. This paragraph is based on Winslow, *Meetinghouse Hill,* 30–45.

4. Bruce P. Stark, in his two histories of Connecticut communities, provides the best qualitative treatment of the creation of new societies: see Stark, "Lebanon, Connecticut: A Study of Society and Politics in the Eighteenth Century" (Ph.D. diss., University of Connecticut, 1970), 28–97, and *Lyme, Connecticut: From Founding to Independence* (Old Lyme, Conn., 1976), 9–14. See also J. M. Bumsted, "Revivalism and Separatism in New England: The First Society of Norwich as a Case Study," *William and Mary Quarterly,* 24 (October, 1967), 597; and James Walsh, "The Great Awakening in the First Congregational Church of Woodbury, Connecticut," *William and Mary Quarterly,* 28 (October, 1971), 555–60.

5. M. Louise Greene, *The Development of Religious Liberty in Connecticut* (Boston, 1905), 191.

6. Paul R. Lucas, *Valley of Discord: Church and Society Along the Connecticut*

River, 1636–1725 (Hanover, N.H., 1976), 31–42, 74–75 and *passim*.

7. E. Edwards Beardsley, *The History of the Episcopal Church in Connecticut* (Boston, 1883), 126, 127; Nelson Burr, *The Story of the Diocese of Connecticut* (Hartford, 1962), 41; John Ledyard Denison, *Some Items of Baptist History in Connecticut from 1674 to 1900* (Philadelphia, 1900), 11; A. H. Newman, *A History of the Baptist Church in the United States* (Philadelphia, 1898), 244, 245; O. Seymour, *The Beginnings of the Episcopal Church in Connecticut*, XXX, *Connecticut Tercentenary Series* (New Haven, 1930), 8–10.

8. Nelson R. Burr, "The Quakers in Connecticut: A Neglected Phase of History," *Bulletin of the Friends Historical Association*, 31 (Spring, 1942), 11–24; Roland Osterweis, *Three Centuries of New Haven, 1638–1938* (New Haven, 1953), 90.

9. Denison, *Some Items of Baptist History*, 6, 7, 14; C. C. Goen, *Revivalism and Separatism in New England, 1740–1800: Strict Congregationalists and Separate Baptists in the Great Awakening* (New Haven, 1962), 192, 193; Seymour, *The Beginnings of the Episcopal Church*, 2; Burr, *The Story of the Diocese*, 11, 23, 43; Bruce Steiner, *Samuel Seabury: A Study in the High Church Tradition* (Athens, Ohio, 1971), 2, 34; Beardsley, *The History of the Episcopal Church*, 28, 29; James P. Walsh, "The Pure Church in Eighteenth-Century Connecticut" (Ph.D. diss., Columbia University, 1967), 80, 81.

10. A cogent summary of the literature on the role of deprivation in forming religion can be found in Charles Y. Glock, "The Role of Deprivation in the Origin and Evolution of Religious Groups," *Religion and Social Conflict*, eds. Robert Lee and Martin Marty (New York, 1964), 24–36. See also H. R. Niebuhr, *The Social Sources of Denominationalism* (New York, 1929), 29–38.

11. Greene, *Development of Religious Liberty*, provides a full and rich discussion of the rise of toleration through the various General Assembly enactments. Bruce E. Steiner, "Anglican Officeholding in Pre-Revolutionary Connecticut: The Parameters of New England Community," *William and Mary Quarterly* 31 (July, 1974), 403; and Ellen Larned, *The History of Windham County*, 2 vols. (Chester, Conn., 1976), I, 483, discuss Anglican and Separatist attempts to secure society status.

12. Greene, *Development of Religious Liberty*, 339.

13. Based on calculations on Steiner, "Anglican Officeholding," 370; and Walsh, "The Pure Church," 128, 129.

14. J. Hammond Trumbull and Charles Hoadley (eds.), *The Public Records of the Colony of Connecticut*, 15 vols. (Hartford, 1850–90), VII, 211 (hereafter cited as *Col. Recs.*); Estelle Feinstein, *Stamford: From Puritan to Patriot, 1641–1774* (Stamford, Conn., 1976), 139; Samuel Rankin, Jr., "Conservatism and the Problem of Change in the Congregational Churches of Connecticut, 1660–1760" (Ph.D. diss., Kent State University, 1971), 142.

15. Walsh, "The Pure Church," 19, 37; Larned, *Windham County,* I, 407–10; Stark, "Lebanon," 85, 88–92.

16. I have augmented the rich secondary sources on societies by analyzing the governments of twenty of them from differing parts of the colony. The discussion in the following paragraphs is therefore based on both extensive primary and secondary sources. The records of the societies used here are all found in the Connecticut State Library, Hartford. See table 14 above for the societies in the sample of twenty.

17. Feinstein, *Stamford,* 140–41; Stark, "Lebanon," 354; Frances Manwaring Caulkins, *A History of New London, Connecticut* (New London, 1895), 397.

18. Larned, *Windham County,* I, 372.

19. Middletown First Society Records, January, 1745; Preston Second Society Records, March, 1771; Litchfield First Society Records, December, 1779.

20. See Caulkins, *New London,* 395, for a discussion of schoolmasters and schoolmistresses. The compromise was worked out in the Guilford First Society. See Guilford First Society Records, October, 1759.

21. Walsh, "The Pure Church," 22.

22. Mansfield Second Society Records, March, 1784.

23. Feinstein, *Stamford,* 139.

24. William Chauncey Fowler, *History of Durham, Connecticut, From the First Grant of Land in 1662 to 1866* (Durham, Conn., 1790), 33. The need for unanimity is stressed in many secondary sources. See Caulkins, *New London,* 195; A. G. Hibbard, *History of the Town of Goshen, Connecticut* (Hartford, 1897), 83; Jane Eliza Johnson, *Newtown's History and Historian* (Newtown, Conn., 1917), 54; J. L. Rockey (ed.), *History of New Haven County, Connecticut,* 2 vols. (New York, 1892), II, 42–43; Walsh, "The Pure Church," 22.

25. For the Voluntown and Pomfret examples see Larned, *Windham County,* I, 248–49, 371. Rockey, *New Haven County,* II, 43–45, shows the problems some societies could have in attracting ministers. See Farmington First Society Records, May, 1702.

26. Walsh, "The Pure Church," 22; Rockey, *New Haven County,* II, 42–43; and Quincy Blakely, *Farmington, One of the Mother Towns of Connecticut,* 38, *Connecticut Tercentenary Series* (New Haven, 1935), provide the examples for Colchester, Branford, and Farmington. Stark, "Lebanon," 88–92, and James Montgomery Bailey, *History of Danbury, Connecticut, 1684–1896* (New York, 1896), discuss the impact of a search for a minister on a society.

27. The best secondary account of the negotiation process is in Walsh, "The Pure Church," 16–18. See also Ezra Stiles, *Extracts from the Itineraries and Other Miscellanies of Ezra Stiles,* ed. Franklin Bowditch Dexter (New

Haven, 1916), 331–33. The negotiation process can be followed in detail in
Greenfield Hills Society Records, 1725, 1756–57; Glastonbury First Society
Records, 1759; Hadlyme Society Records, 1745; and Hartford First Soci-
ety Records, 1748.

28. For a general account see Walsh, "The Pure Church," 17–18. For
Bulkeley's troubles see Caulkins, *New London,* 137–39. For an in-depth
analysis of salary disputes in the societies of one town see Stark, "Lebanon," chap. 2.

29. Thomas Lewis, Jr., "From Suffield to Saybrook: An Historical
Geography of the Connecticut River Valley in Connecticut prior to 1800"
(Ph.D. diss., Rutgers University, 1976), 108; Winslow, *Meetinghouse Hill,*
54–65. A good general description of early Connecticut meetinghouses
can be found in J. Frederick Kelly, *Early Connecticut Meetinghouses* (New
York, 1948). Most town histories contain descriptions of local meetinghouses and many contain illustrations.

30. *Col. Recs.,* VII, 334–35, IX, 134–37, X, 372, XI, 460. See Winslow,
Meetinghouse Hill, 128–29; and Stark, "Lebanon," chap 2, for a general
account of disputes. See Walsh, "The Pure Church," for Simsbury's troubles.

31. Larned, *Windham County,* discusses the building of many meetinghouses, and my account is based heavily upon her work. See *Windham
County,* I, 230, for the account of Ashford. See also Johnson, *Newtown,*
34–38. The process can be followed in minute detail in the records of the
meetings of the Hartford First Society, 1727–39.

32. Larned, *Windham County,* I, 86–94, 209, 230, 367, discusses the seat-
ing process in several towns. See also Caulkins, *New London,* 132; Theron
W. Crissey (comp.), *History of Norfolk, Litchfield County, Connecticut* (Everett,
Mass., 1900), 70; Feinstein, *Stamford,* 127–28; Rockey, *New Haven County,* I,
129; and Charles M. Tainter, *Extracts from the Records of Colchester*
(Hartford, 1864), 14. See Larned, *Windham County,* II, 57–58, for the attempt to sell pews. See Kenneth Scott, "Rude and Profane Behavior in the
Litchfield Meeting House in 1764," *Bulletin of the Connecticut Historical Society,* 19 (June, 1954), 93–95, for the controversy over blacks. See Glastonbury First Society Records, August, 1739; Norfield Society Records, May,
1785; and Greenfield Hills Society Records, September, 1743, for the respective examples cited.

33. Walsh, "The Pure Church," 33–42; and Rankin, "Conservatism and
Change," 54, 110–14, 154–65, 316–23, make the most thorough analyses
of society-colony relations; they are in perfect accord on the independent
spirit of societies. The societies' desire to guard their prerogatives bristles
in both society records and the records of the General Assembly. See also
Larned, *Windham County,* I, 332–38, 341, 374; and Winslow, *Meetinghouse
Hill,* 128–29.

34. *Col. Recs.,* IX, 120. For examples of towns electing officers by societies, see Farmington Town Meeting Minutes, Farmington Town Hall, December, 1722, 1723, 1748; "Hartford Town Votes, 1675–1700," Connecticut Historical Society, *Collections,* VI (Hartford, 1897), *passim;* Larned, *Windham County,* I, 229; Waterbury Town Meeting Minutes, Waterbury City Hall, December, 1748; John J. Waters, "Patrimony, Succession, and Social Stability: Guilford, Connecticut in the Eighteenth Century," *Perspectives in American History,* 10 (1976), 142. For examples of a society meeting nominating town officers, see Greenfield Hills Society Records, 1757–90, *passim;* and Norfield Society Records, 1785–90, *passim.*

35. Burr, *The Story of the Diocese,* 9.

36. That unity, concord, and harmony were *goals* of all New England colonists is agreed upon by almost all historians. For a penetrating discussion of these values in eighteenth-century New England, see Richard D. Brown, *Revolutionary Politics in Massachusetts: The Boston Committee of Correspondence and the Towns, 1772–1774* (Cambridge, Mass., 1970), 9–10; and Stephen Patterson, *Political Parties in Revolutionary Massachusetts* (Madison, Wis., 1973), chap 1. Michael Zuckerman in his book on Massachusetts towns agrees with Brown and Patterson, but unlike them he argues that the colonists were successful in realizing these goals. See Zuckerman, *Peaceable Kingdoms: New England Towns in the Eighteenth Century* (New York, 1970), *passim.*

37. For a discussion of religious pluralism and the independence and individualism it produces, see Robert Nisbet, "The Impact of Technology on Ethical Decision-Making," *Religion and Social Conflict,* eds. Lee and Marty, 13–15.

CHAPTER V. THE PROLIFERATION OF LOCAL INSTITUTIONS

1. The standard and most valuable source for the proprietors of New England is Roy Akagi, *The Town Proprietors of the New England Colonies* (Gloucester, Mass., 1965). See Charles Andrews, *The River Towns of Connecticut* (Baltimore, 1889), 65–72, for a discussion of the proprietors in the River Towns. For examples of the blending of functions between the town and the proprietors, see Percy Bidwell and John Falconer, *History of Agriculture in the Northern United States, 1620–1860* (Washington, D.C., 1925), 54–55; Erna Green, "The Public Land System of Norwalk, Connecticut, 1645–1704: A Structural Analysis of Economic and Political Relationships" (M.A. thesis, University of Bridgeport, 1972), 65–66; "Hartford Town Votes, 1635–1716," Connecticut Historical Society, *Collections,* VI (Hartford, 1897), March, 1640; Middletown Town Meeting Minutes, Middletown City Hall, I, *passim;* and *Some Early Records of and Documents*

Relating to the Town of Windsor, Connecticut, 1639–1703 (Hartford, 1930), 107. See Dorothy Deming, *The Settlement of the Connecticut Towns*, VI, *Connecticut Tercentenary Series* (New Haven, 1933), 51, for a discussion of the bachelor lots.

2. Bidwell and Falconer, *History of Agriculture*, 53–54; Green, "Norwalk," 41–42; Leonard Labaree, *The Early Development of a Town as Shown in Its Land Records*, XIII, *Connecticut Tercentenary Series* (New Haven, 1933), 4, 5, 9, 10; Samuel Orcutt and Ambroise Beardsley, *The History of the Old Town of Derby, Connecticut* (Springfield, Mass., 1880), 20; Susan Reik, "Genesis of a New England Town: The Growth of Farmington, Connecticut, 1645–1700" (M.A. thesis, Columbia University, 1972), 13; J. L. Rockey (ed.), *History of New Haven County, Connecticut*, 2 vols. (New York, 1892), I, 243, 344; Bernard Steiner, *A History of the Plantation of Menunkatuck and of the Original Town of Guilford, Connecticut* (Baltimore, 1897), 49–55.

3. Bidwell and Falconer, *History of Agriculture*, 54; Green, "Norwalk," 45, 67; Labaree, *The Early Development*, 4, 9; Orcutt and Beardsley, *Derby*, 20; Reik, "Farmington," 13; Rockey, *New Haven County*, I, 344; Steiner, *Guilford*, 49–55. See George Homans, *English Villagers of the Thirteenth Century* (New York, 1975), 90–91, for a discussion of late medieval village land practices.

4. William Deloss Love, *The Colonial History of Hartford* (Chester, Conn., 1974), 125; Orcutt and Beardsley, *Derby*, 38; Rockey, *New Haven County*, II, 10–11; Green, "Norwalk," 70; Joan Ballen, "Fairfield, Connecticut, 1661–1691: A Demographic Study of the Economic, Political, and Social Life of a New England Community" (M.A. thesis, University of Bridgeport, 1970), 157–62; Labaree, *The Early Development*, 21.

5. "Hartford Town Votes," 21, 32; Estelle Feinstein, *Stamford: From Puritan to Patriot, 1641–1774* (Stamford, Conn., 1976), 107; Steiner, *Guilford*, 174–75; Labaree, *The Early Development*, 21; Frances Manwaring Caulkins, *A History of New London, Connecticut* (New London, 1895), 259–62.

6. Branford Town Meeting Votes, Branford Town Hall, 1690–1700; Bruce P. Stark, *Lyme, Connecticut: From Founding to Independence* (Old Lyme, Conn., 1976), 4; Middletown Town Meeting Minutes, February, 1680, December, 1715, 1717; Middletown Proprietor Records, Middletown City Hall, 1734, *passim.*

7. Norwich Town Meeting Minutes, Norwich City Hall, December, 1717, May, 1718; Farmington Proprietor Records, in Farmington Town Meeting Minutes, Farmington Town Hall, I, April, 1727, December, 1736; J. Hammond Trumbull and Charles J. Hoadley (eds.), *The Public Records of the Colony of Connecticut*, 15 vols. (Hartford, 1850–90), VII, 137, 379 (hereafter cited as *Col. Recs.*); Feinstein, *Stamford*, 107; Hartford Town Meeting Minutes, Hartford City Hall, May, 1729.

8. *Col. Recs.*, VII, 137, 379; Akagi, *Town Proprietors*, 63–66.

9. Akagi, *Town Proprietors*, 46; Richard Bushman, *From Puritan to Yankee: Character and the Social Order in Connecticut, 1690–1765* (Cambridge, Mass., 1967), 83–85.

10. Deming, *Connecticut Towns*, 48; William Chauncey Fowler, *History of Durham, Connecticut, from the First Grant of Land in 1662 to 1866* (Durham, Conn., 1970), 27–28; Ellen Larned, *History of Windham County, Connecticut*, 2 vols. (Chester, Conn., 1976), I, 203–4; Bruce P. Stark, "Lebanon, Connecticut: A Study of Society and Politics in the Eighteenth Century" (Ph.D. diss., University of Connecticut, 1970), 349.

11. Anthony Garvan, *Architecture and Town Planning in Colonial Connecticut* (New Haven, 1951), 61–65; Charles Hammond, *The History of Union, Connecticut* (New Haven, 1893), 40–41; Jane Eliza Johnson, *Newtown's History and Historian* (Newtown, Conn., 1917), 14, 26; Alan C. White (comp.), *The History of the Town of Litchfield, Connecticut, 1720–1920* (Litchfield, Conn., 1920), 15, 310; Fowler, *Durham*, 27–28; Stark, "Lebanon," 349; Larned, *Windham County*, I, 22–26.

12. Feinstein, *Stamford*, 105–106; Stark, *Lyme*, 4; Steiner, *Guilford*, 175; Farmington Proprietor Records, 1730–40, *passim;* Middletown Proprietor Records, 1730–40, *passim;* Caulkins, *New London*, 63; Ezra Stiles, *Extracts from the Itineraries and Other Miscellanies of Ezra Stiles*, ed. Franklin Bowditch Dexter (New Haven, 1916), 189; Labaree, *The Early Development*, 22–23.

13. Garvan, *Architecture*, 69–77; Charles Grant, *Democracy in the Connecticut Frontier Town of Kent* (New York, 1972), 15, 23–27, 56–62; *Sketches of the People and Places of New Hartford* (New Hartford, Conn., 1883), 2; *History of Litchfield County* (Philadelphia, 1881), 237, 274–75; Stanley Ranson, *The History of Hartland, the 69th Town in the Colony of Connecticut* (Hartland, Conn., 1961), 7; Edward C. Starr, *A History of Cornwall, Connecticut: A Typical New England Town* (New Haven, 1926), 35.

14. Starr, *Cornwall*, 35; Ranson, *Hartland*, 7; Richard Wheeler and George Hilton (eds.), *Barkhamsted Heritage: Custom and Industry in a Rural Connecticut Town* (Barkhamsted, Conn., 1975), 6; Garvan, *Architecture*, 68–77; A. G. Hibbard, *A History of the Town of Goshen, Connecticut* (Hartford, 1897), 31.

15. Albert McKinley, *The Suffrage Requirements in the Thirteen English Colonies in America* (Philadelphia, 1905), 382–406; *Col. Recs.*, II, 112.

16. Charles Hoadley (ed.), *Records of the Colony and Plantation of New Haven*, 2 vols. (Hartford, 1857), I, 13–15, 137–39, II, 403–4, 407.

17. This paragraph is based on David Fowler, "Connecticut's Freemen: The First Forty Years," *William and Mary Quarterly*, 15 (July, 1958), 312–33.

18. *Col. Recs.*, III, 24, VII, 250. The process of admitting freemen is described in Grant, *Kent*, 109. Since it was not a requirement for a town selectman to be a freeman, a non-freeman selectman could theoretically

recommend someone for freemanship. It is doubtful, however, that any selectman was ever not a freeman.

19. Many of the low estimates of freemanship stem from historians' acceptance of Ezra Stiles's remark that only one out of nine Connecticut men could vote. See Oscar Zeichner, *Connecticut's Years of Controversy* (Chapel Hill, N.C., 1948), 8; and George Groce, Jr., *William Samuel Johnson, Maker of the Constitution* (New York, 1937), 54. Lawrence Henry Gipson, *Jared Ingersoll: A Study of American Loyalism in Relation to British Colonial Government* (New Haven, 1920), 19, rejected Stile's estimate and suggested that freemen may have numbered slightly more than 25 percent of the adult white male population. See appendix seven above for data on freemanship.

20. A detailed study by Bruce Stark shows the relationship between distance and freemanship: see Stark, "Freemenship in Lebanon, Connecticut: A Case Study," *Connecticut History* (January, 1975), 27–48. See appendix seven above for correlation tests and consistency tables for medians.

21. Grant, *Kent*, iii, estimates that at least 70 percent of the adult white males had enough property to qualify. Stark, "Lebanon," 208–9, agrees with Grant's conclusion. Work I have done in the probate records of Connecticut suggest that this was a minimum number: see Bruce C. Daniels, "Money-Value Definitions of Economic Classes in Colonial Connecticut, 1700–1776," *Histoire Sociale—Social History* (November, 1974), 346–52.

22. Middletown Town Meeting Minutes, March, 1974; Sharon Town Meeting Minutes, Sharon Town Hall, October, 1975; Hartford Town Meeting Minutes, September, 1783. The call for published lists of votes was first made in the *Connecticut Courant* during the Stamp Act crisis and was repeated intermittently. See *Connecticut Courant*, September 23, 1765.

23. The whole process is described in *Col. Recs.*, IV, 11, 12.

24. Robert Dinkin, "Elections in Colonial Connecticut," *Bulletin of the Connecticut Historical Society*, 37 (January, 1972), 17–20; Caulkins, *New London*, 409; Fowler, *Durham*, 165.

25. For three such cases in one year involving Newtown, Ridgefield, and Ashford, see *Col. Recs.*, VI, 556–57, 558.

26. The "steady habits" cliché is discussed perceptively by Christopher Collier, "Steady Habits Considered and Reconsidered," *Connecticut Review*, 5 (April, 1972), 28–37; and the oligarchical pattern of deputy officeholding is discussed in Bruce C. Daniels, "Democracy and Oligarchy in Connecticut Towns: General Assembly Officeholding, 1701–1790," *Social Science Quarterly* (December, 1975), 460–75. The "gimmickry" is discussed in various aspects by Grant, *Kent*, 122–27; Robert Dinkin, "The Nomination of Governors and Assistants in Colonial Connecticut," *Bulletin of the Connecticut Historical Society*, 36 (July, 1971), 92; Richard Purcell, *Connecticut in Transition: 1775–1818* (Middletown, Conn., 1963), 125–27; and Jackson

Turner Main, *The Upper House in Revolutionary America* (Madison, Wis., 1967), 81. Bruce P. Stark, "The Upper House in Early Connecticut," *A Lyme Miscellany*, ed. George Willauer (Middletown, Conn., 1977), shows the limits of the voting procedure's ability to influence the freemen's choice.

27. Richard H. Marcus, "The Militia of Colonial Connecticut, 1639–1775: An Institutional Study" (Ph.D. diss., University of Colorado, 1965), 61, 66. The following section on the militia is heavily dependent on Marcus's thesis and on another thesis by Stewart L. Gates, "Disorder and Social Organization: The Militia in Connecticut Public Life, 1660–1860" (Ph.D. diss., University of Connecticut, 1975).

28. *Col. Recs.* I, "Code of 1650," 542–43; Andrews, *River Towns*, 110; Gates, "Disorder and Social Organization," 80.

29. Gates, "Disorder and Social Organization," 17, 75; Marcus, "The Militia of Connecticut," 253–57. For an account of training days see Caulkins, *New London*, 406–7.

30. Gates, "Disorder and Social Organization," 23, 80.

31. *Ibid.*, 57, 60–62, 72; Marcus, "The Militia of Connecticut," 241–42, 252–53.

32. Gates, "Disorder and Social Organization," 68–69.

33. The two lists are found in the Connecticut Archives, Militia, Connecticut State Library, Hartford, Series I, vol. I, 1–32, and vol. II, 1–31, respectively. For 1774 and 1790 the number of trainbands is estimated by multiplying the number of regiments by thirteen. Normally, each regiment was composed of twelve trainbands, but in several instances a regiment contained more than twelve because of administrative difficulties and geographic factors. In one case a regiment contained sixteen trainbands, and enough regiments had thirteen, fourteen, or fifteen so that it seems safe to assume that the average number of trainbands per regiment was raised to approximately thirteen. The number of regiments can be determined by examining the appointments of officers at the end of a session of the General Assembly, which are listed in the Connecticut Archives indices.

34. Marcus, "The Militia of Connecticut," 352; Gates, "Disorder and Social Organization," 12–13, 136–39.

35. The number of justices for most years can be determined by looking at the lists of appointments after the spring session of the General Assembly. Checklist of Probate Records in the Connecticut State Library, ms., Connecticut State Library, Hartford.

36. Leonard Labaree, A. E. Van Dusen, Christopher Collier, *et al.* (eds.), *The Records of the State of Connecticut*, 9 vols. (Hartford, 1894–1967), V, 257–77, 343–73, contains the acts of incorporation. See chapter one above for the forces behind incorporation.

CHAPTER VI. THE EMERGENCE OF CENTRAL PLACES

1. This overview of the economy is based primarily upon Percy Wells Bidwell and John Falconer, *History of Agriculture in the Northern United States, 1629–1860* (Washington, D.C., 1925); Chester Destler, *Connecticut: The Provisions State*, V, *Connecticut Bicentennial Series* (Chester, Conn., 1973); Albert Olson, *Agricultural Economy and the Population in Eighteenth-Century Connecticut*, XL, *Connecticut Tercentenary Series* (New Haven, 1935); Gaspare Saladino, "The Economic Revolution in Eighteenth-Century Connecticut" (Ph.D. diss., University of Wisconsin, 1964); Albert E. Van Dusen, "The Trade of Revolutionary Connecticut" (Ph.D. diss., University of Pennsylvania, 1948); and Glenn Weaver, "Some Aspects of Early Eighteenth-Century Connecticut Trade," *Bulletin of the Connecticut Historical Society*, 22 (January, 1957). I am currently preparing for publication an essay that summarizes economic trends in colonial Connecticut.

2. See M. G. Smith, "Complexity, Size and Urbanization," *Urban Settlements: The Process of Urbanization in Archaeological Settlements*, ed. Ruth Tringham (Andover, Mass., 1973), 567–74; and Paul Wheatley, "The Concept of Urbanism," *Urban Settlements*, ed. Tringham, 620–21. The aggregate population that is clustered together is usually a good rough guide to urbanization, but the population of an area grouped into a local governmental unit is not. See Brian Berry and William Garrison, "The Functional Bases of the Central Place Hierarchy," *Economic Geography*, 34 (April, 1958), 149, 153–54. If the population of a city as it appears in the official census were a guide to urbanization, my home city of Winnipeg, Manitoba, would have doubled its urbanization development with the stroke of a pen when the provincial government changed its boundaries and doubled the population officially residing in the city.

3. This assertion is accepted by most local historians. See Roland G. Osterweis, *Three Centuries of New Haven, 1638–1938* (New Haven, 1953), III; Saladino, "The Economic Revolution," 16–20; Robert Decker, "The New London Merchants: 1645–1901: The Rise and Decline of a Connecticut Port" (Ph.D. diss., University of Connecticut, 1970), 51; William D. Love, *The Colonial History of Hartford* (Chester, Conn., 1974), 254; Carl Bridenbaugh, *Cities in Revolt: Urban Life in America, 1743–1776* (New York, 1955; reprint ed., New York 1970), chap. 5; Edward E. Atwater (ed.), *History of the City of New Haven by an Association of Writers* (New York, 1887), chaps. 13, 14.

4. Wheatley, "The Concept of Urbanism," 603–5; Smith, "Complexity, Size and Urbanism," 570–73.

5. Richard Bushman, *From Puritan to Yankee: Character and the Social Order in Connecticut, 1690–1765* (Cambridge, Mass., 1967), provides the best account of dispersion, although he does not locate the process in any

context larger than Connecticut. The "least effort" principle and its effects on population distribution are brilliantly discussed in George Kingsley Zipf, *Human Behavior and the Principle of Least Effort* (Cambridge, Mass., 1949), 355.

6. Michael Chisholm, *Rural Settlement and Land Use: An Essay in Location* (London, 1962), 53, 70–73, 126–27, 144–45, chap. 3. There were examples in England of dispersed farming populations as early as the thirteenth century, but this model of living was in a small minority position. See George Homans, *English Villagers of the Thirteenth Century* (New York, 1975), 20–21.

7. Chisholm, *Rural Settlement*, 57–58, 144–45, chap. 3. Kenneth Lockridge, *A New England Town: The First Hundred Years* (New York, 1970), 135, argues that the dispersal of the population was the crucial factor that shattered the political and social unity.

8. Wheatley, "The Concept of Urbanism," 615–17; Brian Blouet, "Factors Influencing the Evolution of Settlement Patterns," *Urban Settlements*, ed. Tringham, 5; Edward Ullman, "A Theory of Location for Cities," *American Journal of Sociology*, 46 (May, 1941), 853–64. Charles Fobes, "Path of the Settlement and Distribution of Population in Maine," *Economic Geography*, 20 (January, 1944), 65–69, shows in a case study the crucial role of transportation for central places.

9. Wheatley, "The Concept of Urbanism," 615. See Berry and Garrison, "Central Place Hierarchy," 147, for an empirical validation of this ratio.

10. For a contemporary account of the importance of secondary rivers, see Robert Hunter, Jr., *Quebec to Carolina in 1785–1786; Being the Travel Diary and Observations of Robert Hunter Jr., a Young Merchant of London*, eds. Louis B. Wright and Marion Tinling (San Marino, Calif., 1943), 143. For historians' accounts of their importance, see Van Dusen, "The Trade of Connecticut," 55; Margaret E. Martin, *Merchants and Trade in the Connecticut River Valley, 1750–1820*, XXIV, *Smith College Studies in History* (Northampton, Mass. 1939), 8; and Winifred Kotchian, *The Quinnipiac: The Story of a River* (New Haven, 1976, 14–20. The remark on New London harbor was made in 1680 in a report of the colony to the Board of Trade. See J. Hammond Trumbull and Charles Hoadley (eds.), *The Public Records of the Colony of Connecticut*, 15 vols. (Hartford, 1850–90), III, 297 (hereafter cited as *Col. Recs.*). See Decker, "The New London Merchants" for a brief discussion of harbors. For the importance of distance in developing central places see James Lemon, "Urbanization and Development of Eighteenth-Century Southeastern Pennsylvania and Adjacent Delaware," *William and Mary Quarterly*, 24 (October, 1967), 520–24. Lemon shows that Philadelphia's gravitational pull extended for a thirty-mile radius, destroyed the commerce of any nearby town, and prevented the establishment of other central places within the radius.

11. Van Dusen, "The Trade of Connecticut," 118, 253; Frances M. Caulkins, *A History of Norwich, Connecticut* (Hartford, 1866), 310–11, 397–98; Decker, "The New London Merchants," 55–56; Love, *Hartford,* 313–18; Map of Middletown in 1783, copy in Connecticut State Library, Hartford; Map of Hartford in 1760 in Ezra Stiles, *Extracts from the Itineraries and Other Miscellanies of Ezra Stiles,* ed. Franklin Bowditch Dexter (New Haven, 1916), 84; Map of New London in 1776 in Trumbull Papers, XXIV, Doc. 18, Connecticut State Library; Saladino, "The Economic Revolution," appendices 29, 30.

12. Martin, *Merchants and Trade,* 13, 14, 74–82, 103–4, 140, 144; Van Dusen, "The Trade of Connecticut," 262.

13. Stiles, *Itineraries,* 265; Map of New Haven in 1748, copy in Connecticut State Library.

14. Map of Main Street of Middletown in 1776 in Van Dusen, "The Trade of Connecticut," 118; Map of Main Street of Hartford in 1776 in William Henney, *Hartford: Three Hundred Illustrations* (Hartford, 1906).

15. Stiles, *Itineraries,* 265, 395; Map of Middletown in 1783.

16. Osterweis, *New Haven,* 76.

17. J. P. Brissot De Warville, *New Travels in the United States of America, 1788,* ed. Durand Echeverria (Cambridge, Mass., 1964), 118; Caulkins, *Norwich,* 325, 332, 333; Decker, "The New London Merchants," 333; Hunter, *Quebec to Carolina,* 145–146; Love, *Hartford,* 232–40, 245; Joan Nafie, *To the Beat of a Drum: A History of Norwich, Connecticut during the American Revolution* (Norwich, Conn., 1976), 28; William B. Weeden, *An Economic and Social History of New England, 1620–1789,* 2 vols. (New York, 1890; reprint ed., New York, 1963), II, 695, 741, 790.

18. J. William Frost, *Connecticut Education during the Revolutionary Era,* VII, *Connecticut Bicentennial Series* (Chester, Conn., 1974), 14; Sidney Kobre, *The Development of the Colonial Newspaper* (Gloucester, Mass., 1960), 97, 174, 177; Albert E. Van Dusen, *Connecticut* (New York, 1961) 121; Love, *Hartford,* 229–30.

19. Caulkins, *Norwich,* 299.

20. Louis Leonard Tucker, *Connecticut's Seminary of Sedition: Yale College,* VIII, *Connecticut Bicentennial Series* (Chester, Conn., 1974), 12.

21. Decker, "The New London Merchants," 40; C. C. Goen, *Revivalism and Separatism in New England, 1740–1800: Strict Congregationalists and Separate Baptists in the Great Awakening* (New Haven, 1962), 68–90, 115, 302–9; Bruce E. Steiner, "Anglican Officeholding in Pre-Revolutionary Connecticut: The Parameters of New England Community," *William and Mary Quarterly,* 31 (July, 1974), 374, 375; Osterweis, *New Haven,* 90, 111.

22. Elizabeth Schenck, *The History of Fairfield,* 2 vols. (New York, 1889), II, 393; Map of Fairfield in Louis Middlebrook, *Maritime Connecticut During the American Revolution,* 2 vols. (Salem, Mass., 1925), I, 57; Map of Guilford,

1639–1810, by Lois North, copy in Connecticut State Library; Map of Greenwich in 1773 in Spencer Mead, *Ye Historie of Ye Town of Greenwich* (New York, 1911), 86; and Map of Lebanon in 1772, copy in Connecticut State Library.

23. Bruce P. Stark, *Lyme, Connecticut: From Founding to Independence* (Old Lyme, Conn., 1976), 50–51; Jackson Turner Main, "The Economic and Social Structure of Early Lyme," *A Lyme Miscellany,* ed., George Willauer (Middletown, Conn., 1977), 45; Estelle F. Feinstein, *Stamford: From Puritan to Patriot, 1641–1774* (Stamford, Conn., 1976), 117; Marjorie Grant McNulty, *Glastonbury: From Settlement to Suburb* (Glastonbury, Conn., 1975), 48; Stiles, *Itineraries,* 550–53; Bernard Steiner, *A History of the Plantation of Menunkatuck and of the Original Town of Guilford, Connecticut* (Baltimore, 1897), 250.

24. William F. Willingham, "Windham, Connecticut: Profile of a Revolutionary Community, 1755–1818" (Ph.D. diss., Northwestern University, 1972), 93; James Montgomery Bailey, *History of Danbury, Connecticut 1684–1896* (New York, 1896), 30, 173; Van Dusen, "The Trade of Connecticut," 253; Bruce P. Stark, "Lebanon, Connecticut: A Study of Society and Politics in the Eighteenth Century" (Ph.D. diss., University of Connecticut, 1970), 158; Glenn Weaver, *Jonathan Trumbull: Merchant Magistrate* (Hartford, 1956), *passim.*

25. *Col. Recs.,* IX, 513–95, XI, 622–23, 628–31, XIV, 498–99; Robert Decker, *The Whaling City* (Chester, Conn., 1976), 23; Hunter, *Quebec to Carolina,* 153; Stiles, *Itineraries,* 550–53; McNulty, *Glastonbury,* 47; Weaver, *Trumbull,* 113; Robert Alcorn, *The Biography of a Town: Suffield, Connecticut, 1670–1870* (Suffield, Conn., 1970), 88–90; Feinstein, *Stamford,* 117.

26. Weaver, *Trumbull,* 43, 113; Alcorn, *Suffield,* 88–90; Preston Historical Society, *Preston in Review* (Preston, Conn., 1971), 129.

27. See Chisholm, *Rural Settlement,* 165, for a discussion of the advantages of being the first-settled part of an area; Ellen Larned, *History of Windham County, Connecticut,* 2 vols. (Worcester, Mass., 1874; reprint ed., Chester, Conn., 1976), II, 468; and Franklin Bowditch Dexter, *Biographical Sketches of Graduates of Yale College,* 6 vols. (New York, 1885–1912), II, 137. For the information on Litchfield I am indebted to Marvin Thompson. Norwalk tried to wrest the county seat from Fairfield in a well-publicized battle of the 1760s. See the *Connecticut Courant,* September 12, 1768, September 19, 1768, and January 2, 1769. County seats were often a matter of contention elsewhere in New England. See Robert Gross, *The Minutemen and Their World* (New York, 1976), 39, 53. See also James Lemon, *The Best Poor Man's Country: A Geographical Study of Early Southeastern Pennsylvania* (New York, 1976), 119–20, for a discussion of how government activity and commercial activity reinforce each other and contribute to growth and centrality.

28. See Weaver, *Trumbull, passim;* and Stark, "Lebanon," chap. 4. For the information on Lebanon's mercantile structure and Jonathan Trumbull's business ability I am indebted to Albert E. Van Dusen, who is editing the papers of Trumbull, and to the "Report on Ledgers E and F of Jonathan Trumbull" by Caroline Norman, ms., Connecticut State Library, which Professor Van Dusen brought to my attention.

29. Bailey, *Danbury,* 28, 83, 84, 174; Saladino, "The Economic Revolution," 46.

30. Ullman, "A Theory of Location," 856–57.

31. Map of Sharon, 1739–76, copy in Connecticut State Library; Map of Simsbury in 1736, original in Connecticut State Library; Map of Voluntown in 1737, copy in Connecticut State Library; Map of Hebron in 1774, in Connecticut Archives, Ecclesiastical, Connecticut State Library, Series I, vol. VII, 351; Van Dusen, "The Trade of Connecticut," 253; Charles Grant, *Democracy in the Connecticut Frontier Town of Kent* (New York, 1961; reprint ed., New York, 1972), 43.

32. Weaver, "Connecticut Trade," 25; Weaver, *Trumbull,* 119–20; J. L. Rockey (ed.), *History of New Haven County, Connecticut,* 2 vols. (New York, 1892), II, 378–79; Martin, *Merchants and Trade,* 81–82.

33. Weaver, "Connecticut Trade," 25.

34. See chapter four above.

35. See chapter seven and appendix eight above.

36. See appendix nine for list of physicians. Stiles, *Itineraries,* 193–94; Jane Eliza Johnson, *Newtown's History and Historian* (Newtown, Conn., 1917), 204; William Chauncey Fowler, *History of Durham, Connecticut, from the First Grant of Land in 1662 to 1866* (Durham, Conn., 1866; reprint ed., Durham, Conn., 1970), 192, 194; and Salisbury Town Meeting Minutes, Salisbury Town Hall, June, 1762.

37. Stiles, *Itineraries,* 193–94; Connecticut Archives, Finance and Currency, Connecticut State Library, Series I, vol. V, 214a; Feinstein, *Stamford,* 19.

38. See chapter two above.

39. See especially Bruce C. Daniels, "Long-Range Trends of Wealth Distribution in Eighteenth-Century New England," *Explorations in Economic History,* xi (Winter, 1973–74), 123–35; and Jackson Turner Main, *The Social Structure of Revolutionary America* (Princeton, N.J., 1965), chap. 1. For Connecticut see also Frances Manwaring Caulkins, *A History of New London, Connecticut* (New London, 1895), 475; Feinstein, *Stamford,* 121; Grant, *Kent,* chaps. 5 and 6; and Willingham, "Windham," 77. For the growing maldistribution of wealth in general in New England, see Alice Hanson Jones, "Wealth Estimates for the NewEngland Colonies about 1770," *Journal of Economic History,* 32 (March, 1972); 98–127; Allan Kulikoff, "The Progress of Inequality in Revolutionary Boston," *William and Mary Quar-*

terly, 28 (July, 1971), 375–412; James Henretta, "Economic Development and Social Structure in Colonial Boston," *William and Mary Quarterly*, 22 (January, 1965), 75–105; and Henretta, *The Evolution of American Society, 1700–1815: An Interdisciplinary Analysis* (Lexington, Mass., 1973), 80–81.

40. This paragraph is based on Jackson Turner Main, "The Distribution of Property in Colonial Connecticut," *The Human Dimension of Nation Making: Essays on Colonial and Revolutionary America*, ed. James Kirby Martin (Madison, Wis., 1970), 54–104; and Main, "Early Lyme," 29–47. See also John Waters, "Patrimony, Succession, and Social Stability: Guilford, Connecticut in the Eighteenth Century," *Perspectives in American History*, 10 (1976), 131–60.

41. For the leading military figures see North Callahan, *Connecticut's Revolutionary War Leaders*, III, *Connecticut Bicentennial Series* (Chester, Conn., 1973), *passim*.

42. Edward Cook, Jr., *The Fathers of the Towns: Leadership and Community Structure in Eighteenth-Century New England* (Baltimore, 1976), chap. 6, shows the propensity of the most important towns in the New England colonies to supply the bulk of colony leadership. See also Bruce C. Daniels, "Family Dynasties in Connecticut's Largest Towns, 1701–1760," *Canadian Journal of History*, 8 (September, 1973), 99–111. Bruce Stark is preparing a monograph on the elections for assistants and governors, a précis of which can be found in *Lyme Miscellany*.

43. See appendices eleven and twelve for the data these conclusions are based upon. See also Bruce C. Daniels, "Democracy and Oligarchy in Connecticut Towns: General Assembly Officeholding, 1701–1790," *Social Science Quarterly* (December, 1975), 460–76.

44. Cook, *The Fathers of the Towns*, 165–184.

45. See appendix eleven and Daniels, "Democracy and Oligarchy," 460–76.

46. Hunter, *Quebec to Carolina*, 149; Brissot De Warville, *New Travels in the United States*, 117.

47. Blouet, "Factors Influencing the Evolution," 1–10.

48. See Carl Bridenbaugh, *The Colonial Craftsman* (New York, 1950), chap. 4; Henretta, *The Evolution of Society*, 80–81; Lemon, "Urbanization and the Development," 520–24; Main, *Social Structure*, 34; Robert Coakley, "Virginia Commerce during the American Revolution" (Ph.D. diss., University of Virginia, 1949), *passim*; James H. Soltow, "The Role of Williamsburg in the Virginia Economy," *William and Mary Quarterly*, 15 (October, 1958), 468; and Joseph A. Ernst and H. Roy Merrens, "Camden's Turrets Pierce the Skies! The Urban Process in the Southern Colonies during the Eighteenth Century," *William and Mary Quarterly*, 30 (October, 1973), 549–74. Ernst and Merren's position that the South was developing urban villages is challenged by Hermann Wellenreuther, "Urbanization in

the Colonial South: A Critique," *William and Mary Quarterly,* 31 (October, 1974), 653–68, but ably defended by their rebuttal in the same issue. Stephanie Grauman Wolf, *Urban Village: Population, Community, and Family Structure in Germantown, Pennsylvania, 1683–1800* (Princeton, N.J., 1976), shows the many service functions of an urban area that even a reasonably small village could provide.

49. Virginia in her most decentralized stage tried purposefully to build central places through a series of town acts and was singularly unsuccessful. See Edward M. Riley, "The Town Acts of Colonial Virginia," *Journal of Southern History,* 16 (August, 1950), 306–23. For the typicality of these social conditions to a normative process, see Wheatley, "The Concept of Urbanism," 608–13; and Smith, "Complexity, Size and Urbanism," 570–72. See also Horace Miner, "Community-Society Continua," *International Encyclopedia of the Social Sciences,* 3, 174–81, for a discussion of folk versus urban values and economic development.

CHAPTER VII. URBANIZATION AND EARLY NEW ENGLAND SOCIETY

1. Richard Bushman, *From Puritan to Yankee: Character and the Social Order in Connecticut, 1690–1765* (Cambridge, Mass., 1967); Kenneth Lockridge, *A New England Town: The First Hundred Years* (New York, 1970); Richard Gildrie, *Salem, Massachusetts, 1626–1683: A Covenant Community* (Charlottesville, Va., 1975); Charles Grant, *Democracy in the Connecticut Frontier Town of Kent* (New York, 1961); Philip Greven, Jr., *Four Generations: Population, Land, and Family in Colonial Andover, Massachusetts* (Ithaca, N.Y., 1970); T. H. Breen and Stephen Foster, "The Puritans' Greatest Achievement: A Study of Social Cohesion in Seventeenth-Century Massachusetts," *Journal of American History,* 60 (June, 1973), 5–22; Darrett Rutman, *Winthrop's Boston: A portrait of a Puritan Town* (Chapel Hill, N.C., 1965); Sumner Chilton Powell, *Puritan Village: The Formation of A New England Town* (Middletown, Conn., 1963); John Demos, *A Little Commonwealth: Family Life in Plymouth Colony* (New York, 1970); Paul Lucas, *Valley of Discord: Church and Society along the Connecticut River, 1636–1725* (Hanover, N.H., 1976); Michael Zuckerman, *Peaceable Kingdoms: New England Towns in the Eighteenth Century* (New York, 1970). This evolution, called "modernization" by recent historians, is perceptively discussed and placed in a theoretical framework by Richard D. Brown, *Modernization: The Transformation of American Life, 1600–1865* (New York, 1976); see especially chaps. 3 and 4. See also Jesse Bernard, "Community Disorganization," *International Encyclopedia of the Social Sciences,* 3, 163–69, for a theoretical discussion of this kind of evolution by a sociologist. Much of this debate was launched with the publication of Robert Brown's *Middle-*

Class Democracy and the Revolution in Massachusetts, 1691–1780 (Ithaca, N.Y., 1955). Few historians accept Brown's substantive conclusions and fewer still accept his methodology, but the debate he unleashed, although taking new forms and reaching a much more sophisticated conceptual state, lives on. See John Cary, "Statistical Method and the Brown Thesis on Colonial Democracy," *William and Mary Quarterly,* 20 (April, 1963), 251–57; and J. R. Pole, "Historians and the Problem of Early American Democracy," *American Historical Review,* 67 (April, 1962), 626–46.

2. The greatest fear of John Winthrop, the dominant figure of the founding of New England, was that the colonists would transfer their loyalties from England and Puritanism to their towns and selves. His fears were well founded. See Edmund S. Morgan, *The Puritan Dilemma: The Story of John Winthrop* (Boston, 1958), *passim;* and Morgan, *The Puritan Family: Religion and Domestic Relations in Seventeenth Century New England* (Boston, 1944), chap. 7.

A BRIEF NOTE ON SOURCES

Such a wealth of primary and secondary sources exists for the study of Connecticut's towns that it defies minute description in a short note. The specific ones I used can be found in my footnote citations, and I will describe in the following paragraphs only general classes of sources, in some cases giving a few examples of the best of these.

The basic place to study town history is in the local records themselves. With only a few exceptions, the greatest of the local sources, town-meeting minutes, have survived intact in every community. A few sets of minutes are published, and copies of a dozen or so can be found in the Connecticut State Library in Hartford, but the vast bulk are housed in town and city halls. Seldom more than three volumes in length and usually less, the colonial and Revolutionary town-meeting minutes are little used by scholars or the public, and it not infrequently takes a town clerk a half hour or more to locate them. These minutes contain all the resolutions passed by the town meeting and record all the officeholders it elected. They unfortunately do not contain substantive debates, but one can infer much about debates from the preambles that often accompany enactments.

Proprietor records have not survived as well as town-meeting records, nor are they as easy to locate. Probably one-half of the towns have extensive extant proprietor records, but it is not unusual for a given town's to be missing. Proprietor records are occasionally interspersed with town-meeting records or the early land records, although most commonly they compose a single volume of their own; because proprietors met infrequently and dealt only with land and land-related matters, the proprietor records seldom are more than seventy-five pages. Still, they, and the early town-meeting records, are the essential sources for early land policy. They can be found in town and city halls, local historical societies, and in some central repositories such as the Connecticut State Library, Connecticut Historical Society, Hartford, and New Haven Colony Historical Society, New Haven.

The minutes of the ecclesiastical society meetings nearly rival those of the town meetings in importance to the historian and exceed them in bulk. Happily for scholars, they are all centrally located in the Connecticut State Library. Although they are not always complete and are occasionally mistakenly catalogued under church meetings, the vast majority of society-meeting minutes are extant. They usually are contained in one or two volumes and are interspersed with parish registries, vital statistics, and church meetings. Although I did not use these latter three types of church records, they are potentially valuable sources for both church and demographic history.

All towns were forced by the constitutional arrangements of the colony and state to deal frequently with the central government; hence the published records of the colony and state and the archives of each are indispensable for local history. The published records contain all the resolutions passed by the General Court and General Assembly; the archives, located in the Connecticut State Library, contain the petitions, counterpetitions, committee reports, and other details behind each resolution. Most of the towns have several hundred entries in the archives, all of which are easily found through a thorough index.

Travelers' accounts of life in early Connecticut are valuable but unfortunately are not abundant for the colonial and Revolutionary periods. About a dozen of them have been published, and more exist in manuscript form. Ezra Stiles's journal is one of the most remarkable sources to exist for pre-Revolutionary Connecticut; Stiles had a penchant for counting and diagraming that has left the profession of history much richer. J. P. Brissot De Warville's and the Marquis De Chastellux's accounts are the two best ones for Revolutionary Connecticut, although they are nowhere near as detailed and useful as Stiles's.

Maps are one of the most potentially valuable sources for local history but for some curious reason have been little used by historians. Most towns have several extant maps for the colonial and Revolutionary periods, showing such things as land allotments, highway layouts, commercial development, society boundaries, and house locations. Several hundred of these maps are in the Connecticut State Library map collection, dozens are scattered throughout the archives, and many local historical societies have some.

There are four important collections of sources that I have not used extensively in this book but that would lend themselves well to quantitative analysis of the town: land records, probate records, tax lists, and genealogies.

Land records, usually comprising several dozen volumes per town for the period prior to 1790, list all land transfers and usually describe the property. These volumes are located in town and city halls today and are indexed by grantor and grantee.

Probate records, containing inventories and distributions of estates, wills, and bonds of indebtedness, exist for from 40 to 90 percent of the male population—the figure varies by date and region. These are all centralized in the Connecticut State Library for the period before 1790 and are the best sources for early Connecticut social and economic history.

Probate records can be supplemented with local tax records, which list the assessed wealth of each taxpayer in the town; tax lists, however, have not survived well, and only a small proportion of them are extant for the colonial and Revolutionary periods. Some are in central repositories and a few in local historical societies, but most are in town and city halls. A few exceptional towns have fairly complete runs, but in most towns only three or four lists survive.

Almost all colonial families have had some genealogical work performed on them, and the majority are the subject of published genealogies. Individuals and their family connections, births, deaths, and frequently occupations can be identified from them.

It hardly need be said that all these groups of sources can be supplemented with the primary ones historians traditionally use: correspondence, newspapers, business records, diaries, and so on. They exist in copious supply for early Connecticut.

The most valuable secondary sources for the study of the town are the hundreds of town histories and the dozen or so county histories. Every town and county in Connecticut has had at least one history written of it, and most have had more. The town histories are of two broad types: those by antiquarians and those by professionals. By labeling them antiquarian I do not wish to demean the first type; they are invariably useful in some way, and frequently literate and well researched. Ones such as Frances M. Caulkins, *A History of Norwich, Connecticut* (Hartford, 1866), and Bernard Steiner, *A History of the Plantation of Menunkatuck and of the Original Town of Guilford, Connecticut* (Baltimore, 1889), are models of exhaustive research and intelligent thought. This present book could not have been written without the antiquarian histories. Of the town histories written by professional historians, two stand out by their quality: Charles Grant, *Democracy in the Connecticut Frontier Town of Kent* (New York, 1961), and Estelle Feinstein, *Stamford: From Puritan to Patriot, 1641–1774* (Stamford, Conn., 1976). Generally, the county histories, while valuable, are not as useful as individual town studies; the great exception to this pattern is Ellen Larned, *The History of Windham County, Connecticut*, 2 vols. (Worcester, Mass., 1874), which is a product of a lifetime of research and an extraordinarily valuable piece of work.

The list of doctoral dissertations and master's theses on Connecticut has grown tremendously in the last decade, and I have used about thirty of them in the writing of this book. Undoubtedly, some others have escaped my attention. Few subjects have not been dealt with in some manner by these dissertations and theses; they do, of course, vary greatly in quality. In particular, I owe a heavy intellectual debt to four outstanding dissertations: Stewart Lewis Gates, "Disorder and Social Organization: The Militia in Connecticut Public Life, 1660–1860" (University of Connecticut, 1975); Samuel Rankin, Jr., "Conservatism and the Problem of Change in the Congregational Churches of Connecticut, 1660–1760" (Kent State University, 1971); Gaspare Saladino, "The Economic Revolution in Late Eighteenth-Century Connecticut" (University of Wisconsin, 1964); and James P. Walsh, "The Pure Church in Eighteenth-Century Connecticut" (Columbia University, 1967).

Before starting this book I had little idea of how many specialized studies existed of specific areas of Connecticut's past. Whether one wants to learn about tinsmithing, newspapers, Baptists, roads, clockmaking, farming, or some other subject, usually some previous historical work will be able to provide much of the information needed or serve as a guide to the primary materials. As with town histories, these specialized studies are frequently written by nonprofessionals who have a special love of and therefore a special commitment to their subjects.

There is a large secondary literature on early Connecticut written by professionals that is also indispensable for a study of the town. The best overall reference book on Connecticut is Albert E. Van Dusen, *Connecticut* (New York, 1961). The major works on seventeenth-century Connecticut are Charles Andrews, *The River Towns of Connecticut* (Baltimore, 1889); Robert C. Black, *The Younger John Winthrop* (New York, 1966); and Richard Dunn, *Puritans and Yankees: The Winthrop Dynasty of New England, 1630–1717* (Princeton, N.J., 1962). The major ones on eighteenth-century Connecticut are Richard Bushman, *From Puritan to Yankee: Character and the Social Order in Connecticut, 1690–1765* (Cambridge, Mass., 1967); Christopher Collier, *Roger Sherman's Connecticut: Yankee Politics and the American Revolution* (Middletown, Conn., 1971); Lawrence Henry Gipson, *Jared Ingersoll: A Study of American Loyalism in Relation to British Colonial Government* (New Haven, 1920); M. Louise Greene, *The Development of Religious Liberty in Connecticut* (Boston and New York, 1905); Bruce Steiner, *Samuel Seabury: A Study in the High Church Tradition* (Athens, Ohio, 1971); Glenn Weaver, *Jonathan Trumbull: Merchant Magistrate* (Hartford, 1956); and Oscar Zeichner, *Connecticut's Years of Controversy, 1750–1776* (Chapel Hill, N.C., 1949). Of course, these citations merely scratch the surface, and many other useful books have been written about early Connecticut. Two lengthy series of short monographs—the *Connecticut Tercentenary Series,* published 1933–36 and numbering sixty volumes, and the *Connecticut Bicentennial Series,* published beginning in 1973, which will number forty volumes when completed in 1980—provide a wealth of material on Connecticut's seventeenth- and eighteenth-century history. Added to book-length works are the hundreds of articles in periodicals ranging from local Connecticut journals to those of national scope.

Finally, I would call the extensive literature in the social sciences to the attention of any serious student of the town's past. In particular, anthropologists, economists, geographers, and sociologists have developed a vast body of knowledge about local communities and provide both tools for analysis of data and conceptual frameworks in which historians can place their conclusions. My own debt to the social sciences is indicated in both the text and the notes of this book.

INDEX